The Rise of Cass Business School

Also by Allan P.O. Williams

USING PERSONNEL RESEARCH (*Editor*) Gower, 1983

CHANGING CULTURE: New Organisational Approaches (*Co-author*) Institute of Personnel Management, 2nd Edition, 1993

THE COMPETITIVE CONSULTANT: A Client-orientated Approach for Achieving Superior Performance (*Co-author*) Palgrave Macmillan, 1994

MANAGING CHANGE SUCCESSFULLY: Using Theory and Experience to Implement Change (*Co-author*) Thomson, 2002

The Rise of Cass Business School

The Journey to World-Class: 1966 Onwards

Allan P.O. Williams

palgrave
macmillan

First published in 2006 by
PALGRAVE MACMILLAN
Houndmills, Basingstoke, Hampshire RG21 6XS and
175 Fifth Avenue, New York, N.Y. 10010
Companies and representatives throughout the world.

PALGRAVE MACMILLAN is the global academic imprint of the Palgrave Macmillan division of St. Martin's Press, LLC and of Palgrave Macmillan Ltd. Macmillan® is a registered trademark in the United States, United Kingdom and other countries. Palgrave is a registered trademark in the European Union and other countries.

ISBN-13: 978–1–4039–9867–5 hardback
ISBN-10: 1–4039–9867–1 hardback

This book is printed on paper suitable for recycling and made from fully managed and sustained forest sources.

A catalogue record for this book is available from the British Library.

Library of Congress Cataloging-in-Publication Data

Williams, Allan P. O.
The rise of Cass Business School : the journey to world-class : 1966 onwards / by Allan P.O. Williams.
p. cm.
Includes bibliographical references and index.
ISBN 1–4039–9867–1 (cloth)
1. Sir John Cass Business School – History. 2. Business schools – England – London – History. 3. Business education – England – London – History. I. Title.

HF1142.L8W55 2006
650′.071′14212—dc22 2005053498

10 9 8 7 6 5 4 3 2 1
15 14 13 12 11 10 09 08 07 06

Printed and bound in Great Britain by
Antony Rowe Ltd, Chippenham and Eastbourne

Contents

List of Figures

List of Boxes

Preface and Acknowledgements

Business schools are largely a phenomenon of the twentieth century, and it was only in the 1960s that they took root in the United Kingdom. The history of two business schools that were established at that time have been written, that is, London Business School and Manchester Business School. The Franks Report is usually identified as the main factor that led to their establishment. This report was the conduit through which a number of forces were synchronised and unleashed on British industry and the government of the day. These same forces led a number of universities, particularly those that were about to be transformed from colleges of advanced technology to universities, to make serious in-roads into the management/business education field. The Northampton College of Advanced Technology was one of these. Given that 2006 is the fortieth anniversary of the City University and the establishment of its Department of Management, it is timely to tell the story of Cass Business School.

The stôry of how a relatively under-resourced business school in 1966 managed to achieve its current international standing is worth sharing with others involved in leading and changing similar structures in a highly competitive industry. While every business school and their environments are unique, there exist sufficient commonalities to learn something from each other. This is particularly true when similarities and differences can be transformed to a common denominator through the use of generally accepted concepts and theories. This academic objective has influenced my approach in researching and writing this book.

A second, and no less important objective, is to recount the historical development of Cass Business School so that all past and future stakeholders have a better understanding of its birth, maturation and future potential. Meeting these two objectives has not been easy, because of the need to meet academic criteria while maintaining interest and readability. Many histories of organisations are replete with notes and references to underline the authenticity of the research. I have tried to keep such details to a minimum in the interest of readability. This constraint has also meant the events and individuals highlighted are those judged to be critical to the development of the School. This can more easily be done with hindsight; hence more space is given to recording events and individuals from the past rather than the present. My apologies to those academics, administrators, alumni and friends of the School who have not been directly mentioned. Future accounts of the School's history will remedy any flaws that this may have created.

The history of a business school cannot be written without the unstinting support of a great many individuals. The present Dean, Lord Currie, and other colleagues provided the initial impetus for the research. The late Vic Fox, the former University Librarian who took a special interest in the University's archives, provided helpful directions for locating the most relevant material. Current library staff, and Leslie Baldwin in the School's Learning Resource Centre, have proved equally helpful. Useful information and advice have also come from the School's accountant (Marion O'Hara), Alumni Relations (Theresa Dzendrowskyj and July Kean), and the Director of Marketing and Communications (Gemma Lines). I am deeply indebted to the 63 individuals whom I interviewed. These included most of the 'pioneering staff' employed in 1966, together with one of the early supporters of the School from engineering (Professor Ludwig Finkelstein who joined the Production Department in 1957) and from the Students Union (Bob Timms, President 1967–68), several past and present Officers of the University, seven Deans and two Acting Deans, and most of the staff who had held senior academic or administrative positions in the School. A number of individuals have been most helpful in their constructive criticisms of parts of earlier versions of particular chapters (Professors Sid Kessler and Clive Holtham, Drs. Paul Dobson and Mohan Sodhi). I am particularly grateful to the four individuals who read and made constructive comments on an earlier version of the whole manuscript (Adrian Seville, a former Registrar of the University, and the present management team of the School – Lord Currie, Professor Haberman and Henrietta Royle).

Information gleaned from several individuals who have played a part in contributing and/or describing aspects of the history of business schools in the United Kingdom is gratefully acknowledged, including: Dr. Edward Brech (author of *The History of Modern Management*); Professor Andrew Thomson (former Dean of the Open Business School); Professor Bernard Barry (former Director of Research at Ashridge, and now at Monash); Jonathan Slack (CEO of the Association of Business Schools); Peter Calladine at the Association of MBAs. Many thanks also to those who shared with me the information they had accumulated and preserved, including: Professor Leslie Hannah on the early history of Bunhill Row; the Hon. Edward Alport for access to his father's files; Michael O'Hara for his notes on the sequence of events leading up to the new building in Bunhill Row. Grateful thanks to all those at Palgrave

Macmillan for guiding the manuscript through to the finished product, and to Philip Meech the photographer of HM The Queen opening the new building of Cass Business School.

The book is dedicated to all those who have contributed to the successful development of Cass Business School, including: staff, students, associates and those individuals and organisations whose generosity enabled the School to innovate even through difficult times.

Allan P.O. Williams

Part I

Introduction

1
A Story Worth Sharing

Her Majesty the Queen formally opened the splendid new building of Cass Business School at 106 Bunhill Row on 7 May 2003 (see Figure 1.1). At that time few people would have been aware of the many achievements and a few disappointments that peppered the pathway leading up to this grand occasion. They would have been even less aware of how and why this pathway followed the route it did. The story of Cass is the pride of its stakeholders, and should be of interest to all those concerned with the process of leadership in business schools.

Cass has been described as the crown jewels of the City University. Today it is one of the world's major business schools, having been rated 42nd and 60th worldwide by the *Financial Times* (*FT*) for its full-time MBA programme in the last two years (*FT* 24.01.2005). In its first rankings of the top 40 European Business Schools, the *FT* placed Cass 2nd in the United Kingdom (behind London Business School – LBS) and 6th in Europe – behind LBS, Insead (France), IMD (Switzerland), Instituto de Empresa, Iese Business School (Spain), but ahead of Said, Judge and Tanaka (UK) (*FT* 6.09.2004). Its undergraduate Business Studies degree has been consistently ranked by the Guardian as one of the top three in the UK. On the basis of an analysis of the top 16 Finance journals, Cass research productivity was ranked 2nd in the United Kingdom, 2nd in Europe and 4th among academic institutions outside the United States (Chan *et al.* 2002). In the academic year 2004–05 it had 1218 undergraduates, 1436 specialist masters students, 205 MBA students, 118 PhD students, 120 academics, 120 administrative staff plus visiting lecturers. The School's MBA programme has always been accredited by the internationally recognised Association of MBAs (AMBA). In 2001 the School as a whole successfully underwent the rigorous accreditation procedure run by the European Foundation for Management Development – the

Figure 1.1 HM The Queen at the Opening of Cass Business School Building.

European Quality Improvement System (EQUIS). It has one of the largest Finance and Actuarial Science Faculties in Europe and probably has no European rival for the range of high-level, finance-based MScs on offer – a total of 17. It runs a range of professional qualifications in the charity and not-for-profit sector unequalled in any European business school.

These achievements are impressive when viewed in the context of 1966 when Northampton College of Advanced Technology became The City University. At that time the University's orientation was toward manufacturing – the engineering faculty dominated its activities. The story of how the School grew from a 'manufacturing sector orientation' (with an intake of 10 students to its MSc in Administrative Sciences) in 1966/67, to a 'financial sector orientation' (with an extensive profile of degrees, research and management development activities) in 2004/05, is well worth sharing. The detailed history of the School's development, and the main forces affecting this development, will be described in later chapters. However, at this stage the story will be more readily understood through a brief overview of the academic structural changes taking place at the School under successive Deans, and by highlighting the School's links with the City of London.

Successive Deanships and academic structures

Figure 1.2 shows that the School has so far had ten 'formal leaders'. Eight of these were for periods of three years or more. The others were temporary arrangements to allow more time for finding a new Dean: the Triumvirate, the Goodhardt Deanship and (although not shown) the School was run by a four-person Cabinet for six months immediately preceding the appointment of Lord Currie in January 2000. For the sake of clarity some information has been omitted from Figure 1.2, including: Information Science becoming an independent department within the University in 1970; since its establishment in 1971 the Post Experience Unit has had semi-autonomous status under different labels (e.g. Management Development Centre, Cass Executive Education); research centres have been omitted but the first formal research centre (Personnel Research & Enterprise Development 1978–98), and the second (City Institute for Financial & Economic Research 1981–87), were the forerunners of an extensive series of research centres; a number of centres were also built around degrees rather than research (e.g. Centre for Systems Analysis & Design; Centre for Shipping Trade & Finance). The term 'dependent' centre in relation to the structure in 1986 indicates centres with semi-autonomous status within the School (this usually meant that separate financial accounts were produced).

City of London links and site history

The School's building in Bunhill Row is a £50 million masterpiece in design; bringing together the latest know-how in business school architecture, building materials and environmental psychology. The Sir John Cass Foundation generously contributed to the cost of the School's building, hence the change of name to the Sir John Cass Business School ('Cass Business School' for short). Sir John Cass was born in the City of London in 1661 and became both an Alderman and a Sheriff. He was also an MP for the City and knighted in 1713. In his Will all his property went to financing the education of young Londoners. One of the educational organisations that benefited in 1902 was the Sir John Cass Institute. In the early 1960s when negotiations were taking place in preparation for the Northampton College of Advanced Technology to become a university, serious discussions took place for the Sir John Cass College to be incorporated into the new university. One of the attractions for Northampton College was that the College was located in Jewry Street, and this would have provided a ready-made base in the

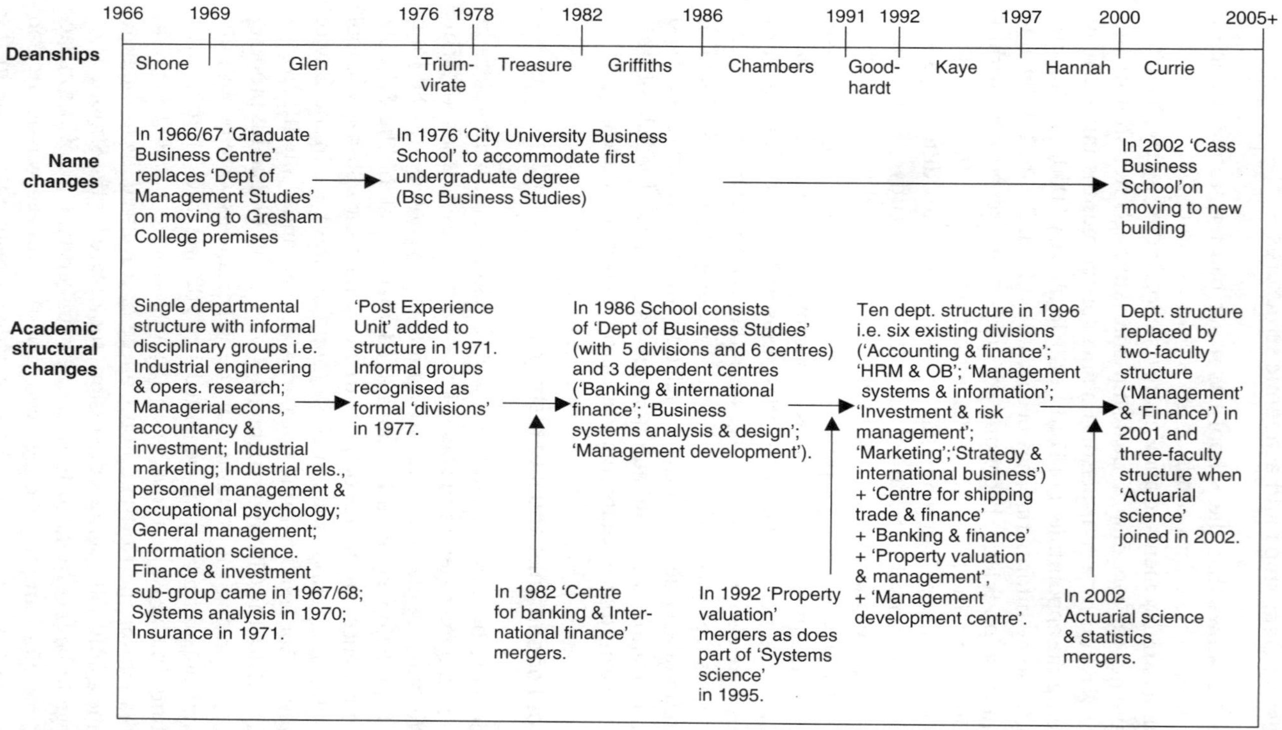

Figure 1.2 Outline profile of the School, 1966–2005+: Deanships (time periods are indicative and not to scale), name changes and academic structural changes.

City for the proposed business school of the new university. However, the terms of the Foundation meant that funds would not have been available for a merger, and it was unlikely that the Ministry of Education would want an additional financial burden to fall upon the University Grants Committee (UGC) when the City University came into being (Teague 1980). Subsequently the College became part of City Polytechnic (now part of London Metropolitan University). It is a remarkable coincidence that 40 years on the Sir John Cass name has become associated with the City University and with its business school.

The School's links with the City of London (i.e. the Corporation or 'City') have been extensive. This is not surprising given the efforts of the first Principal and Vice-Chancellor Sir James Tait (1957–74), and the Chairman of the Board of Governors Oliver Thomson (1956–66) to link the new university to the City. The most visible outcome of this policy was that each Lord Mayor becomes Chancellor of the University during their year in office. A less obvious, but no less important link, is with the City's livery companies. The majority of these are represented on the Court of the University which meets once a year to receive the annual report from the Vice-Chancellor – the University's 'annual shareholders meeting'. The livery companies are intertwined with the City. The remarkable thing about them is how they have survived the fundamental changes that have taken place from the twelfth century to the present day. When first established the livery companies fulfilled the function that our current trade associations, professional bodies and trade unions fulfil. Today their main function is to promote a shared set of values of excellence, comradeship and charitable activities, and thereby help to maintain the health of the City. The University and its students have benefited directly from their charitable funds. The Worshipful Company of Skinners (Chartered in 1327) and the Worshipful Company of Saddlers (1362) were major donors when the Northampton Institute was first formed in 1894, and again when achieving University status in 1966 (hence the 'Skinners Library' and the 'Saddlers Sports Centre'). The Worshipful Company of Mercers (1394) was instrumental in helping the School gain a foothold in the City in 1966. More recently there have developed close links through membership, special lectures, student prizes and bursaries with more modern livery companies such as the Actuaries (1979), Insurers (1979), Marketors (1977), Information Technologists (1992), and Management Consultants (2004).

There are also some tenuous but fascinating historical links associated with the School's new Bunhill Row site. It is worth recounting the rich history of the site and its immediate neighbourhood. In Elizabethan times five windmills stood in the then extensive Bunhill Fields on the north east side of what is now Bunhill Row. One of the Row's most famous residents, John Milton, lived there from 1662 until his death in 1675. It was here that he wrote *Paradise Lost, Paradise Regained.* A scan of maps and historical documents will show that Bunhill Row had changed from the farmland of Elizabethan times to the craftsmen, manufacturers and business traders of the eighteenth, nineteenth and early twentieth centuries. Many of the guilds and livery companies of the City Corporation had representatives here at various times, including: dyers, clock and watchmakers, goldsmith and jewellers, curriers and leather cutters, solicitors, bricklayers, tallow chandlers, playing card manufacturers, stationers. In 1894, the year that Northampton Institute was founded, the site on which part of the School now stands was a timber yard, a joinery factory and a cooperage. By 1965 the University's Northampton Hall occupied a large part of the site, and a few years later the City and Islington College of Further Education was built to the north of the Hall – it is actually on this very site that Cass now stands.

In 1834 a new business partnership (De La Rue, James and Rudd) moved into Bunhill Row and occupied the stretch of road adjacent to Lambs Passage and the Cass building. They were listed as 'Cardmakers, Embosses and Wholesale Fancy Stationers'. By 1835 Thomas De La Rue was the sole owner, and it was here that he founded his house and dynasty, and built up the fortunes of De La Rue & Company. Bunhill Row became a distinguished part of London with De La Rue on the west side and the headquarters of the Honourable Artillery Company (oldest Regiment in the British Army) and the historic burial grounds of Bunhill Fields on the East side. Bunhill Fields is now a tourist attraction to those who want to visit the tombs of John Bunyan who wrote *Pilgrim's Progress*, Daniel Defoe who wrote *Robinson Crusoe*, Thomas Bayes who created *Bayes' Theorem*, and William Blake who wrote *Jerusalem.* Opposite one of the entrances to Bunhill Fields is the statue of John Wesley on horseback commemorating where he lived, preached and is buried. The imposing building of De La Rue was destroyed by the blitz in 1940/41, as were most of the buildings in Bunhill Row. The Artillery Arms on the corner of Bunhill Row and Dufferin Street is one of the few buildings to retain its original purpose – drinking, socialising, scheming!

Although the De La Rue Company relocated to the west of London after the War, its symbolic significance to the School is threefold. First, Thomas De La Rue was a very successful entrepreneur and businessman. He was innovative in the design and production of playing cards, a product that brought a fortune to his stationery business. Apart from inventing the modern English playing card, he is also accredited as being the father of the English visiting card. During the nineteenth century the firm continued to be innovative and timely in the printing of stamps; we are told that before a president or king was cold in his coffin, the company was ready to initiate a correspondence for the successor's new stamps. A major breakthrough came when the company was invited to print the first banknotes for one of the colonies – Mauritius. This was a new product for them. They built a major clientele on the back of this one opportunity, and subsequently catered for the needs of many countries and indeed the Bank of England.

Second, a series of coincidences link the School with De La Rue personnel. For several years Jack Davies, a former director of the Bank of England, was a director of the De La Rue Company. At the same time he was on the Councils of the University and the School, and held the position of Deputy Pro-Chancellor of the University. A further coincidence was when Brandon Gough (a former senior partner of Coopers & Lybrand) became Chairman of De La Rue. Sir Brandon Gough (as he now is) was on the School's Council for several years, and was Chairman for part of this time. Until recently he retained a link through his membership of the School's International Board of Advisors.

Third, a justification for straying into the De La Rue story is an email correspondence the author had with former Dean Leslie Hannah. He pointed out 'it did strike me that the fact the School was training the world's financial services experts, and that in an earlier age when physical capital was more important than intellectual capital, the same site had also provided the world's banknotes, did have a certain poetic ring to it!'

The entrepreneurial spirit of Thomas De La Rue has been amply reproduced in the School's own history to date, through many of its educational activities and through its alumni such as Stelios Haji-Ioannou of EasyJet fame. The entrepreneurial and business skills shown by the De La Rue family over a century and a half ago are what successive governments have been trying to encourage through the development of a more effective partnership between business and higher education (Lambert 2002), and on which the School is delivering. It is apposite that one of the first Government Ministers to visit the School in its new premises was Patricia Hewitt, the Secretary of State for Trade and Industry. She came to officially launch SIMFONEC (Science Ideas to Market Focussed on Enterprise and Commercialisation) in March 2003. This centre is a partnership of four London universities/colleges aiming to increase the level of entrepreneurship coming out of universities.

One result of this collaboration is an MSc in Science Entrepreneurship, designed to teach students to recognise, finance and market their scientific ideas. The School's Centre for New Technologies, Innovation and Entrepreneurship (CENTIVE), launched in June 2004, is further evidence of this entrepreneurial spirit. Through both these centres the School creates learning and research opportunities for stimulating successful entrepreneurship.

Further links with the City will be elaborated upon in the following chapters. One of the most interesting themes in the School's story is its developing relationship with City institutions and businesses. The mix of factors that facilitated and delayed the maturing of this relationship lies at the heart of this story. The methods used in researching the School's history are aimed at unravelling this mix of factors. The important point to make at this juncture is that the City is on the doorstep of the School, and the School is on the doorstep of the City. The School's perception of this has occasionally been blurred. It is worth quoting what Michael Cassidy (an alumni of the MBA programme and former Chairman of the Corporation's Policy and Resources Committee) said in the University's Centenary Magazine in 1994:

> The City is like a big village and you can virtually guarantee that walking down the street you will meet somebody and that's how ideas start. City University is part of that village and many of the students tend to be drawn from businesses active in the area. That is why the University's location is so important because the companies in the City feel comfortable to send their bright young people to study somewhere close and somewhere that they know.

The village idea fits in well with the current Dean Lord Currie's aspiration for the School – to be the intellectual hub of the City of London.

Comparable histories of business schools

Several histories of universities (Teague 1980; Dahrendorf 1995; Pullan and Abendstern 2000) and business schools (Barnes 1989; Wilson 1992; Servan-Schreiber 1994; Barsoux 2000) have been published. Each of these histories reflects the orientation of their authors. Thus Dahrendorf's account of London School of Economics (LSE) is that of a social scientist, Barsoux's INSEAD study is that of an international business academic, Wilson's book on Manchester Business School is that of an economic historian.

The two case histories that are most relevant to the present one are those of LBS and Manchester Business School. But apart from similar environmental events relating to management education in the United Kingdom in the 1960s, their histories are quite different. Both the London and Manchester Schools were the products of the Franks' Report (Franks 1963), and as such started life with significant financial help from industry and government. They were in the privileged situation of having a large degree of freedom in planning their development, recruiting the 'right' professorial staff for implementing the plan, and thereby creating an appropriate 'culture'. Within a few years they were also able to occupy purpose-built premises.

The LBS history covers the period 1964–89, and the Manchester Business School history 1965–90. These histories go into some detail into the background to management education and the immediate events leading up to their establishment. They both give an account of the developments that took place in their respective institutions, and the main individuals and events that influenced their development. Wilson (a lecturer in economic history at Manchester at that time) framed the MBS story as an experiment (his title was 'The Manchester Experiment: a history of MBS'), partly because the university was embarking on something different but also because they were innovative in their approach to management education (i.e. emphasising the benefits of action learning or project-based learning) and academic structure (i.e. a democratic, non-departmental structure loosely co-ordinated at the top). Barnes (formerly a Civil Servant and Secretary of LBS), was less concerned with teaching approaches and organisational structure and more concerned in discussing the potential impact of LBS on management (his title was 'Managerial Catalyst: the story of LBS').

Aims of present case history. The author had two primary aims in researching the history of Cass Business School. The first was to help current and future stakeholders understand how the institution that they identify with, help and benefit from, developed from the efforts of others. The second was to extract knowledge from the developments identified, and to share this knowledge, with those who are involved in leading similar institutions in a highly competitive world. The fulfilment of both aims proved more challenging than anticipated: the former because of the need to be selective in dealing with a mass of data; the latter because of the wide choice of frameworks available for interpreting and reporting findings. Readers will judge for themselves the extent to which these challenges have been met.

Methodology. The present study has some affinities to the London and Manchester studies, and an important difference – more attention is paid to methodology in this study. Reporting the 'facts of history' is coloured by the interpretations of the researcher. This is even more likely to happen where the researcher is an 'actor' in the unfolding events being recounted. Moreover, the memories of the other 'actors' who helped to create those 'facts' are subject to various distortions. This means that obtaining corroborative evidence is needed where critical events or individual achievements are concerned. It is therefore important for the author to share with his readership those theoretical frameworks that have influenced data collection and interpretations. Readers will then be in a better position to judge the soundness of the conclusions drawn and the generalisations made. A discussion of methodology is found in Appendix 1.

Contents. This introductory chapter in Part I has tried to set the scene by contrasting the present standing of Cass Business School with its humble beginnings in 1966, and by indicating the School's major changing structures under successive Deans. At the same time historical and current links with the City of London have been touched upon in order to emphasise the uniqueness of the School. The twin aims listed provide the rationale for the rest of the book. Part II is the core of the book. It follows a chronological profile in the development of Cass. Critical events, structures and personnel are identified and appropriate comments made. The material breaks down into five chapters, named after their characteristic theme: The awakening spirit of management education, 1957–66; Pioneers in management education, 1966–82; Strengthening the City of London orientation, 1982–92; Towards a business-like business school, 1992–97; Premises to match world-class aspirations, 1997–2005. A quick overview of the milestones in this unfolding history will be found in Appendix 2.

Part III adopts an analytical rather than chronological approach. The contextual factors that impinged on the School are brought together in Chapter 7. The next five chapters are devoted to the different strategies followed by the School. These are presented under the headings: the evolution of a mission and vision; growth through innovation and expansion; differentiation and orientation; development of a quality culture; premises: the meandering pathway to a state-of-the-art building. Chapter 13 in Part III is devoted to exploring the effects of these strategies in terms of quantitative trends and external assessments stretching from 1966 to 2005. These include: degrees offered; number of students awarded each of these degrees; current alumni profile; number of professors in post at the end of each Deanship (differentiating between external and internal appointments); external assessments (e.g. the Quality Assessment Agency and the Research Assessment Exercise of the Higher Education Funding Council) and media rankings (e.g. *FT* top 100 business schools worldwide).

Part IV examines the Cass story in terms of leadership. Chapter 14 develops an open systems framework for exploring leadership, with emphasis on those organisational elements that have strategic significance. Chapter 15 explores the drivers and constrainers of change, recognising the differential leadership roles of academics and Deans and the influence of culture. A number of concepts already prominent in the management literature are used in developing the theme of strategic leadership, including: School/Environmental fit, mental models, and power.

Part II

A Chronological Profile of Changes and Critical Events

2
The Awakening Spirit of Management Education: 1957–66

The City University was granted its Charter in 1966. It was founded in 1894 as Northampton Institute, the site between St. John Street and Northampton Square being gifted by the then Marquess of Northampton. The other founding benefactors were the City Parochial Foundation, and the Skinners' and Saddlers' Livery Companies. In 1900 it was re-named Northampton Engineering College to reflect its orientation. By 1924 the college was called the Northampton Polytechnic Institute. In 1957 it was one of the polytechnics given the status of a College of Advanced Technology, thus recognising the academic qualities it had developed over the years. Until this time, management and business played little part in the curricula of the courses on offer. Only a minor element was taught by the Production Engineering Department to satisfy the requirements of one of the professional engineering institutions.

The vision of Dr James Tait and others

Dr James Tait was appointed the first Principal in 1957 of the Northampton College of Advanced Technology (Northampton CAT). He had previously been Principal of Woolwich Polytechnic (now University of the South Bank), and before that he had been Head of the Electrical Engineering Department at Northampton Polytechnic. As a result of an instruction at this time from the National Council for Technological Awards, the College had to initiate courses in liberal studies and the principles of industrial administration and include them in its recognised qualifications. Tait recruited Alvin Leyton to head this venture in 1957. In March 1961 Tait informed the Governing Body of the College that, after discussions with the Ministry of Education and the London

County Council (LCC), a request had been sent to the Education Officer of the LCC to establish a Department of Social and Industrial Studies from September 1961. At the May meeting of the Governing Body it was reported that approval had been received, and that the go ahead for a staff establishment of a head and 14 academics had been approved. An application had also been made to the Ministry of Education for approval to run a course for the Diploma in Management Studies.

The following extract from the May 1961 meeting of the Governing Body is well worth quoting:

> Sir Walter Puckey (the representative of the London County Council) said he thought it most important that the duties of the new Department should be clearly defined and that the study of management should not necessarily be as an appendage to a Department of Social & Industrial Studies. The importance of management as a subject of scientific study and research was now universally accepted and a national body had been set up to launch students for this and other postgraduate qualifications. He thought it desirable to include the word 'management' in the title of the department dealing with the subject. Dr. Tait replied that the word 'management' had been avoided in the title of the new department because of the inferior courses labelled 'management' which had been given in various institutions up and down the country. It was the intention at the Northampton to develop management studies to the highest level and it was for this reason that the recent increase in establishment of upper grade appointments had been approved. It was essential to conduct research in this field and he hoped a number of research students would be employed in the department. In Circular 1/90 the Minister (of Education) expressed the opinion that post-graduate courses of the type envisaged should be concentrated in the CATs and a small number of other colleges so that an appropriate full-time staff, well qualified in the economic, physical and social services and able to conduct research and consultancy work, could be recruited.

Leyton was appointed to head the new Department of Social and Industrial Studies – in competition with five external applicants. He was a South African and a qualified lawyer who had practised at the South African Bar. Prior to coming to the College in 1957, to be Reader in Communication and Organiser of Liberal Studies, he had held managerial posts in the area of training and executive development. He was a member of the British Institute of Management and was greatly in demand as a speaker on communications to management audiences. When making this appointment the Governing Body also resolved 'That an Advisory Committee be formed to give consideration to all matters relating to Management and Liberal Studies in the college, and that the Principal (Tait) and Chairman (Oliver Thompson) in consultation with Sir Walter Puckey invite appropriate persons to serve on this Advisory Committee.'

In January 1962 the first meeting of this Advisory Committee met. The members were: Sir Walter Puckey (Chairman), Mr Pearson, Dr D. Bramley (formerly of the Urwick Management Centre and subsequently with the firm of George Salter & Co, West Bromwich), John Marsh (Director of the British Institute of Management), A. Richards (Managing Director of Universal Matthey Products). Tait, Leyton and the College Secretary also attended. It was agreed that the future market for postgraduate management students was substantial, and this meant the need to recruit staff mostly at senior levels and to draw on part-time experts in the field. 'The main development in the Department should be in the field of Management, although it was realised that this would include a study of the human sciences, such as Politics, Economics, Sociology, Philosophy and Psychology. The committee therefore advised that specialisation in Management Studies should be accepted as the objective in the future development of the Department, whose work throughout should be coloured by this objective, with the aim of establishing a Postgraduate School of Management Studies of the highest standard. It was decided to recommend that the title of the Department should reflect this objective more closely than the one at present in use.' The title of Department of Management and Social Sciences was subsequently agreed and implemented.

In connection with Sir Walter Puckey it is worth mentioning that he, along with Professor Alec Rodger (who was incidentally the author's PhD supervisor at Birkbeck), Edward Brech (remarkably still active as a Senior Visiting Fellow at Cass) and others, had formed the groundbreaking company Management Selection Limited (MSL) in the 1950s. The significance of MSL was that it was the first management consultancy in the United Kingdom to apply a scientific approach to the selection of managers (based on the pioneering work of Alec Rodger *et al.* at the National Institute of Industrial Psychology and at the Admiralty). Puckey's experience in helping organisations select managers had made him well aware of the need to raise the standards of management in the United Kingdom, hence his enthusiasm in promoting management at Northampton CAT.

The first senior appointment made to the newly named department was a Reader in Industrial Sociology – Ronald Stansfield. He was a Cambridge graduate in physics who had been employed as a researcher in physics and in operations research before moving into the Department of Scientific and Industrial Research to head different units concerned with the human sciences in industry. The external advisor to the interviewing panel was the sociologist Professor D.G. MacRae of LSE. However, Stansfield made no contribution to management education; while a candidate who was not appointed subsequently contributed to management teaching at the College as a Consultant Lecturer. The fact that Rosemary Stewart was not appointed to the full-time post is surprising given her relevant research and experience as a director of the Acton Trust, and her later distinguished contribution to the management literature as an academic at the Oxford Centre for Management Studies, Templeton College (Stewart 1967, 1970).

In the development of management education, Leyton had the strong support of Tait and also of David Manning (a member of the Production Engineering Department) whose Army career had introduced him to the practical aspects of management. In 1963 two post-graduate diploma courses in management were launched – the 30-week-long College's Diploma in Industrial Administration and Business Systems, and a 26-week course leading to the award of the Ministry of Education and British Institute of Management's Diploma in Management Studies. In September 1963 David Manning moved into the department, and at the same time Douglas Vaughan (an Industrial Economist) and the author (an Industrial/Occupational Psychologist) were recruited. Vaughan was recruited to direct the Diploma in Management Studies.

It is relevant to point out that up to that time the City and its financial institutions had little influence in the development of management in the College. A potential breakthrough came when in June 1963 Sir Michael Turner, formerly Chairman of the Hong Kong & Shanghai Banking Corporation, joined the College's Governing Body. In 1966 he was appointed to various influential positions – Deputy Pro-Chancellor and Vice Chairman of Council and other committees (e.g. Finance and General Purposes Committee) that were formed as the College transferred to university status.

Over the next two years (i.e. 1964 and 1965) the department initiated plans and recruited staff for two new postgraduate degrees in anticipation of university status: an MSc in Administrative Sciences and a Diploma/MSc in Information Science. The core multidisciplinary team for management studies now consisted of David Manning (production management), Douglas Vaughan (managerial economics); Peter Grinyer (operations research), Jock Scholefield (general management); Oliver Vesey-Holt (marketing); Sidney Kessler (industrial relations); John Lewis (accountancy); and the author (occupational psychology). During this period the Diploma in Industrial Administration and Business Systems was terminated and its leader, Dick Prescott, resigned to take up a lecturing appointment elsewhere. A further individual (Bob Green) who had moved with Manning from Production tragically died soon after his transfer.

While the management team prepared proposals for an MSc in Administrative Sciences, the social science team (as the lead psychologist at the College the author was a member of both teams) worked on proposals for a BSc in Social Sciences. The pioneering management team were committed to develop management as a separate structure within the college/university, recognising the need for independence from the more basic disciplines so as to be closer to the management market. This aspiration was supported by those guiding Northampton CAT to university status. A significant boost to this aspiration was obtained when the Corporation's Court of Common Council approved a motion in June 1965 that 'In connection with the new City University, the Corporation would welcome the establishment of a Faculty of Business Management and a Hostel for Students within the boundaries of the City of London, and that it be referred to the Special Committee and the Barbican Committee in consultation with the Governors of the Northampton College of Advanced Technology, to examine and to report thereon.'

3
Pioneers in Management Education: 1966–82

Kenneth Shone's Headship

A memorandum from Tate dated 19 April 1966 informed staff that following a decision of the Governing Body (re-named Council on achieving university status) to divide the Department of Management and Social Science, the Academic Board (re-named Senate) approved the suggestion that the department should run in two sections pending the appointment of new Heads of Department – Social Science and Humanities to be led by Ron Stansfield (Reader in Charge) and Management Studies by David Manning (Senior Lecturer in charge). By the time the inaugural ceremonies of the City University were celebrated in October 1966 the Department of Management and Social Science had split into two departments. In those days university departments were expected to be headed by someone of professorial standing. Other departments in the new university were well established, and there was no problem in appointing an internal candidate to the headship and a chair at the same time. The new department of Social Science and Humanities had to wait for an external appointment to be made. This was done in September 1967 when the distinguished educationalist and humanitarian, Sir Robert Birley, took up the reins (Leyton had retired in 1966 as a result of ill-health). In November 1966 Kenneth Shone was recruited from outside to be the first professor to head the new Department of Management Studies. He had been Visiting Professor at the School of Management of Bath University and at the Carnegie Mellon Graduate School of Industrial Administration in the United States. Prior to these honorary appointments he had had experience in manufacturing industry, been a head of department at Strathclyde and been on secondment to the United Nations.

Although 'management studies' was given a firm base in 1963, it was in 1966 that the management department was formally created. This makes 1966 the appropriate year for locating the birth of Cass Business School at City University. The preceding years of 1957–66 represent the period of gestation. The divergence in interest between management and social studies was symbolically emphasised in 1964 by the former being located five minutes down St. John Street in Wigton House (before re-development it was adjacent to Walmsley House and Paramount Building), and the latter in the main building. This temporary accommodation was in fact a converted warehouse – a source of 'amusement' to the students attending the part-time Diploma in Management Studies (they could not resist telling their fellow managers at work that they were being taught in a converted warehouse!)

As part of the new structure the powers that be also decided that information science should be part of management rather than social science. An evening part-time diploma in the subject had been introduced in 1961 to meet the growing need in organisations and their information services for expertise in collecting and communicating scientific information. A four-year DSIR grant to Leyton enabled Jason Farradane (up to that time a part-time lecturer) to be appointed as a Senior Research Fellow for Information Science in September 1963 to develop new methods of information retrieval and to test their efficiency. A subsequent Office for Scientific and Technical Information grant in 1966 was awarded to Farradane for 'a psychological investigation of logical jumps made in the expression of information'. An MSc in Information Science was introduced in 1967, the first such qualification in a UK university. The continuing success of this area, both in terms of research and numbers of students, led to the formation of an independent centre in information science in 1970 with Farradane as its first director. In the same year he retired and the centre became a fully fledged department of the University. This aspect of the history is worth mentioning because it was a success story even though it was regarded as a peripheral activity by many and consequently played little part in the development of the Business School. However the first PhDs were in this area, as were the first research grants. Indeed, the first student to be awarded a PhD (Mrs S. Datta in 1968/69) was in this area, and was probably the first doctorate in information science in a UK university.

Gresham College premises in Basinghall Street

There were multiple forces at work to bring about a 'business school' in the City University that would serve the City of London. In 1963 both the Robbins' Report and the Franks' Report drew attention to the lack of business schools in the United Kingdom (Franks 1963; Robbins 1963). The Franks' Report resulted in the setting up of two prestigious business schools – (LBS) and Manchester Business School (MBS). However, by revealing the need for better management education to strengthen Britain's competitiveness, these reports stimulated the new and the old universities to launch their own schools. This message was reinforced by a report from the National Economic Development Council (NEDC 1963). The Robbins' Report had certainly influenced the thinking of the academics who subsequently formed the Department of Management Studies, and no doubt influenced the thinking of the University's Academic Advisory Committee. Both groups recognised the importance of being closely linked to the City, and this led to a search for premises in the City of London itself. This search was reinforced by the Corporation agreeing that the new university should be named 'The City University', and that each Lord Mayor was to become the Chancellor of the University. The search was successful in the 1966/67 session when, with the help of the Worshipful Company of Mercers and the City Corporation, it became possible to rent the hall and two floors of Gresham College in Basinghall Street. A foothold adjacent to the Guildhall, and within a stone's throw of the Bank of England, was a real marketing asset.

It is worth digressing for a moment to give some background to Gresham College (Chartres and Vermont 1998). The origins go back to 1575 and the Will of Sir Thomas Gresham. Although best known in academic circles for Gresham's Law 'bad money tends to drive out good', and for his hand in the development of the Royal Exchange, his travels to Antwerp and other trading cities on the continent had made him aware of the educational backwardness of the City of London. He was a Mercer and son of a Lord Mayor, and a successful entrepreneur to three sovereigns in fulfilling his duties 'to negotiate loans for the crown with wealthy merchants of Germany and the Netherlands and to supply the State with any foreign products that were required – and to keep the Privy Council informed of all matters of importance passing abroad'. His Will envisaged a college in the City, and he left part of the revenues of the Royal Exchange property in trust to the Lord Mayor and Corporation and to the Mercers' Company for the purpose of establishing and supporting Gresham College. It was intended that the college would have seven professors – four to be nominated by the Corporation (those in Divinity, Astronomy, Geometry and Music), and three by the Mercers' Company (Law, Physic and Rhetoric). The history of Gresham

College has been a mixture of good (it was the forerunner of the Royal Society), bad (some of the early professors abused their privileges for their own ends rather than for the benefit of the citizens of London), and indifferent (the trustees were not always vigilant in ensuring that the spirit of the Will of its founder was preserved). Gresham's imposing mansion in Bishopsgate (the site now occupied by the NatWest Tower) was the college's first location. The Great Fire of 1666 destroyed the Royal Exchange, and pressure was put on the Gresham Committee to develop the site in Bishopgate so as to help finance the re-building of the Royal Exchange. It was not until 1768 that the Gresham College Bill went through parliament and destroyed the physical presence of Gresham College. The Gresham professors continued to deliver their lectures. In one such lecture that was given by the Professor of Music in the City of London School in 1838, Edward Taylor decried the 'ruthless barbarism' of the 1768 Act. The agitation he aroused ensured that the rebuilding of the third Royal Exchange (a fire had destroyed the expensively built second building) was accompanied by a tailor-made building for Gresham College in 1842. It is this building at the corner of Gresham Street and Basinghall Street that was occupied by the Graduate Business Centre (GBC) in 1967.

During the period 1965/66 Tait saw an opportunity of developing a closer link with the City by developing a formal alliance with Gresham College. Becoming the 'parent body' of the college had advantages to the new University (e.g. historical links, additional income) and to Gresham College (e.g. the professorial lectures would be well attended since the audience would consist of University students plus members of the general public). The arrangements forged by Tait had mixed success, and the close link was terminated in 1987, although the University's Vice-Chancellor was to remain a member of the College Council. Even though the School occupied part of the Gresham College building, it was not directly involved in these arrangements since the nature of its activities were not compatible with the core goals of the College – educating all in the City of London including the unqualified. The academic links were with the University's departments of Arts Administration and Continuing Education which were more in keeping with the Will of Sir Thomas Gresham. Prior to this decision it is not surprising to learn that the faculty of the School did seriously explore the possibility of the School becoming the new Gresham College and thereby inheriting a history to rival Oxbridge!

Professor Shone, and the staff most closely associated with the MSc in Administrative Sciences, were re-located in Gresham College. Office space was at a premium, as evidenced by three lecturers (i.e. Kessler, Lewis and the author) sharing an office of about 15 by 15 feet; but the superior furnishings and location made a welcome change from the factory-like setting of Wigton House! The postgraduate nature of the activities at Gresham College was emphasised when the name 'Graduate Business Centre' was introduced in the 1966–67 session, although in terms of the formal structure of the University the School was still the Department of Management Studies.

MSc in Administrative Sciences

> A press release distributed on 1 August 1966 included the following: Some Management courses aim to train managing directors of the future in the skills of general management. The City University Department of Management believes that such courses are valuable. However, having analysed the role appropriate to a technological university serving the City of London and the London area, they have adopted a different approach ... A graduate who aspires to reach a senior post in general management must first prove himself as a departmental manager. At this initial stage, therefore, he needs a thorough grounding in his special field of management development in such a way that it is always seen in relation to the rest of the business and not as an end in itself. To achieve this, students on the City University full-time Master of Science programme will specialise in one of four areas of management ...

The label MSc in Administrative Sciences conformed to nomenclature of the day, but was in fact indistinguishable from an MBA in terms of content and methods of teaching. Indeed it changed to an MBA 12 years later along with most competitors in the national and international markets. The design of the degree reflected what the core team felt should be included in a degree for those students who would be entering a managerial role on graduation. The main differences between this degree and the MScs at LBS and MBS were twofold: it broke away from the American pattern by being a one year (i.e. 12 months) as opposed to a two year (i.e. 18 months) degree; and it was designed to allow for functional specialisation. The assumptions being made were that the curriculum could be covered in a shorter time than previously thought, and that since employers were more likely to recruit graduates to fill functional managerial roles rather than general managerial roles, encouraging specialisation would make them more immediately useful and acceptable to employers.

The first cohort of ten students registered on the MSc in October 1966; this number was quickly exceeded in subsequent years. Students had the choice of specialising in one of four areas: Industrial Engineering and Operational Research Techniques (with majors in industrial engineering and production, statistical and mathematical techniques of operational research), Managerial Economics (with majors in managerial accountancy and financial control, managerial economics, statistical and operational research in managerial economics), Industrial Marketing (with majors in industrial marketing, international economics and comparative law, language studies), Industrial Relations and Personnel Policy (industrial relations, personnel management, occupational psychology). In addition to their specialist areas or majors, students were required to take four supporting subsidiary courses (an appreciation rather than an in-depth study of the areas not covered in their majors but nevertheless contributing to the total business system), and a course in Integrating Studies consisting mainly of case studies and business games. This latter course was very much the general management 'plenary element' that brought all the students together to integrate their specialist knowledge in tackling managerial-type problems. The design of the MSc was sufficiently flexible so that part-time students could complete it over two years. It was also possible for individuals with appropriate qualifications and experience (e.g. a first degree in economics) to attend courses as part of their company's management development programme without obtaining a degree. This latter option was rarely taken up by companies, probably because it was not encouraged by lecturers who found it difficult to integrate these 'occasional' students into relatively cohesive student groups.

Shaping the culture

Schein's observations of the influence of the founding fathers on organisational culture is reflected in the history of the school – particularly the first 15 years (Schein 1992). When the Management and Social Sciences Department split into two sections on 25 April 1966 there were nine full time academics involved in designing the MSc in Administrative Sciences, and only one had completed a PhD. All had relevant degrees and, more significantly, all had practitioner experience in the area in which they provided academic leadership. Thus David Manning was a chartered engineer, a Fellow of the Institute of Production Engineers, and had been awarded an OBE for his achievements in the industrial-based departments of the Ministry of Supply.

Oliver Vesey-Holt had been with the National Coal Board in the marketing and finance departments, and had been Personal Assistant to the Deputy Chairman before taking up a lecturing appointment at the Polytechnic, Regent Street. Douglas Vaughan had been in several government departments (including HM Treasury) where he was concerned with organisational and planning problems, general administration and economic research. Peter Grinyer had had experience as a buyer for the United Africa Company and had managed the production planning and stock control in another company, before lecturing at Hendon College of Technology. Before his academic posts Kenneth Shone had worked as an industrial engineer in Proctor and Gamble and in management development in British Steel and Reed Paper. Sidney Kessler had been Head of the Economic Research Department of the National Union of Mineworkers. After graduating in economics, John Lewis served articles with a firm of chartered accountants and gained practical experience in industry, and then went on to lecture at the Wolverhampton and Staffordshire College of Technology. Jock Scholefield had begun his career as a development chemist before becoming production manager and general manager in his family firm. After studying and researching in occupational psychology the author worked as a psychologist and research head at Marplan – the research arm of the American advertising agency McCann Erickson.

Given the size and composition of this initial team, and the new challenge of tackling management studies as an academic discipline at Masters level, it is not surprising that: (1) the team was very cohesive and supportive, (2) the structure of the innovative degree reflected the interests and expertise of the faculty, (3) a teaching orientation, linked to a strong concern to meet student needs, dominated the activities of the team. Research tended to be treated as a luxury to accompany academic life – encouraged to do but not disadvantaged for not doing.

One of the problems created by this situation emerged with the appointment of Kenneth Shone as Head of Department. He joined a highly motivated team, several of whom had made financial sacrifices to be there because of their strong belief in management education and the need for it to be based on a sound academic footing. While he was academically acceptable, Shone's managerial and negotiating skills did not meet the high standards that staff expected from their representative in the University and the external world. He tried but failed to be accepted as an 'insider'. It took a confrontation with a delegation of staff before he decided to resign the Headship and to continue his professorship. This whole episode was diplomatically smoothed over by Tait – Shone took a period of secondment to the United Nations, and on his return the department was restructured and the name of GBC was introduced. In those days Heads were appointed until retirement, and it was almost impossible for Vice-Chancellors to remove their Headships.

The short courses that the School ran during the years 1965–67 were mainly law related. This may have been due to the fact that Alvin Leyton was a qualified lawyer and that he had appointed the energetic Peter Ford as a part-time lecturer to meet this market need. Thus we find that during this period five of the six short courses were related to law – 'Patent law and administration', 'Introduction to American business law', 'Copyright law and administration', 'Law of copyright and registered designs', 'Trade mark law and administration'. The sixth course was a series of seminars for senior production executives led by Peter Grinyer, who at that time was Lecturer in Industrial Engineering. That these executives should be the target for the first management oriented short course of the School is no surprise given the composition of the 'pioneering team'. The seminars were run at monthly intervals and a paper, giving a comprehensive treatment of a subject that potential participants had themselves suggested, was circulated beforehand. Seminars were held from 18.30 to 20.30 in the Senior Common Room (i.e. the 'library') of the GBC. The programme for the third series of seminars is reproduced in Box 3.1.

Vision of the School at November 1966

A paper discussed at the Board of Studies attempted to set a programme for a City business school that would take on a new name (i.e. the GBC)

Box 3.1 Seminars for senior production executives (18 October 1967–20 March 1968).

'The effective use of management science as an aid to innovation'
K.J. Shone, MA, C.Eng, MIMarE, MEIC
'Productivity bargaining'
S. Kessler, BSc (Econ)
'Strategic and tactical planning'
D.E. Manning, OBE, BSc, CEng, MIProdE
'Contributions of managerial economics to productivity'
G.D. Vaughan, BSc (Econ)
'Management by objectives'
A.J.B. Scholefield, MA, BSc
'Appraisal and promotion of middle managers'
A.P.O. Williams, BA, MA, PhD

in order to differentiate it from other business schools. It was recognised that the character of the School would be dictated by its objectives, the special position it had as a department of a university noted for technology, and the geographic and professional influence that the City would have on it.

The proposal was to expand the current set-up because 'current management studies are based on eight years' experience at Northampton College and a substantial Department of Management Studies is already in existence.' A significant growth rate over the next five years was envisaged. 'We aim to ensure fall-out of City expertise and knowledge for the benefit of technological studies, also fall-out from technology to benefit City institutions.' At this time the School, and colleagues in the rest of the University, saw the GBC as forming a bridge between financial institutions and manufacturing industry, a bridge that would facilitate a mutual understanding to the benefit of the British economy. It is important to realise that for many years the School remained responsible for the teaching of management to most of the University's undergraduate degrees in engineering. In the light of future developments it is worth noting that an additional area identified for growth through new appointments was Actuarial Science and Insurance. The main objective of the paper was to persuade the University to support a strategy for growth, and to provide the necessary resources for this to be realised.

In May 1968 Kenneth Shone made a presentation to the University Council. He pointed out that when he joined in 1966 the only impact the department was making was via the undergraduate programmes for the engineering departments. It was therefore no surprise that up to that time we were ignored by the Foundation for Management Education (unlike LBS, MBS, Warwick and a few others). However, the MSc programmes (in Administrative Sciences and in Information Technology) had persuaded the University that the ambitions of developing a foothold within the boundaries of the City were worth supporting. The result was Senate's recommendation in June 1967 that a GBC should be set-up, and based at Gresham College in Basinghall Street. He showed that the current year of 1967/68 had seen an increase of postgraduate students from 17 to 75, and that the arrival of Sir Robert Shone and two grant-assisted appointments had enabled an expansion of the post-experience courses and the introduction of an additional specialisation on the MSc in Administrative Sciences – investment analysis and portfolio management. Moreover, in April 1968 the Centre had been offered finance for an Esmee Fairbairn Chair/Readership in Investment and Finance.

Looking to the future it was envisaged that postgraduate and post-experience courses would expand, the servicing of undergraduate courses in the University would remain stable, and that significant developments would be needed in the administrative structures and premises of the Centre. Limited space in Gresham College meant that some activities would still have to be undertaken in Wigton House. This meant that separate administrative support would have to be arranged for undergraduate, postgraduate and post-experience activities. Also it was clear that UGC expected post-experience courses to be self-financing, and that a pricing policy and customer service would have to be put into operation that would be completely new to the University. In order to build a scenario whereby more than a tiny element of the University's work was of direct relevance to the City, and in order to take advantage of the explosive development of management studies likely to accompany the operation of the Industrial Training Boards from 1969/70, it was imperative to direct more resources to the Centre. It was pointed out that in 1968 the Centre would present two-thirds of the University's students for higher degrees, and one-seventh of all degrees. In doing so it would use only 3 per cent of the University's floor area and 6 per cent of all academic staff. Fortunately, the UGC had indicated that they would allocate an additional amount for management studies from 1969. Such facts are relevant to the story of the School since they draw attention to an inherent conflict between the ambitious aspirations of the School and the tight resources and dominant culture of the University.

The rise of Finance

One important event that Kenneth Shone facilitated was to introduce his prestigious brother, Sir Robert Shone, to the School. Sir Robert was the first Director General of the NEDC, a Fellow of Nuffield College Oxford, and director of a number of companies. He was made Visiting Professor of Applied Economics as from 1 May 1967 – the first such appointment in the history of the School. Sir Robert's presence cannot be over-estimated because he played a key role in initiating products of direct interest to financiers in the City by launching a series of five seminars on the economics of investment. In April 1967 it was announced that the Esmee Fairbairn Charitable Trust would finance a Research Fellow to work under his supervision on 'Problems of investment and taxation'. Additional research money was obtained from the British Iron and Steel Federation to employ a research assistant to work under him on pricing policy. The significance of the Fellowship was that it enabled the GBC to make its first full-time appointment of someone who had actually worked in the City. Basil Taylor came in July 1967 on leaving his post as Deputy Investment Manager with the Midland Bank (his manager at Midland's was Harold Rose who moved to a Chair at LBS).

By 1967/68 session the GBC had six informal groupings of staff: the new 'Finance and Investment' group; 'Applied Economics'; 'General Management'; 'Industrial Engineering and Operational Research'; 'Industrial Relations and Personnel Management'; 'Marketing'. The number of full-time academic staff had now expanded to 13; in addition there were 3 (part-time) consultant lecturers and 4 research students who did a limited amount of teaching (3 of whom were former students of the department). One of the consultant lecturers contributing to the Integrating Studies course on the MSc was David Glen – a future Dean.

1968 Developmental Appeal

Lord Poole (Chairman of Lazard Brothers) was the Chairman of a distinguished Fund Raising Campaign Committee to help the University complete its development programme. One of the main projects for the Appeal was for a new building for the GBC in the Minories (by the Tower of London). It is worth quoting extracts from the briefing document prepared by the School for Lord Poole – it conveys the perceived ambition and mission at that time:

> The exciting proposals for development on the Minories site offer a unique opportunity such as only occurs when from time to time people and circumstances combine to produce educational institutions of special importance. In the field of education the French Grandes Ecoles, the German Technical High Schools and the American Business Schools are examples. The unique feature of their foundation was that they were unconventional responses to clearly identifiable needs, not then adequately catered for within the existing educational system. The Grandes Ecoles arose from the belief that practical matters should be studied scientifically, the Technical High Schools from the refusal of the traditional universities to accept engineering as a discipline, and the US Business Schools from the reluctance of existing faculties to study business problems. The association of the City of London with a technological university, offers the opportunity to found a centre which could make a similar impact on management education in this country.
>
> The present technological era and the changing place of the UK in world affairs demands a professional approach to business management in general, and in particular to harnessing the latest technological

> developments to the utilisation of the nation's resources. The new managers will need to be financially skilled, trained in the art of management and capable of exploiting the innovations of science and technology in industry and business for the advancement of the economy as a whole. These developments are of particular importance to meet the challenge of further penetration of the markets of the world. To achieve such an end there must be a close association of proved practical achievement with valid theoretical study. The new University working in conjunction with the practising business and industrial experts of the City of London would be in a unique position to achieve this synthesis.
>
> ... The conjunction of a technological university and the City of London provides the opportunity to develop a centre which will be different in character from any elsewhere in the country. The City is concerned with finance and commerce in the broadest sense and on an international scale; it is not so directly concerned with manufacturing industry. The university is concerned with the development of science and technology at the highest level. The work of the Graduate Business Centre will therefore be based first on the application of scientific method to management of finance and commerce, and second the increasing dependence of modern business on the integration of financial and technological expertise.

In the brochure for the Appeal the following paragraph appeared:

> Gresham College, from its vantage point between the Guildhall and the Bank of England, has become the University's Graduate Business Centre for post-experience studies and short courses for the City businessman. The Centre has professors in management studies and in applied economics and fiscal policy, and a third chair in investment and finance has been created in 1968 through the generous action of The Esmee Fairbairn Trust. Further expansion is planned on an imaginative scale. The technological and scientific resources of the University are becoming of increasing significance to the City's business activity as financial decisions at every level are taken more and more against the background of technological developments.

One-and-a-half million pounds had already been raised towards the target of three-and-a-half million pounds when the Development Fund was officially launched at Mansion House in November 1968. A new building for the School was clearly the main incentive for donors.

Dr Thompson, the Pro-Chancellor, pointed out that if more progress had been made in the development of the School then the Governor of the Bank of England (Sir Leslie O'Brien) might not have suffered criticisms for employing the services of McKinsey. Both Thompson and Tait (Vice-Chancellor) had visited the United States a few months before and had become aware of the yawning gap between their capabilities and our capabilities. Lord Poole added that the training that Lazard's young executives received at Stanford should be available nearer home. A model of the proposed new building for the School was on show for the 250 guests of leading businessmen and industrialists. Despite these efforts and their favourable reporting in the Press (e.g. *The Times*, 27.11.1968), the difficulties encountered in finding suitable and affordable premises for the GBC (to be expanded later on) meant that the Development Fund was largely used for other University projects not funded by the UGC. These included a large lecture theatre in the new building for the Civil and Mechanical Engineering Departments, the Saddlers Sports Centre and the Health Centre. The Fund became dormant after 1973/74 and ceased to be mentioned in the University's annual reports.

David Glen's Deanship

Re-structuring

The first major re-structuring had been the separation of Management Studies from Social Science and the Humanities. The second coincided with the resignation of Shone as Head of Department and his continuation as a professor. Moreover, as a result of the visit of the UGC Advisory Panel on Business Management Studies a special grant was made to the Department of Management Studies to facilitate its re-structuring and planned expansion. Senate and Council subsequently approved proposals for the long-term expansion of the Department as a GBC under the direction of a Dean. In June 1969 the new structure became operational. David Glen became Dean. For the past year or so he had been contributing to the integrating studies module on the MSc degree, and prior to that he had been doing some part-time lecturing on business strategy at Manchester Business School. Glen had obtained a First in Mathematics at Cambridge in 1935 and spent the rest of his career in Shell, except for war service (he rose to the rank of Lieutenant Colonel in the Royal Signals, and was subsequently awarded an OBE). Before retiring from Shell he had been concerned with long-term planning and marketing for the whole of the Shell Group. He was a natural choice for the School, having already demonstrated his competence with students in the strategy area, he had good contacts in business (a director of four companies and on the Council of the London Chamber of Commerce), and he was liked by faculty. He was the first non-academic to be appointed Head of a department of the University. There was no surprise when he said in the press release accompanying his appointment: 'I intend to have a market orientated approach, giving industry and business what they need'. In an interview with a *Times* reporter he said: 'We want to be a centre where City people who think in academic terms – and increasing numbers do – can come and discuss their problems and can come for their research' (The *Times*, 17.11.1969).

Since Glen's appointment as Dean was intended to be a part-time appointment (at his request), it was accompanied by a number of other internal appointments to positions of responsibility. These new positions helped to add status to the roles of a number of individuals in return for their co-operation and commitment. Kenneth Shone was made director of post-experience courses, and Manning was made director of formal courses and research programmes and also Deputy Dean. The latter was supported by Vaughan who became senior tutor. Vesey-Holt was made sub-Dean for planning and publicity, and an administrative officer was appointed. Scholefield became senior tutor for undergraduate courses, and Grinyer co-ordinator for research programmes. The new structure enabled those not already at senior lecturer level to be promoted to senior lecturer. Basil Taylor became Reader in portfolio investment (the first readership in the School).

There is a need to add something here about the undergraduate programme before the School introduced its own BSc. Unfortunately several staff who lectured on these 'service courses' regarded this aspect of their job as a distraction from the School's MSc degree. While engineering faculty regarded the management input as important, many of their students did not see the courses as being critical to their degree or to their career. Student reactions, combined with the 'service element', had a de-motivating effect on School lecturers. An implication of this unsatisfactory state of affairs was that in the early history of the School matters relating to its development were sometimes met with a lukewarm reception (or even hostility) at University Senate. Less obvious, but perhaps just as critical, was the effect of the undergraduate service programme on the time available for research. The format of the 'sandwich' pattern of courses adopted by many of the undergraduate degrees meant that staff only had one clear month when they were not required to lecture – this was in August when family holidays had to be taken.

This squeeze on research time was exacerbated by the design of the MSc in Administrative Sciences being a twelve-month programme!

In September 1969 David Glen was invited to make a short report to the University Council. He felt able to say that the GBC could fairly claim that it was already a major business school in the United Kingdom in terms of the numbers graduating in the MSc in Administrative Sciences (over 50 full-time students on this degree). In terms of research there were 33 ongoing projects. These included a data bank of Stock Exchange prices (supported by a firm of stock brokers), and a project on small firms led by Jonathan Boswell and supported by the Social Science Research Council (Boswell 1973). Development on the post-experience front had been less dramatic, but well represented in law, investment and economic policy. He pointed out the serious constraints on space that were prejudicing growth. Additional accommodation would have to be found but not at the expense of losing Gresham College since 'its perfect central position and its appropriate atmosphere will remain our "front door" to the City of London'. The value of this location had already been demonstrated when over 70 partners in Stock Exchange firms responded to the Vice-Chancellor's invitation to visit the GBC, to hear what was being done and to meet staff and students. A second invitation to the insurance industry was equally successful.

Looking into the future Glen recognised the difficulties of obtaining first-class staff, given the rapid expansion of management education in the United Kingdom. He identified two solutions: to grow our own staff through doctoral and fellowship programmes, preferably on an international basis; and utilising the wealth of part-time talent on the doorstep of Gresham College. He expressed the intention of setting up an advisory body to help the School develop in the right direction.

> Indeed it is central to our conception of the nature of the work which should be done at the Graduate Business Centre that it must proceed as a joint enterprise between the University, the City and Industry. By this I do not only mean that we need money but that an essential element is the tripartite interaction of financial and commercial expertise in the City, technological and business acumen of Industry, and teaching and research at the Graduate Business Centre, set in an international context appropriate to this country's place in world trade.

The policy of moving closer to the City was already well underway when Glen made his report to Council. This strategy became even more pronounced as the years went by. Early expressions of this, in addition to events already mentioned, were the appointment of Leslie Pressnell to the Esmee Fairbairn Chair of Finance and Investment in October 1970, and the introduction of an annual course in 1970/71 for new entrants to the City in conjunction with the *FT*. Pressnell came to the School from LSE where he was a Reader with special interests in monetary economics and monetary history. The City/*FT* courses were an introduction to City institutions. They took place on Thursday afternoons in the Gresham Hall during the autumn term, and normally involved two speakers from City institutions. 150 participants were attracted to the first course.

Lionel Denny House

There was an urgent need for additional premises to cater for the growing School before a more permanent home could be built. This led the University to rent property in Goswell Road near to the Barbican in 1970. The building was named after the first Chancellor of the University, Sir Lionel Denny. It was fully occupied when he returned to formally open it in May 1971. The Gresham College building continued to be used; the Dean's office remained there, and the short courses run by the Post Experience Unit operated from there.

By 1970 there were 67 students on the MSc Administrative Sciences, and it included a specialisation in Investment (Portfolio) Analysis – the first development in the degree specifically aimed at the City. This was an interesting example (to be repeated in the future) whereby sponsorship for a fellowship enabled an individual to carry out research free from teaching duties, the individual then switching to a teaching role, using his research as the basis for a new course. It was in Lionel Denny House that the School first introduced two computer terminals to operate through the telephone network thus giving access to the online facilities of a large computer bureau to supplement the facilities available from the University's own computer.

A new venture that developed was a short course in systems analysis designed specifically for the Civil Service Department. Owen Hanson was recruited by Kenneth Shone to run it in July 1970. This self-financing course subsequently developed into a diploma (1973) and an MSc (1979). The staff recruited to teach in this area formed a centre within the School structure in 1983, a department in 1988 and achieved independent status within the University in 1989. The self-financing nature of this programme gave the dedicated staff a fair amount of autonomy and this, together with their emphasis on teaching as opposed to research, made it difficult for them to be properly integrated into the

School. This pattern mirrored that of the Information Science Centre mentioned earlier; they were also only loosely integrated into the School, although their research record was good.

Early research in management and finance

One of the implications of recruiting initial staff with significant practitioner but limited academic experience, was that research output was slow to appear both in terms of the award of research degrees and publications in academic journals. A handful of academic journal publications (as opposed to conference papers) began to appear in the years 1967–70. Thus Farradane had papers on 'Concept organisation for retrieval', 'The problems of input and their implications in mechanization', and 'Standards in education in information science'; Sir Robert Shone had a paper on 'Planning and fiscal policy'; Taylor on 'Financial tables and the future', 'The N.E.D.C. after six years', 'Portfolio investment in perspective', and with Albert Russell 'Investment uncertainties and British equities', 'Investment analysis and portfolio management – readings from British publications'; Kessler and Grinyer one on 'The systematic evaluation of methods of wage payment'; Scholefield one on 'The effectiveness of senior executives'; and the author on 'Increasing the value of management appraisal schemes: an organisational learning approach'. The last three papers all appeared in the *Journal of Management Studies* – edited by Professor Tom Lupton and the only British academic journal devoted to management in the 1960s.

In February 1971 an SSRC research grant enabled a senior research fellow to be appointed to investigate 'Investment and technical change'. In May 1971 another research fellow joined the School, financed by the insurance industry. This was Hugh Cockerell who had retired from his post of Secretary of the Chartered Insurance Institute. The intention was that he should carry out the necessary research on which to build an insurance specialisation for the MSc in Administrative Sciences (this was duly introduced in 1972/73). By 1971 the GBC had 50 research students to add to the 84 students on the MSc in Administrative Sciences.

The Laurie Milbank Centenary Lectures

An innovation that set a precedent for the future was holding annual lectures given by distinguished individuals. The first example of this was initiated by Laurie Milbank and Company who offered, as part of their centenary celebrations, to set up a trust fund for a series of annual lectures at the School given by distinguished persons on some aspect of finance of interest to the City. The first lecture was given by Sir George

Bolton, President of Bank of London and South America Ltd, on 'Overseas banking in South America', in the Livery Hall of Guildhall in January 1971. In October 1973 the speaker was the Deputy Governor of the Banque de France, and over 300 eminent members of City institutions and School staff attended; 'How the City of London looks from Paris' was chaired by the Vice-Chancellor Sir James Tait in Plaisterers Hall. The lectures continued to attract good audiences and prominent speakers (e.g. the fifth lecture was given by Lord Robens).

The Minories and the old Stock Exchange

The University continued the search for new premises for the School. The latest proposal was to build a hall of residence and a business school in the Minories overlooking the Pool and Tower of London, but this had met with difficulties. The Department of the Environment had objected to the proposed height of the twin towers that would form the hall of residence on grounds of dominating the skyline behind the Tower. With the generous help of the City Architect's Department it was possible to adjust the plans to meet their objection. James Tait wrote in his 1970/71 annual report: 'The Dean and his team have created an enviable reputation and as we move into the Common Market era we feel that there is an enormous job to be done. It can only be done by providing the best teachers with suitable buildings in the right environment. We must build the Minories complex somehow.'

Depressingly a year later Tait had to inform the Court of the University that the cost of the island site in front of the twin towers, on which it was proposed to build a new GBC, had escalated beyond the University's means. The financial position of the University at this time was precarious. This had partly been brought about by over-estimating the expected increase in undergraduate numbers for the quinquennium 1967/68 to 1972/73. 'Unfortunately, it is not possible to transfer staff who can teach, say, electrical engineering or physics to fill vacancies in graduate business studies or computer science, and there has consequently been some imbalance in departmental student/staff ratios.' The problems of engineering and the physical sciences at the University have a long history, and the remnants remain although in a much reduced form as a result of management action (e.g. the closing of the physics and chemistry departments and the restructuring of engineering). The inflexibility of transferring staff from one department to another is one of the constraints that universities face that is not shared by most other organisations, and slows down the speed of adapting to environmental changes.

The raising and dashing of expectations with respect to new premises was a recurring theme. A new Stock Exchange building meant that some use had to be found for the old building. The Court of Common Council commissioned two architects to prepare outline sketch plans to provide greater possible use of the old building. Here was an opportunity for the School to link even more strongly with City history. As already mentioned, Sir Thomas Gresham erected the first Royal Exchange building 400 years previously, and in his Will in 1575 he left his house for the purposes of providing a college (that would offer free lectures for all) and the Royal Exchange as an endowment. The University had already benefited from his Will. The Grand Gresham Committee had agreed that the Gresham Professors should deliver their lectures at the University when it had obtained its Royal Charter in 1966, and enabled 'the University to rent part of Gresham College to establish its Graduate Business Centre where it should be – at the heart of the City.' Unfortunately the space requirements for the Centre were such that the Old Stock Exchange building was impractical, and the proposal never got beyond the preliminary stage.

Optimistic signs

Despite the setback on premises the GBC felt able to give an encouraging and optimistic report for 1971/72.

> The University had always considered that as the City University it should develop a business school distinctly different from any other ... the distinctive difference derives from accepting that a university should evolve in response to the structure of the environment in which it functions. Evolution for the Graduate Business Centre has meant developing from a tradition of studies in Industrial Administration, and responding to the stimulus of the environment by developments deliberately oriented towards the City, with its financial, commercial and international interests. This is the strategic analysis ... which has been made within the Centre and steadily pursued for the last five years. As a result of this conscious planning process and of the excellent teamwork which has been an outstanding feature of the Centre's work, we have created one of the leading business schools in the country. The figures speak for themselves: a full-time teaching and research staff of thirty supported by an extensive and growing network of part-time and consultant staff, ninety postgraduate students on the Master's degree programme, with a record number of Social Science Research Council awards to students, over fifty research students, and a rapidly expanding programme of post-experience courses.

The Centre had always believed that post-experience activities should be an important aspect of its work. During 1971/72 a more determined attempt to develop these activities was undertaken. Accordingly, a part-time adviser was appointed, an Advisory Panel formed, and a course management unit created. John Bruce Lockhart, CB, CMG, OBE, MA, was appointed adviser and John Bell course manager. After resigning from the Foreign Office in 1965 Bruce Lockhart became Head of the Central Staff Department for the Courtaulds Group before joining the GBC. When it came to networking in the City he was a goldmine – he had access to top management in many City organisations. Most of his colleagues at the Centre were aware that this was probably the result of the contacts he had made while being in the Secret Intelligence Service (M16). It was only on reading his Obituary in the *Times* of 10 May 1995 that his former colleagues became fully aware of his outstanding record in that Service. He was in fact the Services senior director and often acted as head until he retired in 1965. Bruce Lockhart was an active member of the School (primarily through the Post Experience Unit) until 1980. The many external appointments he held during this time reflected his standing in the wider community. For example, he was the first Chairman of the British Educational Council and a member of several bodies such as: Naval Education Advisory Committee, National Advisory Council on Industrial and Commercial Education, Schools Council, Council of City and Guilds, London and Home Counties Regional Management Council.

The Advisory Panel that was established for post-experience courses was chaired by Sir Cyril Kleinwort. The priorities agreed by the Panel and the University Senate were to concentrate on City and international subjects. This was exemplified by the School/*FT* courses for continental bankers, and a course in French Business Law for lawyers. Short courses were only one avenue through which the Centre was developing excellent contacts with the City and the professions. Through Dean Glen and other individual members of staff good relations had already been developed with the London Chamber of Commerce and Industry (Glen was on their Council), the British Insurance Association, the Corporation of Insurance Brokers and Lloyd's, the Committee on Invisible Exports, the Institute of Bankers and the Inter-Bank Research Organisation. Two further visiting professorships were made in 1972/73 that were consistent with the School's strategies: J. Wadsworth, formerly Economic Adviser to the Midland Bank, became the first Visiting Professor in Commercial Banking; and G. Morello, Director of the Management School at the University of Palermo, became Visiting Professor in International Marketing.

Short courses on 'Law' topics in the Post Experience Unit

In view of the future developments of Law at the University it is worth mentioning the School's successes in this area. Peter Ford (a consultant lecturer) was the driving force even before 1966, and he continued to contribute until resigning in 1979 on being appointed a member of the Patent Appeals Tribunal of the European Patents Agency in Munich. In the early 1970s another part-time member of the School made outstanding contributions in this area over many years. This was Clive Schmitthoff, Visiting Professor of International Business Law. In 1975 he was awarded the Grand Cross of Merit (approximately equivalent to the CBE) by the President of the German Confederal Republic for his work in furthering Anglo-Germany relations. By 1977 he had been awarded honorary degrees by several British and European universities. The UGC started to recognise the School's activities in this area when in 1973 it made a special grant for starting a collection on EEC law and laws of member states in the Lionel Denny Library.

Professor Edward Parkes appointed Vice-Chancellor

Tait gave unquestioned support to the development of the School while heading Northampton CAT and the University. He retired in 1974 as Sir James Tait. Parkes continued this support, even though he had reservations over the academic merits of the School (coming from heading engineering at one of the 'elite' universities his standards of comparison were not based on former CATs). He took over when universities were still operating under severe financial constraints. Solvency was achieved only by postponing the filling of academic posts and reducing departmental budgets. As mentioned previously a contributory factor to this situation was that the swing away from science and technology had meant that the University was substantially over-staffed for its student population. Despite this adverse climate the GBC continued its development in line with its mission and strategies, and in 1975 the UGC gave its provisional approval for the University to acquire a long-term lease of part of the 'horseshoe' shaped building in the Barbican (i.e. Frobisher Crescent), the construction of which was due to begin in 1976. Again the hope was that this building would provide a 'permanent' home for the School.

1974/75 saw many new developments in the School. Contributions were made to two new degrees within the University: a BSc in Chemical and Administrative Sciences that was to be introduced in 1975/76 (based in the Department of Chemistry); and a BSc in International

Banking and Finance, based in the independent Centre of that name (see next). An increased demand for service teaching from other departments meant that the School had to defer its plans for running a BSc in Management Studies despite the market potential. By now there were 89 full-time students on the MSc and 18 part-time students. During the year Senate approved the introduction of a new MSc in Finance. This was based mainly on the modules of the MSc in Administrative Sciences, but as a separate degree it could be promoted as more City oriented.

In January 1974 the Foundation for Management Education visited the School and was particularly impressed by three of the School's proposals. The visit resulted in substantial grants for the Library (for the development of a learning resources unit), the European Business Law Unit, and for a Chair in business strategy. Peter Grinyer, an internal candidate whose work in the business strategy field was becoming internationally recognised, was appointed to the Chair in 1975 – the first internal appointment to a Chair.

Studies in internal auditing developed as a result of the Leverhulme Trust financing a senior research fellowship. The incumbent, Andrew Chambers, carried out the necessary research to include the subject in the 1975/76 MSc Administrative Sciences degree. He also developed courses, in consultation with the Society of Internal Auditors, for the Post Experience Unit. Numbers on this Unit's courses increased by some 30 per cent in 1974/75. They included several innovative courses such as two senior management seminars on 'International monetary problems' (Chaired by Sir Jeremy Morse of Lloyds Bank), and one between City and Whitehall (Chaired by Sir Philip de Zulueta); and a tailor-made series of courses for Barclays Bank designed to help them adapt to the new environmental conditions surrounding industrial relations and personnel management (see Chapter 10 for further details). The City/Whitehall seminars became an annual event right into the 1990s, and were consistently well received. Numbers were limited to eight from City institutions and eight from government departments. The first seminar in January 1976 included the following institutions: Legal & General, Kleinwort Benson, Samuel Montagu, Midland, Panmure Gordon, Lazard, Prudential, Barclays; and the following departments: HM Treasury, Employment, Defence, Scottish Office, Energy, Prices and Consumer Protection, Industry.

A further innovation in 1974/75 was the introduction of a Placement Service for graduands, jointly organised by Bruce Lockhart and the University's careers adviser. Although this added to the strain on administrative resources it was greatly valued by the students. It was at this time that the Advisory Panel became the City Advisory Panel, and a new panel was created – the Industrial Advisory Panel that was chaired by B.H. Wilson, Town Clerk and Chief Executive of the London Borough of Camden. Malcolm Wilcox, Chief General Manager of Midland Bank, succeeded Sir Cyril Kleinwort as Chairman of the City Panel. The City Advisory Panel extended their sphere of interest and influence to cover the MSc and the embryonic BSc, but their main function continued to focus on the post-experience programme aimed to meet the needs of the City. The potential value of these panels is evident from their membership (see Appendix 3).

It is worth noting, particularly in the light of the indifferent financial performance of executive development short courses in the 1990s that the surplus generated by the Post Experience Unit provided wholly or in part for the salaries of 15 full-time and part-time academic and administrative staff, excluding those engaged in running the Unit. After these commitments had been met the surplus went to supporting research in the School. An example of one such research project was carried out by Kessler and the author into the practices of Industrial Democracy in European banks. This was very topical at the time since UK organisations were under pressure to implement practices prevalent on the Continent (Williams *et al.* 1976; Kessler and Williams 1978). This study stimulated the banking industry to carry out their own more extensive study of the issue.

The Dunn working party

1975/76 saw the retirement of Glen as Dean. Achievements under his leadership, particularly in relation to the City, were recognised by all. The University saw this as an opportunity to initiate a review of the future development of the School. Professor Dunn, Head of the Ophthalmic Optics Department, chaired the working party. The recommendations (Box 3.2) were largely approved by the staff of the School and by Senate.

The change of name was required because of the proposal to introduce a BSc in Business Studies in October 1977. The subject groupings (i.e. divisions) that had arisen were in fact synonymous with the streams on the MSc in Administrative Sciences. These divisions were not large enough to form departments. But there were two other possible reasons for not making them departments: it was the norm for a professor to head departments, and as yet internal staff would have found it difficult to meet the traditional academic criteria for Chairs; the School would

Box 3.2 Recommendations of the Dunn Working Party that were agreed by Senate.

- The Graduate Business Centre should be recognised as a School of the University and be renamed 'The City University Business School'.
- The informal subject groupings that had arisen should not as yet be given the status of departments, but the nomenclature of 'divisions' could be used (this was allowed for in the Charter).
- Using the title of 'Director' of Postgraduate courses, Undergraduate courses and Post-experience courses was acceptable but the holders should not necessarily be appointed at senior lecturer level or above.
- Support (e.g. in terms of priority in the allocation of resources) should be given to the School to extend its activities, particularly in connection with (a) financial and business interests associated with the City of London, and (b) technological management and assessment.
- The proposal to incorporate the International Banking and Finance Unit in the School should be deferred until the newly appointed head had been consulted.
- Urgent consideration should continue to be given to the accommodation requirements of the School (it was accepted that accommodation in the Barbican would not be until 1981 at the earliest).
- The appointment of a full-time Dean was urgent, and while it was important for the Dean 'to be a capable administrator who could also foster links with the City, it was even more important that he should be a person of high academic standing'.

have increased its voting power and therefore its potential to influence decisions on Senate. The significance of this last point could be seen in relation to the power battles that surrounded the location of the International Banking and Finance Unit between the School and the Social Science and Humanities Department, with their growing number of economists. In the end one of the economists (Geoffrey Wood) moved over from Social Science to the Unit, a professorial Director was appointed in January 1977 (Brian Griffiths from LSE), and the Unit was established as an independent Centre within the University.

International Banking and Finance Unit

Something more on the background to the formation of the Unit is worth recounting. Thanks to the thoughtfulness of Edward Alport (an alumnus of the School's Day MBA) it has been possible to access Lord Alport's personal file on the relevant Lord Mayor's Appeal. It is traditional for each Lord Mayor to have an Appeal, and Lord Mais clearly saw the need for a structure that brought the University and the City closer together. The Unit was the outcome of the Appeal that was launched in

June 1973. The Distinguished Appeal Committee formed a working party from its members, all but one of whom held a position in the University: Lord Mais (Chancellor), Lord Alport (Pro-Chancellor), Sir James Tait (Vice-Chancellor), John Bruce Lockhart (Advisor to the Post Experience Unit), and Jack Davies (Executive Director of the Bank of England) as the Honorary Treasurer of the Appeal (this was of particular interest to the author since at that time he was Honorary Treasurer to the British Psychological Society, a position that Jack Davies occupied with distinction several years later).

The target for the Appeal was £350,000 and intended to finance a Chair of International Banking and Finance, a research assistant for the professor, a readership in 'The City of London Capital and Money Markets', a research fellowship in 'City/Industry/Government Relations', and a second one in 'Harmonisation of European Common Market Fiscal Systems', and two lectureships in international banking and financial subjects. It is clear from the Appeal brochure that the Unit was to carry out research projects for City institutions in co-operation with their own research organisations, to establish undergraduate teaching in Banking and Finance in the University, to build on the existing activities of the GBC by introducing a specialism on international banking and finance in the MSc in Administrative Sciences, and by increasing the courses of the Post Experience Unit for City executives working in London and for 'bankers and finance men from overseas'. From the correspondence it appears that a number of different views had to be reconciled in drafting the letter for the Appeal, particularly in relation to a first degree. Also there was concern that institutions that had already contributed to the University's Development Appeal (which was still open) would be reluctant to participate in a further appeal. While success in coming close to the target figure was undoubtedly due to the standing of the mayoralty and the generosity of individuals and institutions, the importance of the working party's knowledge of the City and the organising and diplomatic skills of Bruce Lockhart cannot be overestimated.

The file includes a lengthy but very perceptive note from Bruce Lockhart to Lord Alport and Jack Davies about the need for the 'lay guardians to decide about the framework within which this new Unit will work'. The implied assumption was that without such a framework 'the academic predators will soon be on the move' (no doubt a diplomatic way of saying that the University's Senate was likely to hijack anything that helped to increase its undergraduate intake). The note points out a number of home truths that were probably a fair reflection of the

City's image of the University at that time, and are therefore worth noting, for example: the University has little affinity with the City given its Northampton CAT tradition; the GBC had little contact with the City until the post-experience courses were started, and it is these courses that have given a degree of credibility in the financial institutions of the City; academics are not known for their administrative ability and any plans for the Unit would have to include an element of creative administrative backing (such as that provided by John Bell as manager of the Post Experience Unit); the accent on the GBC's successful MSc course has been on industrial techniques and not City skills, and its greatest single asset is the location of Gresham College ('In the minds of senior City executives, St. John Street might as well be in Birmingham'). These observations highlight the uphill battle that the School had to face in 'breaking through' City attitudes. While most institutions contributed positively to the Appeal, some needed a follow-up letter from Lord Mais before responding. Fortunately the following extract that accompanied the reluctant contribution of the Chairman of a merchant bank was atypical: 'I must say quite frankly that there is little enthusiasm in the City for multiplying academics. Their role in our difficulties has long been causing concern.'

One of the benefits of the Appeal was the publicity surrounding it. The two lists of subscribers that were published in the Press included the majority of home and overseas institutions operating in the City. The commitment of the University and the GBC to develop further by serving the interests of the City was more firmly communicated than ever before.

Triumvirateship

Following the resignation of David Glen, the School was run by a triumvirate until a suitable replacement could be found. Its members were Vaughan (an economist and as the most senior person he represented the School on Senate), Russell (Operations Research) and Jones (Systems Analysis). This period lasted from October 1976 to December 1977 – longer than anticipated. The solution of the triumvirate was arrived at since no internal staff member was seen to have the necessary stature to lead a major business school (this reflected the view of the University Officers and most of the School). Membership was determined by a very democratic process, that is, nominations and voting by academics in the School, and approved by the University. During the interregnum it was very much 'business as usual'. There were 90 on the

MSc Administrative Sciences, 30 on the MSc Finance, and 14 on the Diploma in Systems Analysis. A proposal by the Institute of Export for a Chair in export management was approved, and the Institute and the School set out to acquire the necessary funds. The Federation of Commodity Associations provided funds for two senior research fellowships, and Lloyds funded a research fellowship in insurance. Three new lectureships were filled in preparation for the start of the BSc Business Studies course in October 1977. The short course programme continued to flourish. Newcomers included a two-week Summer School on 'Accounting for non-financial executives' in association with the *FT*, and 'Economics for dealers' for City financial institutions. These developments occurred despite the continual emergence of financial obstacles, particularly the decision by the Government to impose a fourfold increase in the fees for full-time attendance on postgraduate courses. Fortunately the School's courses were sufficiently attractive for recruitment to be maintained, and even increased.

Dr John Treasure's Deanship

In January 1978 John Treasure was appointed Dean and Professor of Marketing. He was formerly the UK Chairman and the worldwide Vice-Chairman of J. Walter Thomson, the major advertising agency. As with Glen he brought with him a network of contacts and a reputation of someone who would understand the world of business and industry. He had been President of the Market Research Society and of the Institute of Practitioners in Advertising. Unlike Glen he was also seen by many as being an academic by nature – the clues for this included his doctorate at Cambridge after studying economics at University College Cardiff, and his early career in market research. Staff looked forward to continued growth under his leadership. A number of things that had been initiated before Treasure arrived soon came to fruition. For example: the efforts of the Institute for Export and the School resulted in Midland Bank International funding a Chair in Export Management; Kessler's personal Chair in Industrial Relations recognised his national reputation in the field; the BSc in Business Studies was successfully launched with 25 students with average 'A' level grades of BBB; the Personnel Research Unit (later renamed Centre for Personnel Research and Enterprise Development) was established with the author as the Director, initial funds coming from the University, the Foundation for Management Education and the Social Science Research Council (now the ESRC).

During 1978/79 a number of noteworthy developments took place. The final agreement was reached with the UGC on the rental of Frobisher Crescent – the two top floors would be occupied by the School and the Centre for Banking and International Finance, but only three quarters of the space would be funded by the UGC. The year also saw the retirement of Manning, who had played a prominent part in the early years of the School but whose influence decreased as the years went by as a result of poor health. Grinyer, who joined in 1965, resigned to take up the Headship of the Department of Economics at St. Andrews. The first exchange scheme agreement for the School was reached with Northeastern University, Massachusetts, thus enabling five second-year students on the BSc Business Studies to spend part of their degree studying abroad. Dr Hugh Murray from the LBS was appointed to the Midland Bank Chair of Export Management in December 1979. A third Advisory Panel was established – the Insurance Industry Panel reflected the growing relationship with that industry. The interests of the School and the Actuarial Science section of the Mathematics Department were catered for by this Panel. It took another 25 years before Actuarial Science itself was integrated into the School!

Treasure was keen on the School re-launching the MSc in Administrative Sciences and the MSc in Finance as the MBA degree. The objectives, design and content of the programme were the same. The only difference was that all those wanting to specialise in finance now had to join students in the other specialisms for integrating studies (i.e. the general management element of the MBA). This change of name to the MBA followed a trend occurring elsewhere in the United Kingdom, and reflected the global influence of American business schools. The specialisms mirrored the divisional structure of the School (i.e. Finance, Marketing, Industrial Relations and Personnel Management, and Management Science). A further division was formed when in October 1980 Export Management and International Business was added to the specialisms open to students. The academics in the General Management division were the only ones not to have direct ownership of a group of students. Each one of the other divisions was responsible for the initial selection, overall monitoring and guidance of their students. This structural arrangement created conflict between general management and the other divisions. The highly motivated general management team needed a greater share of the student's own time (working in small groups on cases and projects) to achieve their learning objectives, and this encroached on the time available for the specialist areas. But the fact that individual students could identify with a smaller specialist group, rather than the mass of MBA students, did bring benefits in student morale and support.

It was in 1979/80 that the first graduates emerged from the BSc Business Studies – a degree that has proved highly successful to the present day. The School's commitment to research took a step forward when the School Secretary and administrator (Dr Carol Williams) shared the load of organising the research seminars with the Chairman of the Research Committee – a role that the author took over in 1979. By now a research culture was becoming more visible. John Treasure was aware of the need to put additional resources into improving the research effort, hence more help was available in producing a working paper series and in running research seminars. Apart from Carol Williams, part-time help in producing the working paper series was provided by Lesley Baldwin (currently the School's Librarian!) and Mary Harris (currently programme manager in the Centre for Charity Effectiveness!). But the process of bringing in research income still rested with individual academics, as did publications. There were now several research oriented non-professorial staff including: J.C. Spender, Rob Grant, Andrew Chambers, Gerry Dickinson, Gordon Gemmill, Richard Taffler, Axel Johne and the author – all of whom were subsequently promoted to Chairs at the School or in top American business schools.

Professor Raoul Franklin succeeded Edward Parkes in 1978, when the latter left to become Vice-Chancellor of Leeds and then Chairman of the UGC. When Franklin joined, engineering and science formed 49 per cent of the University, and as an engineer/physicist he was expected to maintain the historical base and to build on the more promising parts of the University. The anticipated effects of adverse government policies towards the universities led the Vice-Chancellor to write in the 1980/81 annual report:

> It is clear that to adjust to a reduction of income of some 15% over the next three years some painful and some harmful decisions will have to be taken. The space occupied by the University will have to be reduced, repairs and maintenance will be forgone and level of staffing in all categories must fall. This process is one to which the management structure of the University is not well adapted and there will be inevitable strains on it, as well as on specific individuals ... I end as I began, emphasising that the University is entering a period of uncertainty and difficulty greater by far than anything it has yet had to face. I hope that we are able to prevent what has been steadily and painstakingly built up over the past fifteen years from being destroyed in three.

Despite this pessimistic climate the School continued its academic development. In May 1981 Gerald Goodhardt was appointed to the Chair in Consumer Studies. This endowed Chair was financed by the Sir John and Lady Cohen Foundation – probably the first Chair in this subject in the United Kingdom. There are two different accounts as to how the Chair arose. Treasure recounts that his first meeting with Jack Cohen was on a train journey, and that Cohen had said he would like J. Walter Thomson (JWT) to take care of Tesco's advertising. This did not work out as Tesco was aiming too down market for JWT. However, when they met again Treasure had relinquished his Chairmanship of JWT and, as Dean of the School, he asked Cohen to fund a chair in marketing. Cohen was not interested in marketing, but he said he would fund one in Consumer Studies. The second version is provided by Gerald Goodhardt. When Jack Cohen died, his interest in retailing led his family to give sizeable sums of money to universities, particularly in Israel. They approached Kenneth Cork a former Lord Mayor and Chancellor of the University, he put them in touch with John Treasure. Whichever version is correct is not important, what is important is that both versions underline the importance of networking. This is reinforced by the establishment of a second chair to which Michael Beenstock was appointed in April 1981. According to Treasure he played golf on one occasion with an individual who turned out to be the director of the Esmee Fairbairn Trust. When he found out what his job was he asked if the Trust would sponsor a chair in finance. This triggered a series of events resulting in the Chair in Finance and Economics. Both these appointments carried with them the Headship of their specialism, that is, marketing and finance.

The Next Three Years' Report

In February 1981 Treasure produced a document reviewing the current position of the School and laying down the plans for the next three years. In addition he invited three distinguished externals to study the review and to talk to a number of people inside and outside the School. This independent view of the School formed one of the appendices to the report, and indeed influenced the report itself. He pointed out that despite being starved of resources compared to some other business schools (e.g., only receiving 0.6 per cent of the £11.6 million raised by British industry and commerce in support of management education), and being accommodated in a converted showroom/warehouse (Lionel Denny House), the School's achievements were noteworthy. It offered a range of MBA/MSc degree courses, had a BSc Business Studies degree with higher entry requirements than any of its type in the United Kingdom, had broad-based research activities and a thriving short course programme. There were now 17 senior staff (6 professors, 1 reader, 10 senior lecturers), 17 lecturers, 8 full-time researchers, 12 administrative staff and 21 visiting or part-time staff.

As to strategic aspirations, the report states:

> It has long been recognised that the geographical location of the School provides it with a unique opportunity – indeed an obligation – to develop as a major business school serving the needs of business and management in the City of London. Despite the increasing difficult economic climate of recent years – with encouragement from the University and support from certain sectors of the City – it has constantly strived to move closer to meeting its objectives ... The fundamental strategic problem facing the School is to manage successfully its role as a department of the City University, together with its role as an 'independent' business school with major links with the City of London. The School has to live in these two very different worlds – a fact which brings with it many advantages and some disadvantages.

Undergraduate plans for the next three years included restricted entry to 40 per year with average BBB grades. This was the pattern up to now, but it was recognised that beyond this period the intake would have to be approaching twice as many. The quality of learning aspired to had not yet been achieved because restrictions on staff appointments had forced the School to seek economies by combining some of the degree courses with other courses given as part of the 'service teaching' provided for degrees in other parts of the university. This meant that instead of having lecture groups of 40 they were often in excess of 80 and even 200 plus. Although a relatively diminishing proportion of the School's work involved 'service teaching' in 1980/81, over 600 students from other departments attended courses provided by the School.

Plans for postgraduate courses pointed out that the MSc in Administrative Sciences had been superseded in October 1979 by a number of specialist orientated, 12 month full-time/24 month part-time, courses. In other words while the MBA covered the same ground as before, the 'specialism' choice of students was recognised by the qualification they received (e.g. MBA in Finance, or Marketing, or Export Management & International Business, or Industrial Relations & Personnel Management, or Management Science). The School continued to offer its MSc/Diploma in Business Systems Analysis & Design.

The SSRC only recognised some of the specialisms for their Quota awards. There was a need to find other ways in which students could finance themselves, otherwise the School would be catering mainly for overseas students. It was pointed out that while the present MBA must remain part of the School's main stream of activities, it must also seek to meet the educational needs of those students who for financial, career or senior organisational position, made it difficult for them to attend a 12 month full-time or 24 month day release part-time course. It was therefore planned to introduce a part-time evening based MBA for graduate or professionally qualified students with at least two years business experience. It was anticipated that demands for the course would be substantial, given the success of such courses in major American cities. During the last two years exploratory work had been carried out by Scholefield with regard to the development of in-house or in company MBA/Management Development courses, and this was ongoing.

Research activities were summarised as follows: currently there were 61 research students (32 full-time and 29 part-time), and the policy over the last two years for focussing on quality rather than on quantity would continue; academic staff carry out their own research in an independent way, the policy of the School was to help and encourage research initiatives by small grants, publishing a research working paper series, holding research seminars and the publication of a research register; research carried out by research fellows or research units are the result of outside sponsorship, and the intention was to add to the current five research fellowships, and to follow the Personnel Research Unit example by setting up marketing and financial research units; it was planned to launch in the next three years something comparable to the LBS Economic Forecasting Unit which has given them such good publicity, one possibility was to support a proposal prepared by Michael Beenstock relating to a medium-term model of the UK economy. Finally, the intention was expressed that the research committee that had been resuscitated 18 months ago should continue and strengthen its role in the coming 3 years. Membership of the committee was: the author (Chairman), Carole Williams (Secretary), Divisional heads, the Librarian and the Dean.

In summarising post-experience activities the report pointed out that a steady development had taken place since the Post Experience Unit had been established in 1971. In 1979/80 the Unit ran 40 courses attended by 1361 participants. It is worth quoting the policy of the Unit as stated in the report:

> The primary objective of the P.E. Unit is to contribute towards the education and training of management at all levels. While many of the courses are aimed at City institutions and concern 'City' skills, the Unit has a substantial role to play in acting as a meeting place between

> the City and the rest of commerce and industry. In addition, partly by virtue of its unique location, it is able to attract considerable numbers of overseas participants to courses. This helps to disseminate knowledge and understanding of the City and assists in building up long-term contacts and business relationships. The policy of the P.E. Unit is to run courses with a high learning content and with active participation from the course members whenever possible. With this aim in view most of the courses are restricted to a maximum number of participants. For courses run in the Lyons Suite the maximum is twenty-four, elsewhere it is likely to be forty. Existing courses have an excellent reputation and are frequently overbooked. It is essential that the high quality of courses is maintained. In the next three years, therefore, the policy of the Unit will be to build on the existing sound base with a steady, rather than rapid development of new courses. Where possible the new courses will be aimed at areas where the Unit is already strong and well established. Competition ... is strong. This competition must be met primarily by the quality of the courses and the marketing but it is also intended to develop ideas that are too specialised to attract the competition. Examples of these are the courses run for overseas bankers and the courses in economics for dealers.

The report acknowledges that the major problem in the next three years would be that of accommodation. The freeholders were likely to be closing Gresham College for refurbishment in December 1982 for 12 months. The increased cost of the accommodation after that would be beyond the means of the self-financing Unit. A central City location was essential for the teaching and catering facilities, and for effective control it was highly desirable for the administrative office to share the same accommodation.

The independent view of the 'three wise men' was written under two headings: (1) assets and limitations, and (2) strategy for the future. The three were: William Clarke, a financial journalist and director of several banks; Sir Leo Pliatzky, a distinguished Civil Servant; and Ladislas Rice, a Harvard MBA and well-known in the City as a director of several companies. They talked to a number of individuals inside and outside the School. The latter included the Deputy Governor of the Bank of England and the Chairman or Deputy Chairman of the following institutions: Lloyds Bank; Barclays; Commercial Union; Committee on Invisible Exports; Kleinwort Benson; Stock Exchange; Morgan Grenfell; Lloyd's of London. The key observations of the three wise men are presented in Box 3.3.

The independent review concluded with a series of specific ideas and proposals stemming from their observations. John Treasure's 'Next Three Years Report' was an important document in the history of the School, and prepared the way for the next phase of development.

Box 3.3 Observations of the three wise men.

Assets and limitations. 'Being so close to the City is a major potential asset, but it has not yet been used to full advantage ... All courses are in demand, but they are of mixed quality ... The fact that the course (MBA) is relatively short and economical is thought to be an attraction and it appears to meet a need. But in the eyes of the City these Masters' courses do not appear to have parity of esteem with some other such courses mainly because there are some important gaps in the teaching staff in areas considered important by the "City" ... The short Post Experience courses, making extensive use of the time and experience of outsiders, appear to have been the most successful activity from the point of view of securing the involvement of the City and gaining its esteem. They also enable the School to staff key posts from their financial surplus ... Some progress has been made in developing research activities, but the Business School does not make a particularly distinctive contribution in fields of research relevant to the City ... The Business School has been fairly successful in distancing itself from its polytechnic origins but it has not yet established as strong an identity as it should have. The Business School as a whole is not yet seen by the City, or not to the extent that would be desirable, as an institution specially oriented towards its own needs and activities. The current shortage of resources makes this orientation more difficult ... The existence of the much smaller City University Centre for Banking and International Finance is probably one minor cause of dilution of the Business School's identity ... The location of the larger part of the Business School (Lionel Denny House) is not such as to capitalise to the maximum on the School's proximity to the City ... The premises are much less than ideal in other respects also. There is nothing in the nature of a Senior Common Room and there is a lack of amenities which would best promote collegiate life and activity.'

The future. 'The City of London is a major centre of financial services and other non-manufacturing industries, which produce invisible earnings on an astonishing scale ... We cannot expect anything like a positive invitation from the City to the Business School to equip itself more fully to help in meeting these objectives of the City. But if the Business School can of its own initiative orientate itself so as increasingly to be of interest to the City and provide education for management which is relevant to the City's needs, it is likely to evoke a response ... The adaptation of courses would be a principal feature of such a change of emphasis. One point to bear in mind in this process is the widespread feeling that full-time postgraduate education is an expensive business and that the proliferation of new full-time Masters' degree courses should not be encouraged. The suggested change of direction would, in general, produce results only over a period of time. But the projected move into the Barbican, if successfully accomplished, could provide an important new point of departure physically and psychologically.'

4
Strengthening the City of London Orientation: 1982–92

Brian Griffiths Deanship

The 1981/82 session saw several important events. The predicted reduction in UGC funding forced the University to reduce its staffing by over 100 employees. John Treasure resigned in January 1982 after being with the School for four years. During this time he had made a substantial contribution to the development of the School. Nevertheless, he had never been completely at ease in the academic setting where his position gave him authority but limited power, and where decisions were made by committees rather than by individuals. Treasure left to launch his own advertising firm, and then went on to become Vice-Chairman of Saatchi and Saatchi. By March 1982 Professor Brian Griffiths became Dean, and Dr Geoffrey Wood replaced him as Director of the Centre for Banking and International Finance. As part of the University's scheme for voluntary early retirement several of the remaining 'old guard' or management education 'pioneers' left. These included Vesey-Holt, Vaughan, Schofield, Russell, and Taylor. By April Carole Williams resigned as School Secretary, and Geoffrey Moulton (Executive Officer) was promoted to School Administrator. The Business Systems Analysis Division that had always had a fair amount of autonomy to run their courses, had this autonomy formally recognised by being made a 'dependent centre' within the School in 1983 under the directorship of Owen Hanson. The next step for them was departmental status within the University structure, and this they achieved in 1989 (after having departmental status within the School for one year).

Frobisher Crescent

A major event that took place in November 1981 was a visit from the UGC Business and Management Sub-committee. The necessary finance to move into Frobisher Crescent depended upon the outcome of this visit. It was a great stimulus to teamwork in the School, with everyone participating in the preparation of reports and presentations for the visit. The University duly received UGC and Treasury consent to enter into a lease for two floors of the Frobisher building in the Barbican. This was a significant improvement over Lionel Denny House, despite its disadvantages inherent in its design (originally intended for high quality flats and therefore there were inadequate lifts and no frontage). Once in Frobisher the UGC sub-committee re-visited the School – the difference in premises was such that they could hardly believe that this was the same business school they had visited a few months before!

Frobisher also preserved something that was important to the School given the pessimistic outlook concerning Gresham College building, that is, accommodation within the boundaries of the City. In order to use these capital assets more efficiently it was now even more important to launch an evening MBA degree that catered for more senior and experienced students than the full-time degree. The School/University established a second research centre during the year – the City Institute for Financial and Economic Research (CIFER). It was the brainchild of Professor Michael Beenstock who had joined from LBS, and reflected a more determined strategy to recruit 'research stars' into the School. The main activity of CIFER was to build a medium-term econometric model of the UK economy, and to publish the results in a new academic journal edited by Beenstock – *The Economic Review*, which was first published in the Spring of 1983. Funds for CIFER came from the Bank of England, London Clearing Banks, NatWest, Institute of Economic Affairs and HM Treasury. Additional research centres were subsequently established within the School without necessarily having the status of a University centre.

Several other significant events took place in the years 1982/84. There was the launch of the Evening MBA with two intakes a year, and the creation of a new Division of Accounting under the leadership of Professor Andrew Chambers so as to improve academic co-ordination and development in the area. A diploma course in Internal Auditing was soon introduced. Professor Grammenos' Centre for Shipping and Shipping Finance was launched at the Baltic Exchange in May 1984 by the Foreign Secretary, Sir Geoffrey Howe. The Centre for the Study of Financial Institutions, under Dr Shiv Mathur, was launched at the Barber Surgeons' Hall in February 1984. Both were externally funded. The Dean, Professor Brian Griffiths, was appointed to the Court of the Bank of England. These, and other developments already referred to, ensured that School reorganisations were becoming part of the culture. Chambers was appointed Administrative Sub-Dean; Murray, Academic Sub-Dean; Taffler, Head of Accounting Division; Ian Jones, Director of the Evening MBA; Zannis Res, Head of the Centre for Banking and International Finance (now part of the School).

In 1984/85 the Senate Committee on Research replaced their 'research unit' scheme with the 'research centre' scheme. Under this new scheme they approved proposals for the establishment of 11 centres, the following 4 being based in the School: Personnel Research and Enterprise Development (previously the Personnel Research Unit, with the author as director); City University Institute for Financial and Economic Research (Beenstock); Study of Financial Institutions (Mathur); Study of Monetary History (Capie and Wood).

1985/86 was the year in which the UGC began to introduce selectivity based on research reputation and performance, and these criteria were to reappear again in a different format in the future. The School's reputation for research was enhanced by the UGC's assessment of its research as above average. It also saw Griffiths resigning as Dean in order to head the Prime Minister's Policy Unit at 10 Downing Street. Andrew Chambers was appointed Dean from June 1986 after serving as Deputy Dean during Griffiths' two-year secondment to the Policy Unit, and a number of School staff were promoted to Personal Chairs: Capie, Wood, Taffler. Colin Mayer joined from Oxford University as the School's first Professor of Corporate Finance – a Chair financed by Price Waterhouse. Financially the School was able to add to its reserves and to create two new support posts – an Assistant to the Administrator, and a Placement/Alumni Officer. By now the School was one of the largest in the country.

Re-defining the School/University relationship: Business School Council

The relationship between the School and the University fluctuated over the years. Many in the School felt that they were not getting a fair share of UGC funding because the School had been more successful than the rest of the University in obtaining outside funding for posts. Government policy towards the universities in the early 1980s had led to constraints on recruitment. The School, with its high aspirations and its ability to attract private funding, continually sought greater autonomy from the University. Brian Griffiths and Hugh Murray felt that there was a case to speed-up the process of the incremental approach to greater autonomy; they promoted the idea that business schools should be privatised. In 1985 their thinking was embodied in a pamphlet of the Institute of Economic Affairs entitled 'Whose Business?' (Griffiths and Murray 1985). This aroused considerable controversy within the School, the University and nationwide. It provoked the Heads of Cranfield and LBS to write letters to the *Times* protesting against the proposed loss of state subsidy. Although this intellectual and political Unilateral Declaration of Independence (UDI) solution to the School's relationship with the University was only supported by a handful of individuals, it had the positive effect of pressurising the University to review its structure in relation to the School.

After heated public discussions at Senate, and heated private discussions elsewhere, a constructive approach was arrived at. A working party was set up at a meeting of School staff at which the Vice-Chancellor, the Academic Registrar (Dr Adrian Seville), Professor Dunn and the President of the Students' Union Society attended as representatives of Senate. The meeting was held to discuss a paper on the future of the School prepared by members of the professorial staff, and a reply prepared by the Academic Registrar. The paper argued that the School was hampered in its development by the nature of its relationship with the University. The reply challenged many of the assumptions of the paper, particularly those relating to the provision of resources. The result of the meeting was the setting up of the working party to 'consider the relationship between the Business School and the University; and to make recommendations on this, initially to a meeting of staff of the Business School, and thereafter to the Board of Studies, Senate and Council'. Brian Griffiths as Dean chaired the working party, the Academic Registrar was secretary, and other members were Gerald Dunn (representing Senate), Hugh Murray, Jack Davies (representing Council), Gill Palmer (elected by the academic staff of the School), Anne Stewart (elected by the administrative staff of the School). The University Secretary and the Finance Officer were present by invitation. The working party's report and the recommendations of Senate were presented to Council in December 1985.

In their original paper the professorial staff had listed three main problems in the relationship with the University. Under the Deanship of Brian Griffiths the professoriate fulfilled the traditional role which was similar to the consultative role that executive committees fulfilled in subsequent Deanships. First, there was the problem of resources: the financial arrangements were felt to be biased against the Business School, so that the School was supporting the Science and Engineering departments at the cost of its own staffing ratios. Second, other business

Box 4.1 Key points of agreement reached by working party.

- The academic relationship required no fundamental change, the 'quality control' provided by Senate and its committees being seen as a necessary part of the validation of degrees.
- As an organisation dependent upon public funds, the School accepts the need for accountability and control.
- There would be advantages in establishing a Business School Council with an influential City membership.
- This Council would be responsible for the School's finance and development, and would have a finance committee reporting to it.
- Contractual positions of staff would not be affected.

schools had, as a governing body, their own Councils on which important people served. Finally, attraction of external funding was being hampered by the fear that the funds might be used to support the UGC account. Although the University had fostered growth, resources had not grown proportionally. Whilst the working party recognised these problems they also noted that the University had made available substantial resources for the development of the School, had supported the move to Frobisher Crescent, and expected the School to make full use of the opportunities that this afforded. Box 4.1 lists the key points on which unanimous agreement was reached by the working party.

As a package these statements were less radical than the proposal that the School should be separately funded by the UGC. However, they represented a considerable change from existing arrangements defining the relationships between the University and its departments. As a result of the working party report, and the ensuing discussions, the recommendations that went to Council from Senate may be summarised as follows: a Business School Council be established as a sub-committee of the Council of the University; a Finance sub-committee of the Business School Council be established; the University's financial model be taken as the basis for the allocation of UGC funds to the School; and that implementation of these recommendations should take place at the beginning of the 1986/87 financial year. It is worth noting that changes made to the financial model may only have marginally benefited the School (e.g. postgraduate students were given more weight, the overhead burden on non-UGC activities was reduced), but the weighted model guaranteed a reasonable share of UGC funding to the School irrespective of the level of external funding raised. The School had therefore gained something from this contretemps. Moreover, through the School Council's Finance sub-committee came the first opportunity to see separate accounts for the School (prior to this they were integrated into the University accounts).

Andrew Chambers' Deanship

The Business School Council came into being in the session 1986/87. External membership of the first Council is listed in Box 4.2.

For the time being both the City Advisory Panel under the Chairmanship of Brandon Gough, and the Insurance Advisory Panel under Tony Ratcliffe (See Appendix 3 for membership), continued to serve the School and University.

In addition to the coming into being of the Business School Council, 1986/87 saw an internal restructuring of the School, the introduction of the Consortium MBA, the establishment of several exciting new Chairs, and more specialist support staff. To date, despite its name, the School had the status of a 'department' of the University. University policy was now to group departments into schools, each headed by a Dean. The new structure of the School consisted of the Department of Business Studies (with its five divisions and six centres), and three dependent centres. The latter were: Centre for Business Systems Analysis and Design; Centre for Banking and International Finance; and the Management Development Centre. The intention was for the first two to achieve departmental status within a year – the first outside, and the second inside, the School (this happened in 1988). CIFER moved into

Box 4.2 External membership of the first Business School Council.

- Sir Peter Graham, Council Chairman; Chairman, Standard Chartered Bank; Chairman, Crown Agents
- Jack Davies, former Director, Bank of England
- Graham Day, Chairman and CEO, Rover Group
- Brandon Gough, Senior Partner, Coopers & Lybrand
- Alistair Graham, Director, The Industrial Society
- Lord Howie of Troon, Pro-Chancellor of City University
- Sir Anthony Jolliffe, Chairman, Walker Greenbank
- Peter Miller, Chairman, Lloyds
- Christopher Norman-Butler, Business in the Community
- Lady Porter, Leader, Westminster City Council
- Christopher Reeves, former CEO and Deputy chairman, Morgan Grenfell
- D. Trevelyan, First Civil Service Commissioner and Deputy Secretary, Cabinet Office.

the Banking Centre when Roy Batchelor (a member of the Banking Centre) replaced Beenstock (a member of the Finance Division of Business Studies) as the director following the latter's resignation on moving to the Hebrew University in Jerusalem.

The driving force behind the new Consortium MBA was Hugh Murray. The two defining characteristics of this innovative programme were its adoption of the action learning model (Revans 1983), and the learning partnership forged between the School and a group of companies. The degree was launched by Geoffrey Holland, director of the Manpower Services Commission, in November 1987. The first group of companies belonging to the Consortium were: American Express, International Stock Exchange and J. Sainsbury. Further details on the Consortium MBA will be found in Chapter 9.

The School had for sometime been aware that its public image did not reflect its achievements relative to competition. A number of high profile public lectures sponsored by Peat Marwick McLintock contributed to putting this right. Among the speakers were Kenneth Clark, Graham Day, Alan Sugar, Anita Roddick, Brenda Dean, Anthony Cleaver, Alistair Morton and Sir Colin Marshall. The School used for the first time public relations consultants, and appointed a full-time Conferences and Press Officer. By now there were 67 full-time academic staff and 44 full-time support staff – one of the largest in the United Kingdom – together with an impressive array of part-time experts. Its full-time equivalent student size was over 1300.

Four new Chairs were filled in 1987/88: the Price Waterhouse Professor of Corporate Finance (Colin Mayer), the Honeywell Bull Professorship in Information Management (Clive Holtham), the Market Research Society Professorship (Martin Collins) and the National Westminster Bank Professorship in Personal Finance (Alec Chrystal). At least two of these Chairs were firsts in the business school setting – Information Management and Personal Finance.

In November 1988 the UGC sub-committee concerned with business management made its next academic audit visit to the School. This was its last visit prior to handing over to its successor the Universities Funding Council (UFC). The previous visit had taken place in 1981. Since then the School had grown threefold: from about 500 to 1500 equivalent full-time students, and from about 30 to 70 full-time academic staff. Over this time the quality of student intake had gone up, as had the numbers of professorial staff. However, when these trends are examined in the context of the overall UK MBA market, some significant changes had taken place in the School's MBA market share. A few years earlier 25 per cent of the UK's MBA holders graduated from the School; but despite an increased output of graduates by 60 per cent, its share of the UK MBA market was down to 10 per cent by 1989. This fall in market share was commented upon by the Business and Management Panel.

A new venture in the PR area was launched. This was the 'Young business writer of the year' competition that was sponsored by the law firm Clifford Chance and the national newspaper *The Independent*. Sixth formers and undergraduates entering were required to write a profile on a local entrepreneur, to provide a summary of business news on a particular day, and to write an essay on one of a number of business topics. Ten cash prizes were awarded by John Banham, Director General of the CBI, in June 1989. This competition continued over the next two years.

The international dimension of the School became very visible in November 1988 when the Greek branch of the alumni association of the Centre for Shipping, Trade and Finance was established in Athens. The occasion was marked by a speech from Sir Graham Day and a banquet for 500 guests including the ambassadors of Britain, United States and Cyprus, MPs and government ministers and CEOs of many Greek companies.

1988/89 was the first year that Banking and Finance was a department as opposed to a centre. In January 1989 Mark Taylor was appointed to the Department's newly created Morgan Grenfell Chair in Financial Markets. Substantial funding from Midland Bank enabled the School to establish a Midland Montagu Research Centre to be headed by Gordon Pepper as an Honorary Visiting Professor. The teaching of the department focused mainly on the undergraduate degree course in Banking and Finance, and a new responsibility was added when the MBA (Finance) transferred from the Business Studies Department. At this point in time the Banking and Finance Department had five full-time professors (Crystal, Mayer, Taylor, Wood, Capie) and a Reader (Batchelor) amongst its eight academics, and this top heavy profile was favourably reflected in its impressive publications record.

1989/90 saw the adoption of the slogan 'Academic excellence in the heart of the City' with the overall strategic objective 'to be recognised internationally as the leading university business school in the UK and amongst the leaders worldwide'. At this point in time the School was probably in the top five in the United Kingdom. The increasing international orientation was emphasised by the co-operative agreement with ESCP (one of France's top three schools), and the widening of the agreement in the following year (see later). The main structural change to occur was the separation of the Deanship from the Headship of the Department of Business Studies. Gerald Goodhardt was appointed to the latter while Chambers continued as Dean. A further research centre was established under visiting professor Martin Mendelsohn with financial support from National Westminster Bank.

The outcome of the University's performance in the 1989 Research Selectivity Exercise showed little improvement from the first such UGC exercise in 1986. In other words, the University as a whole was given a below average rating. This was of great concern, not only because of the relative standing of the University but also because of the impact on the parlous financial situation. From the School's point of view there was some light in the tunnel – its research being rated above average on both occasions, and that of its Department of Banking and Finance was assessed as being of 'national excellence' in 1989. However, this was tempered by other mixed developments. Problems of space and accommodation for undergraduates meant the School was only able to get approval from Senate for launching a BSc in Insurance and Investment, and not one in Accountancy and Management. The Council minutes indicate that they found the School's plans for rapid expansion too ambitious, and recognised that even the modest plans that were approved would put great strain on the School's accommodation. A solution to the accommodation problem that was actively being pursued was to find alternative land for the construction of a Hall of residence, and to include space for the School in the re-development of the Northampton Hall site (referred to as the 'Chiswell Street Development'). The School for its part was preparing a persuasive case for being based in London. A paper prepared by Colin Mayer 'The London Effect' was discussed at the Business School Council meeting of March 1990. This was well received but it was recognised that any re-drafting would need to convince the UFC that the School 'generally performed better than rival institutions outside London'.

The School's aspirations and plans for becoming an internationally recognised business school were presented to the next meeting of the Business School Council (June 1990). This was incorporated in a paper prepared by Dr Paul Raimond (Senior Lecturer in Business Strategy). Again there was the feeling that the School was trying to go too fast on the basis of over-stretched resources. At this time the School's general reserves were at a critical state, due to lower Management Development Centre (MDC) income and under-recruitment on the Day MBA programme.

A further element in the School's international strategy was realised in 1990/91 with the formation of AMSEC (Alliance of Management

Schools in European Capitals). Early members in addition to the School were: ESCP of Paris, Solvay of Brussels, Technische Universitat of Berlin, Libera Universita Internazionale degli Studi of Rome, and Universitad Complutense of Madrid. The intention was that this network should facilitate student and faculty exchanges and eventually to lead to a multi-national MBA. European links were strengthened still further when the School co-operated with three European banking associations to develop a unique financial training programme (parallel courses were run in French and English) aimed at bankers in Luxembourg. The programme commenced in January 1992. This venture was a peripheral activity (e.g. the courses were self-financing and School staff were paid for their contributions) and was administered and run in Luxembourg. The School's participation ceased ten years later when the authorities in Luxembourg took over the responsibility for the academic as well as the administrative elements of the programme.

Gerald Goodhardt's Deanship

Andrew Chambers resigned when his appointment as Dean came to an end in August 1990. Although an external candidate was offered the Deanship subject to certain conditions, the offer was withdrawn after nine weeks of protracted negotiations. Gerald Goodhardt, the Deputy Dean, was appointed Dean for one year while a further search was launched. In that year a new venture for the School came into being with the establishment of the Centre for the Study of Voluntary Sector Management (VOLPROF), under the directorship of Visiting Professor Ian Bruce, Director General of the Royal National Institute for the Blind (see Chapter 9).

In 1990 Higher Education and Funding Council for England (HEFCE) resurrected the old chestnut of a merger between the City University and the City of London Polytechnic. By June 1992 it was clear that the University had little to gain from such a merger, and the School would have much to lose. A merger would have worked against the School's strategy of developing high quality business and professional courses, and improving its research performance. For the second time external pressure for such a merger was successfully fought off. The external pressure originated mainly from the Inner London Education Authority who were in financial difficulty and whose responsibilities included the City of London Polytechnic.

A number of changes in personnel and structure took place around this time. Brandon Gough succeeded Sir Peter Graham as Chairman of the Business School Council, and it was recognised that the City Advisory Panel (that Brandon Gough had been chairing) was now redundant. The School experienced its second de-merger when Systems Analysis and Design became a separate department within the University. A second merger took effect in August 1992. Property Valuation & Management had been set up as a Centre within the University in 1981 with a remit to provide Chartered Surveyors with financial and business skills. Its creation was the result of an appeal to the profession, and a Trust Fund was formed with Sir Nigel Mobbs as Chairman. Its first intake of 22 undergraduate students was in October 1981, subsequently it expanded into postgraduate education, and was given departmental status in 1989. As the department expanded so an increasing overlap developed with the expertise of the School. Professor Venmore-Rowland and his staff were in favour of joining the School. Lack of space at Frobisher meant that the department had to remain in its existing premises in the Parkes Building next to the main campus. The School was already operating from the Parkes building where the administrators for its undergraduate programmes were based.

5
Towards a Business-like Business School: 1992–97

David Kaye's Deanship

David Kaye was appointed Dean in August 1992. He had spent his whole career at Andersons, the consulting firm, and had retired a year earlier. His main knowledge of business schools came as a recruiter of MBAs for Andersons, and he had strong views as an employer as to what business schools should be doing. Kaye came out of retirement to complete five years as Dean. Three main structural changes took place during his first year. First, the School's part-time MBA and executive education programmes were brought together to form the Continuing Management Education and Development Centre, co-ordinated by Hugh Murray. This included: the MDC, the Evening MBA course and the Consortium MBA. A further development of the latter degree was the 'franchising' agreement with the Middle East's largest management education organisation – the consultancy firm TEAM. The agreement enabled TEAM to offer the Consortium MBA programme at its training centres in Egypt and Saudi Arabia.

Second, as a result of a review of the function and composition of the School's Council it was proposed to emphasise its role 'to provide strategic advice, review plans for the development of the School, making representations as necessary on overall resourcing to Council (University), and evaluate performance'; to abolish the School's Finance Committee, but to designate an external member to oversee the financial affairs of the School with the Director of Administration (a new appointment) and other senior officers; to reduce the size of the Council from 24 to 17 (mainly by reducing internal members). The thinking behind the abolition of the Finance Committee was that its existence made it more difficult for the Dean to perform his responsibilities for the financial management of the School as required by the University's Financial Regulations. Replacing the post of Deputy Dean (Administration) – an academic appointment that was held by Georges Selim – by a Director of Administration (an administrative appointment) meant that the Dean could delegate the day-to-day financial management while at the same time increase his influence over matters for which he was responsible. The University's Council approved the changes, but at the same time agreed to examine the structure of the governance of schools in the University to ensure adequate consultation of staff in decision-making. This latter point was made in the context of Kaye's proposal that the School Board should in effect be an extended version of the executive committee, and therefore not strictly conforming to the representational provisions incorporated in School Boards as determined by the University's Ordinances. Third, the MDC was incorporated so that input VAT could be reclaimed. The University treated it as a company from August 1993, the members of the Board being: the Dean (also Company Chairman), the Director of Administration (Donal Walsh), the University Secretary (also Company Secretary, O'Hara), the University Finance Director (Frank Toop), the Directors of the Consortium MBA (Professor Murray) and the MDC (Dr Carla Millar). MDC staff were seconded by the University to the Company, and the Company rented its accommodation from the University.

During this first year of his appointment David Kaye presented a framework for strategy to the Business School Council; this had previously been discussed by the Dean's Executive Committee. The prime task was to improve the research performance of the School so that its 1992 RAE (Research Assessment Exercise) rating of '4' (national excellence) would be a '5' (international excellence) the next time round. A key strategy for bringing this about was to recruit senior staff with strong research capability ahead of several retirements due over the next few years. The cost involved would require the School to find short-term sponsorship for some of the appointments. In 1993/94 a new budgetary provision was made specifically towards the improvement of the research rating. With the departure of Brandon Gough to Chair the Higher Education Funding Council, Robin Fox (Vice-Chairman of Kleinwort Benson) became Chairman of the School Council.

In the process of implementing the RAE strategy the School obtained the agreement of the University to advertise for three professorships. The first two appointed were labelled Centenary Chairs in celebration of the University's Centenary in 1994. Both appointees had impressive research records: Chris Hendry (Organisational Behaviour) who came from Warwick Business School; Charles Baden-Fuller (Business Strategy) from Bath Management School.

With the combined professional and managerial orientation of Kaye and Walsh (who possessed an MBA with distinction from MBS and like Kaye also had management consultancy experience) a start was made in calculating the full cost of each programme delivered by the School. Revenue on self-funding programmes now aimed to cover costs on a fully absorbed basis plus 15 per cent contribution for overheads. On the basis of the 1992/93 accounts and the outlook for 1993/94, and student intake trends, concern was expressed at the Council meeting of November 1993 in relation to the Consortium MBA, the MSc/Diploma in Internal Auditing, some specialisms in the Day MBA, and the MDC. The School was expecting to make an operating deficit in 1993/94, and closure of programmes was an option that would have to be considered in the future. At the same meeting a mission statement (intended to provide a framework for change) was welcomed by the Council.

Council members were informed that the relocation of the School depended on a successful redevelopment of the Northampton Hall site from 1996 (by then a new Hall would be operational), and therefore 1998 was conceivable for relocating the School. Detailed user requirements were produced so as to facilitate the process of evaluating suitable accommodation opportunities. This action was stimulated by the serious consideration of 'Bastion House' (adjacent to the Museum of London) for housing the School. Bastion House was rejected mainly on the grounds of problems in constructing tiered lecture theatres. Prior to this site the Golden Lane Exhibition Halls in the Barbican had already been found to be unsuitable for redevelopment.

In 1994/95 the Dean was able to report to the Business School Council that the previous year had resulted in a better financial performance than expected – that is, a predicted deficit had resulted in a small surplus. The profile of the cost centres emphasised the value in having a range of self-financing 'products' that related to different markets. Thus while the MDC generated a surplus, the Consortium MBA and Evening MBA incurred deficits as did the newly merged Property Valuation and Management Department. The strategy of raising the School's profile with the City and the professions, for whom the School wished to be perceived as the obvious service provider, was well underway.

Discussion concerning accommodation continued around the draft brief of requirements. The University recognised the need for the School to have quality accommodation in order to maintain their competitive position. But this would mean the School having to find some of the funding itself. Much depended upon the self-financing courses making a healthy surplus. The success of the new MSc in Investment Management, which had been well subscribed, showed what could be done, and other MScs were in the pipeline. The continuing deficit on the Consortium MBA led to steps being taken to close it down in an orderly fashion so that the interests of registered students were protected.

From the various minutes of the Business School Council, and from the yearly planning and budget meetings between the School and the University, a number of observations can be made: impressive documentation was being produced by the School; in implementing the mission statement a good financial return was essential, and this should guide the development of courses such as the MSc in Investment Management and the proposed MSc in Mathematical Trading and Finance that was receiving pump-priming money from the Corporation; the future quality and disposition of accommodation space had to take into account needs that were not being met at the moment such as library space, 'break out' space and social space; the University was implementing devolved budgeting in 1995/96 and while this allowed the School to create opportunities for itself, it also placed the responsibility to manage risk more firmly in the lap of the School; there would need to be continuous ongoing management involvement if the School were to reach its targets; marketing effort needed to be upgraded (an External Relations Manager had already been appointed).

Devolved budgeting was introduced in all schools of the University from August 1995. This meant that the School received at the start of the year a fixed income from HEFCE sources (as determined by an agreed formula) and a fixed charge for central services. It would then receive directly all other income that it earned and meet all direct expenditure. The advantage of this system was that the School should be able to react more rapidly in its particular markets. It also meant that there was a need for qualified accounting staff to be located in the School, and for the School to develop a business plan each year that would be discussed and agreed with the University and then incorporated into the latter's strategic plan.

During 1995/96 accommodation for the School again occupied the attention of key individuals. Frobisher Crescent was heavily congested. Search for suitable premises continued. Progress was however being made in the development of the Chiswell Street site – a project manager had been appointed to manage a contract for the demolition and clearance of the site. Every effort was being made (including obtaining planning permission) to increase the marketability of the site. In the five-year business plan for the School to 2000/01 a 24 per cent increase of academic staff was predicted. It was recognised that additional short-term accommodation would be needed for a segment of the School so as to free up some space in Frobisher. The most likely segment was executive education (i.e. the Consortium MBA and the MDC). In the University's strategic plan for 1995 one of the targets set for 1995–99 was 'by means of the Northampton Hall project, to approve firm plans for the re-housing of the business school, so that the present high rate of growth, based on a distinctive and innovative rate of professionally-related courses, can be maintained into the following planning period.'

Strategy within the 'business and management' category included the following:

> The Business School has recently declared its mission: To be a top rated business school serving industry and commerce across the world, and to be the business school of first resort for students and organisations focusing on activity associated with the City of London and the business professions ... The Business School is committed to excellence in research. Following a '4' rating in the last RAE, a priority has been to consolidate and improve its already high performance, assisted by external research grants. The success of the School in mounting high-quality professionally-related postgraduate courses is considerable. Most of this activity relies upon fee income and premium fees are charged even where there is some HEFCE support ... Growth has been dependent on establishing a relationship with the University in which entrepreneurship thrives within an agreed development plan and with central quality assurance. In this, the Business School Council, established in 1986 with a strong representation from the City, continues to play a key part. A major expansion of undergraduate activity ... is now essentially complete. The demand from students remains strong and entry standards are of the highest ... The agenda now is to implement a new academic strategy for the Business School, aimed at consolidating its position in the emerging market for business higher education and generating levels of financial surplus that would underwrite the financial uncertainties of new developments and provide a basis for academic initiatives ... Central to this plan is an ambitious programme of new areas for MSc courses, e.g. Finance, Transport Trade and Finance ... This would add almost 300 fte. A parallel doubling of EMBA numbers is foreseen, together with a substantial increase in research student numbers ... All this would, if fully implemented, have a significant

impact on space planning ... The time scale for provision of a new building is perhaps six years ahead, representing a severe constraint on expansion of courses and preventing the Business School from achieving its mission to secure its leading place in the City's estimation ... From 1992, Property Valuation and Management has been part of the Business School, recognising an increasing synergy of activity. It already represents the largest postgraduate activity in Europe to focus on the area of commercial property, with Masters courses in Property Investment and in Property Valuation and Law; there are strong overseas links ...

Re-affirmation of an important principle

Part of the policy of the University was that independent departments should eventually be incorporated into schools. The Department of Systems Science had set-up a working party to determine their future. The main recommendations of the working party were accepted by Senate in January 1995 and approved by Council in March 1996. At an earlier meeting of Senate (December 1995) the important principle that the School had fought over on earlier occasions was 'that it be accepted as academic policy that it is inappropriate in City University to maintain or create a focus for management outside the Business School'. The School had fought for this principle more than once, particularly in relation to the use of the MBA title. The feeling was that unless the School had control over the use of the degree within the University there was the danger of lowering the quality of the degree to the detriment of the high quality MBA brand that the School was trying to create. The most recent incident had in fact been the Systems Science attempt to label their MSc in Health Service Management an MBA. In the break-up of Systems Science the School was determined to only absorb those staff and degrees that would not dilute its chances of obtaining a '5' rating in the next RAE. This resulted in the Management and Systems BSc becoming part of the School's portfolio in August 1997, but not their MSc in Health Service Management. A further factor in not having the Health Service Management degree was that David Kaye's strategy for the School had intentionally drawn away from servicing the public sector, since this would have meant an additional strain on the already stretched resources catering for the needs of business in the private sector.

Another major re-structuring

An important re-structuring of the School was proposed at the School's Council meeting on May 1996, and subsequently approved by Senate and Council for implementation in August 1996. The Department of Business Studies was the original core of the School and at the time of re-structuring was organised into six divisions and a centre. The re-structuring made these seven into departments. This would give more individuals experience of management, would provide a more effective structure to implement the business plan and help to create the culture needed for the future development of the School. Also these changes could theoretically result in the School exerting more influence within the University, since there were more Heads able to cast a vote when it came to Senate elections. As part of the restructuring the author's role changed from being Head of the Business Studies Department (a role held since 1993 in succession to Goodhardt) to being Deputy Dean (Academic) and Quality Assurance Director from August 1996 to July 2001. All the new Heads were given appointments to July 2001 – this showed good foresight in the light of future developments. The seven new departments (and their heads) are shown in Box 5.1.

The already existing Departments of Banking and Finance (headed by Alec Chrystal), and Property Valuation and Management (Bill Rodney), meant that the School consisted of nine departments plus executive education or MDC that was managed as a limited company. For the School to operate successfully under the departmental structure it was realised that an integrative management mechanism had to be introduced; this was the executive committee which met monthly and was chaired by the Dean and included all Heads, the Deputy Dean, Director of Administration and other key academics such as the director of the MBA programme. It soon became clear that the agenda rarely left sufficient time to discuss strategic and long-term issues. This weakness, together with the fact that it was University policy to encourage newly appointed Heads of Departments to attend a residential course on leadership specially designed for a group of universities, triggered the idea of

Box 5.1 The seven new Departments and their Heads.

- Strategy and International Business (Professor Chong Choi)
- Human Resource Management and Organisational Behaviour (Professor Chris Hendry)
- Marketing (Professor Axel Johne)
- Accounting and Finance (Professor Mario Levis)
- Shipping, Trade and Finance (Professor Costas Grammenos)
- Investment, Risk Management and Insurance (Dr Elias Dinenis)
- Management Systems and Information (Professor Clive Holtham)

asking Professor Ian McNay of Danbury Park Conference Centre (part of Anglia University) to run a course tailor-made for the School. This course was held in two parts: three days in February and two days in July 1997. The outcomes were to generate a shared perception of the School's mission and strategies, to provide an opportunity to explore certain issues that normally would only be given cursory attention at executive meetings, and generally to improve the level of teamwork through more effective 'bonding'. The Danbury course was a precursor to the next two 'executive retreats'; the main differences were that the Dean was a participant, the residential element included only one night, there was no outside facilitator, and new locations were used. From 2000 these gatherings became less a team development experience and more an 'away day' to focus on managerial and strategic issues.

The University for business and the professions: an institutional statement and case for support

The 1996/97 session saw the serious start being made in planning for a University fund-raising campaign with the School as the focus and its relocation as the primary objective. The date for the launch was 1999. It was accepted that leadership would have to come from the newly appointed Dean of the School (Leslie Hannah) when he joined in September 1997, from the new Vice-Chancellor when appointed (David Rhind), senior staff in the School and selected external individuals.

It is worth highlighting some of the contents of a draft paper prepared in January 1997 because it consolidated what in effect had been the University's mission and strategy for a number of years. The paper was intended to demonstrate the valuable contributions made by the University to the City and beyond in order to persuade potential sponsors to support the proposed Appeal. Thus, it states that the University continues to have a clear vision of its distinctive place in higher education: 'It is a university for business and the professions, playing a special part in meeting the needs of the City of London.' The paper points out that Lord Mais used his Lord Mayor's Appeal to establish the banking and finance activity which forms an important pillar of the Business School's work – 'The annual Mais Lecture attracts distinguished speakers including – almost a tradition by now – each new Chancellor of the Exchequer.' Of the five courses used to illustrate the practice of developing courses with the direct involvement and support of external institutions and professional bodies, three were from the School: Mathematical Trading and Finance (Corporation of London); Shipping Trade and Finance (Baltic Exchange); Property Valuation and Management (Royal

Institute of Chartered Surveyors). A fourth was closely linked to the School and is now part of the School – Actuarial Science (Institute of Actuaries). The impressive record of the postgraduate courses in improving employment prospects both of graduates and of those admitted on the basis of experience and professional qualifications, often led Raoul Franklin (the Vice-Chancellor, 1978–98) to observe that 'City University takes in graduates from other universities and makes them employable'.

A generous gift from the Cyril Kleinwort Foundation toward the end of Kaye's Deanship augured well for the future. It made possible the much needed refurbishment of the School's library in Frobisher Crescent.

6
Premises to Match World-class Aspirations: 1997–2005

Leslie Hannah's Deanship

At his first meeting with the Business School Council in the session 1997/98, Leslie Hannah said that he had encountered no major problem except for the deficit of the Management Development Centre. He intended continuing the strategy of David Kaye, and his thoughts were the subject of a favourable article on the School in the *FT* of 20 October 1997. He was confident that London could imitate New York with its two top business schools – Columbia and Stern. In the case of London it would be LBS and City University Business School. Fundraising for relocating the School was critical, but he was aware of the need for a lot more 'friend raising' before launching into fund raising, and this meant developing contacts with alumni. Co-ordinated advertising for appointments in different departments was used in order to sharpen up the public image of the School – for example the 'City Experts' advertisement and web site.

The strong finance faculty was strengthened even further with the recruitment of Professor Mark Salmon. With the help of funds from the School and the University he was encouraged to set-up the Financial Econometrics Research Centre and to appoint two research fellows.

1997/98 saw real progress being made in partnership with a developer for a mixed development of the Northampton Hall site and the adjacent City and Islington College. Hannah, with the full support of School staff, was keen to ensure that any proposed new building would be of a size that would cater for the planned growth. The University, for its part, felt that the current business plan (to 2001) did not support the requested size and wished to retain some of the capital payment for Northampton Hall for other developments. The School was asked to prepare a new ten-year business plan (to 2007) so that a clearer picture of planned growth, and the financing of this growth, would emerge.

Business Plan 1998–2007

The mission of the School and its strategies remained the same, that is:

> To be a top-rated business school serving industry and commerce across the world, and to be the business school of first resort for students and organisations focusing on activity associated with the City of London and the business professions.

In order to give some credibility to the School's capability to achieve its targets a comparison was made of the School's recent and planned performance.

Thus over the four years 1993–1997/98 the following changes in performance took place:

- income increased by 60 per cent (or *c*.44 per cent in real terms);
- overall student numbers increased by 36 per cent;
- the underlying surplus of the School increased from zero (when the trend was toward a deficit) to about £400k pa;
- the School obtained an 'Excellent' QAA rating for its courses;
- the School maintained strongly its '4' rating in the 1996 RAE.

Over the next ten years, the School plans to improve performance on most of the above parameters:

- income to increase by about 102 per cent (about 53 per cent in real terms);
- overall student numbers to increase by 26 per cent, entirely accounted for by postgraduate numbers which are planned to increase by about 63 per cent ...
- the underlying annual operating surplus of the School is planned to increase by about £2.9 m to about £3.2 m;
- improve its strong research rating of '4' to a '5' in the 2000/2001 RAE;
- maintain the equivalent of 'Excellent' ratings for its business and management courses in the HEFCE Quality Assessment next planned for 2000.

It was made clear however that the achievement of these objectives was dependent upon the provision of new premises for the School by

2001. Growth was predicted to occur mainly in the MSc courses, for example, launching part-time versions of present courses and some new ones. Although numbers on the Day MBA had been decreasing, the plan incorporated a further reduction in numbers for an initial period while the quality of intake (in terms of GMAT and previous experience) was enhanced to be on a par with other top schools. The other 'problem' facing the School – Executive Development – was to be tackled by adopting a strategy 'to shift from being a merchanter of technical and junior management orientated courses to an operation more closely integrated with the School, and using its faculty, aiming primarily at the tailored company (in-house) course market.'

To facilitate achieving the research objective of a '5' rating in the next RAE, a system for the allocation of academics' workload that had been developed in the previous Deanship continued to be used to make explicit the provision for both teaching inputs and research outputs. Also the plan recognised the problem that broadly based schools had in the use and marketing of its research resources. The strategy here was to identify potential themes around which some of the leading research could be developed and to facilitate these developments in the allocation of resources (e.g. establish centres in financial markets, knowledge management and learning, corporate governance).

To assist the funding of new premises the School would have to be committed and involved in the funding process. The main elements of strategy here included: an approach which seeks to raise friends and demonstrate the value added (particularly to organisations) which the School can provide; maximum use of the School's alumni (as well as the development of stronger alumni networks over the long run); the use of a professional fund raiser – a Development Director for the Appeal.

By the end of the planning period about 80 per cent of current teaching staff of the School would be aged at least 55 or have retired. It would be difficult to fill these positions in a highly competitive market without adequate incentives – such as competitive salaries, substantial funding for conferences, up-to-date computer equipment, attractive working environment and so on. Apart from these considerations a strategy proposed was to employ more research staff (from 16 per cent to 22 per cent of total academic staff), and to make increasing use of research fellows to teach as well as for the purpose of generating research proposals. One of the dilemmas facing schools was meeting the practical as well as the academic needs of students. A mixed strategy, that the School was in a good position to exploit, was to appoint full-time faculty that would help to deliver the research rating sought in the RAE, while making maximum use of the practitioner experts on the doorstep of the School. Certain assumptions relating to teaching and learning were changing and would change, but these had not been factored into the business plan. These included: the increasing use of new technology to encourage self-directed learning, and the related reduction in direct teaching contact hours per students. Most of the MScs had about 500 contact hours per year as against a UK average of about 300 hours. A strategy to continue to implement this trend would result in more effective learning as well as the more efficient use of resources. The better use of academic resources should also follow if more of the 'administrative' work that had increasingly been put on the shoulders of academics was transferred to non-academics.

The financial plan included the following points: the School's annual income was planned to increase by 53 per cent in real terms, and the planned surplus would be approximately 10.4 per cent of annual income; Funding Council grants were likely to shrink from 19 to 10 per cent of total annual income. In the concluding paragraphs of the Plan it was stressed that the School had the potential for growth but required the appropriate space and premises to realise that potential. A School that sets its sights on a 2001 Frobisher Crescent level of operation would go into relative decline because it would be standing still in a growing market, and lose credibility as an institution of 'first resort'.

The great news by July 1998 was that progress on the various negotiations for the new building had advanced sufficiently for the University to transform the 'Chiswell Street Executive' into the 'Business School Project Group'. More progress a year later led to the new label 'Bunhill Row Project'!

Dean's Review of Business School in 1998/99

Underlying many of the papers and activities during the Hannah Deanship was the need to influence the University to agree to provide the School with a building that would help achieve the School's mission. The majority of the 14-strong executive committee of the School wanted Leslie Hannah to give priority to achieving this goal. He prepared a paper for the University Council meeting of March 1998. It will serve as a useful summary of the position of the School at that time, why it needed to be treated differently from other schools in the University, and the strategy for the future. The following is the main thrust of the paper using much of the actual wording used.

The School resembles the University in many respects: a lively undergraduate programme and a high proportion of postgraduates; it uses the

City University brand and is firmly orientated to business and the professions; it follows similar processes of academic appointments and promotions, student recruitment and maintaining academic quality and degree standards and generally conforms to staff salary levels; its research as measured by the last RAE (a '4' rating) is only slightly better than average for the University. However, there are respects in which the School is different: it is more international (two-thirds of postgraduate students and one-third of faculty are non-British); it is closer to the City and business, and in some areas (e.g. executive education) it operates on more commercial principles (the School could survive independently of the University if required); in the past it has been a net provider of cash flow to the University, but this would change with the University's massive investment in the proposed new building in Bunhill Row; it ranks higher in the national pecking order than the University overall by a variety of criteria and so can be considered as a major jewel in the crown of the University.

Evidence to support the 'jewel in the crown' observation includes: an *FT* survey of the top 50 world business schools on 25 January 1999, placed the School 6 in the United Kingdom; an independent 1998 American survey of global research in finance placed the School top in England; 'A' level entry standards for the main undergraduate business courses are high and being raised to an 'A and 2Bs' to control recruitment quality and quantity; only 16 per cent of the School's income comes from the Funding Council, most of the income is generated by high fees – a low fee (e.g. £6000 per annum) in the School context is a high fee elsewhere in the University, the School's high fees are £18,000 and rising.

The School has done well in the business school market, partly because it was one of the first in the field. In the 1970s it was vying for third place with Bradford and Cranfield, behind LBS and MBS who were heavily favoured by government and industry. In the 1980s and 1990s the attractions of the management education market created new competitors whose parent universities were in the top category of universities (e.g. Oxford, Cambridge, Warwick, Imperial, Lancaster). But the School's location is a powerful competitive advantage, its reputation in finance is very strong, and in some areas (e.g. Shipping Trade and Finance MSc) it is the best in the world. Hannah went on to pose three central strategic questions: (1) Can we leverage our leading positions in particular niches to establish a leading national and international position as convincingly as LBS, despite the rise in new competitors with excellent brand names, better endowed funding and lower (provincial) costs? (2) Can we arrest our relative decline and ensure that we are delivering really high quality courses and offering value for money at the top of the global second league (perhaps aspiring to rank 25–30 rather than, as now, 44, among those other second leaguers, that is, those ranked between 25 and 50 globally)? (3) Or should we continue as at present while others upgrade and offer the quality of teaching and other facilities that are required in the top 50 (in other words perpetuate the gradual relative decline)?

The main threats that may make it difficult for the School to achieve strategy (2) and avoid strategy (3) relate to Facilities and People – they both are linked and both support the high fee strategy. While the Barbican building is generally superior to other accommodation in the University, it is inferior to our closest competitors. The Bunhill Row building will give us more space but the strategy we adopt, that is, whether strategies (1), (2) or (3), will have to be reflected in the quality of the new building. It needs to be borne in mind that the *FT* rankings are significantly determined by students who left the MBA programmes 3 years before; which means that actions taken now will be reflected in the 2003 rankings, and that Bunhill Row will only be fully reflected in the 2006 rankings if the building is occupied in 2002/03. The services we are offered by the University (e.g. computing, careers, library etc.) are often inadequate for high fee paying students. This usually results in our having to hire extra staff – a solution that leads to inefficiencies and not necessarily to a high level of service.

The School is losing some key staff, particularly in the field of finance, because of competition from the City (e.g. recently Alec Chrystal left for the Bank of England and a senior lecturer joined a merchant bank). Some other schools pay higher salaries, and some have opted out of the university salary structure. Thus in 1997/98 LBS paid 15 of their staff over £100,000 and 88 staff over £50,000, while in the whole of City University with far greater numbers of staff none were paid over £100,000 and only 25 paid over £50,000.

One of the conclusions of the paper was: 'The only way to square the circle of substantial capital funding needs and high current expenses that strategy (2) requires is by external fundraising for the Business School to defray part of the costs of the new building, to increase our capacity to attract and retain leading academics in our core areas, and to recruit staff or increase outsourcing to improve services to students. That is why we are asking the University to put the Business School at the heart of the initial fundraising campaign.' The University Council agreed that together with the School it should pursue Strategy (2).

Bunhill Row project

University Council were informed in March 1999 that outline planning permission was given in December 1998, a problem of the 'Rights of Light' relating to St Joseph's Presbytery was resolved (at a hefty financial cost), and Helical Bar had commenced the demolition of Northampton Hall. The University would achieve vacant possession of the City and Islington College in August 2000 (the site for the new building), and the target date for completing the building would be July 2002. The process of selecting the professional team for the project was well underway. A project manager was appointed and Bennett Associates with Rab Bennett as lead director were appointed architect for the duration of the whole project (see Appendix 5 for a blow-by-blow account of this process).

One of the concerns still in the minds of University Officers was the School's ability to service a substantial loan (about £14 m less any income from fundraising). It was pointed out that the School was not projecting a surplus for the current session. For its part the School argued that it was spending income for good reason and that it was still being taxed a substantial amount to support Engineering and other departments in financial difficulty. The School's plans showed substantial increases in surpluses to support loans but only from 2002. By then it was planned that with the temporary additional space rented in 24 Chiswell Street, the high fee executive development courses housed there would be generating an increased income. The University initiated a study by the consultants Pricewaterhouse Coopers to examine the validity of the School's business plan, particularly focusing on its ability to service a loan of some £9 m from its surplus funds.

More structural changes and more building considerations

Two changes took place in the 1998/99 session. The most significant was the dissolution of the Business School Council. The original aims of the Council had changed, there was a need for the School to have closer links with the University's Development Board (the fundraising body), the University was making a substantial investment in the School via the new building, a good deal of autonomy was assured for the School through the University's devolved budgeting policy. There was still a need for an external body to provide advice to meet the requirements of quality management. Such a body was subsequently formed and named the Board of Overseers – no doubt a carry over from Leslie Hannah's time at Harvard! While there was some continuity of membership, the new

Board met the criterion of diversity and at the same time consisted almost entirely of School alumni who had experienced very successful careers in the financial sector. In 2003 the Board was re-named the International Advisory Board and minor changes in membership were introduced (see notes attached to Appendix 3).

The second structural change was a minor adjustment, partly initiated by the staff involved themselves. Some of the new departments in the School were relatively small by University standards. On the resignation of one of the heads (Professor Choi leaving to direct the MBA at the Judge school in Cambridge), the opportunity arose for bringing together under one umbrella the Department of Marketing and the Department of Strategy and International Business. The new Department of Strategy and Marketing came into being in January 1999 under the Headship of Professor Axel Johne.

In September 1999 it was reported to University Council that the outline scheme for the new building included a basement, ground and five floors – this was the School's requirement as per the business plan. There was the possibility of building a sixth and seventh floor, and the cost and funding implications were being explored. The outline scheme had benefited from a benchmarking exercise with similar contemporary buildings and from the study visits to six schools in North America.

> The principles governing the design internally and externally are to provide a building that gives a strong and distinctive identity to the Business School and to which students, employers and others can relate; that is functional in terms of good quality teaching spaces, library, computing facilities and amenities; and which will be adaptable in a cost effective manner. Other factors guiding the design are that the building layout should facilitate circulation and communication and that its structure and services are environmentally responsible. Above all the new building has to be affordable both to the University and the Business School.

A further criterion taken into account was that if the need ever arose the building could be used for other purposes, such as office accommodation, thus protecting the investment value of the property for the University.

The end result of all these activities, including the Pricewaterhouse Coopers review of the School's case, was the go ahead for the construction of the additional floors, the University Council authorising the commitment of funds for the new building; and the School's business plan was approved, particularly the financial targets requiring surplus net income to service the cost of the loans of £19.6 m as a contribution to the new building.

Cabinet management

Leslie Hannah's departure to take up the post of Chief Executive of Ashridge came as a surprise to everyone and caused considerable concern, given the momentum that had been built up for the Appeal and the Bunhill Row building project. The Vice Chancellor David Rhind formed a School Cabinet as an interim management that would be acceptable to the senior staff of the School and keep the momentum moving forward from July 2000 until a new Dean was in place. He asked Costas Grammenos to be Acting Dean and to Chair the Cabinet, Adrian Seville (the University's Academic Registrar) to represent him in the Cabinet, Charles Baden-Fuller to keep an eye on strategic considerations, and the author as Deputy Dean to manage the internal operations of the School. This arrangement worked well for the six months that were needed for the University to make a considered appointment to the Deanship.

David Currie's Deanship

In January 2001 Lord Currie of Marylbone became Dean of the School. His previous post was Deputy Dean of LBS. Before joining LBS he was Dean of Social Studies at Queen Mary's College in London. For a time he was one of the 'wise men' on the Bank of England's monetary policy committee. Leslie Hannah had faced two main challenges during his tenure of the Deanship: ensuring that the School was to be accommodated in a building that would be compatible with a world-class business school; and getting the five finance-related departments to co-operate more in the interest of the School as a whole. The first was well on the way to being achieved when he resigned, but the second only partially so. The latter problem had existed for many years, and was exacerbated in the departmental structure introduced by David Kaye. The main reason for the apparent resistance to change was the factor of 'ownership' – programmes were owned by different departments who were reluctant to lose the control and identity they enjoyed. This applied particularly to the BScs and specialist MScs. The problem with the MBA programmes was rather different in that no single department 'owned' the Day MBA or the Evening MBA. These two programmes had developed independently of one another, and for many years had separate directors. Both

Kaye and Hannah had tried to resolve this by appointing a single director to oversee both programmes. This solution did not solve the problem of giving the director sufficient authority to gain the co-operation of individuals from the different departments. These structural problems faced David Currie when he arrived.

David Currie recognised the potential of the School to work its way up the worldwide rankings. Hannah had clearly recognised this (and no doubt previous Deans as well), and had explicitly named the conditions necessary for this to happen to the University Council. Currie took a similar stance. A high quality, tailor-made building was essential. Also while both recognised the importance of simplifying the decision-making structures and processes in the School, Currie managed to bring this about during his 'honeymoon period'. A major factor contributing toward this was that the appointments to various positions of responsibility were due to end within six months of his appointment (including the author as Deputy Dean as a result of reaching retirement age). This provided a target date for a new structure to be in place by the start of the 2001–02 session.

After due consultation, the solution backed by the majority was to do away with departments altogether and to have two faculties – management and finance. Informal discussions led to one unopposed candidate to head the Faculty of Management – Professor Axel Johne. Not surprisingly, no single unopposed candidate emerged to head the Finance Faculty. Fortunately an acceptable 'neutral' candidate surfaced. This was Alec Chrystal who had left the School to join the Bank of England as its senior Economic Adviser five year before, but now wished to return to an academic post. On appointment he was duly made Head of the Faculty of Finance.

A number of other appointments were made. The position of overall director of the undergraduate programmes had already existed at the time of David Kaye, but had had little effect in building on the potential synergy between the four degrees. In an effort to change things, Kaye incorporated into the role of Deputy Dean responsibility for the undergraduate programme. The committee of undergraduate degree directors became 'a working party for change' and was chaired by the Deputy Dean. The 'ownership' factor again slowed the pace of change, but there was sufficient new thinking in the committee to enlarge the amount of shared teaching, to reduce the contact hours that were noticeably greater than those for similar degrees elsewhere, to develop a co-ordinated marketing approach, and to adopt the good learning practices of colleagues. The potential improvements in efficiency and effectiveness that were emerging through better co-operation across the degrees led Leslie Hannah to reintroduce the role of a separate overall director for the undergraduate programme. The director-designate was filled by Dr Carol Vielba before she chose to become the senior administrator for the School, whereupon the responsibility fell to Professor Elias Dinenis who had already taken the lead in bringing two degrees closer together (i.e. BSc Insurance and Investment, BSc Property Valuation and Finance). From 2003 overall responsibility for the programme has been with Professor Grammenos, as Deputy Dean for the Undergraduate School (in addition to his role as one of the University's Pro-Vice-Chancellors).

Attempts to create a similar over-arching role for the MSc programmes (where the potential for greater synergy was strong) had been made by Leslie Hannah but met with too much opposition from the individual directors. The abolition of departments under Currie changed the dynamics of the situation, and it became possible to make a relatively new member of the School (and therefore seen as a 'neutral' appointment) director of the MSc degrees. This was Professor Philip Booth who had been appointed to head the Department of Property and Management in 2001 – he had previously been a member of the Department of Actuarial Science and Statistics in the University. In 2002 Professor Mario Levis took over responsibility for the MSc programme when Philip Booth went part-time following his appointment as editorial and programme director at the Institute of Economic Affairs.

Currie also introduced a change that followed American practice: instead of using the title 'director' for those who headed School-wide programmes, the title of 'Associate Dean' was introduced. There are now Associate Deans for Research, Teaching and Learning, Academic Quality and Standards, MBA programmes, MSc programmes, Undergraduate programmes, Off-campus programmes, and External Relations and Business Development. The title of director was maintained for those in charge of individual programmes, e.g. director of the Day MBA.

A part-time Dean

In June 2002 the Government announced that Lord Currie was to be the Chairman of OFCOM the new regulatory body for the communications and media industry, a position he was to take up in September 2002. This presented the Vice Chancellor with the opportunity for another 'creative solution'. The agreement with Currie was that he would be a part-time Dean on a one day a week basis. The Deputy Dean (academic) post had remained in abeyance when the author retired in 2001; it was now brought back into play. The post was advertised within the University. The result was that Professor Steven Haberman, Dean of the School of Mathematics, was appointed. He was an academic with an impressive international reputation in actuarial science, and already had close links with the School's faculty in insurance and risk management. The appointment was combined with the Actuarial Science and Statistics Department moving into the School. In 1974 the University had introduced a BSc in Actuarial Science, with the support of insurance companies and the actuarial profession; an MSc followed in 1997. The goal of attracting Actuarial Science to the School, with its strong research record, was something that David Kaye had tried to bring about several years earlier. The merger also helped the University in dealing with the difficulties of maintaining a School of Mathematics when few students were opting to study mathematics. On the downside the merger challenged all the space calculations (offices and lecture space) on which the new Bunhill Row building was planned.

Merger into the School formally occurred in August 2002. It was decided that the School would be organised into three faculties: management, finance, actuarial science and statistics. To have maintained a two faculty structure would have made the very large finance faculty difficult to manage, and the management faculty would have been swamped. At the same time the School officially changed its name from 'City University Business School' to 'Sir John Cass Business School, City of London'. There were a number of versions of the new name before the shortened version of 'Cass Business School' rolled off the tongue. The name change came about in recognition of the generous donation of the Sir John Cass Foundation to the University's Development Fund. The initial donation was for £5 million with the possibility of more to follow in later years. One of the consequences of accepting the donation was it confirmed the School's commitment to continuing undergraduate education (the Foundation being mainly concerned with the education of the young). This is worth mentioning since under Leslie Hannah the School had seriously considered dropping out of the undergraduate market because of the financial disadvantages that it entailed as a result of Government policies.

The new building was completed almost on time. Some of the lecture theatres began to be used in October 2002, and staff moved into their new accommodation from December onwards. On 7 May 2003 the building was officially opened by Her Majesty the Queen, accompanied by the Duke of Edinburgh.

Strategic plan 2003–08

As predicted the new building opened up opportunities for the School while at the same time highlighting the need to service a hefty mortgage. The member of the School who had done as much as anyone to bring the new building about, Donal Walsh the Director of Administration, had resigned in September 2002. Henrietta Royle, who came from the City, replaced him as the Chief Operations Officer for the School. These factors, together with the other changes that had taken place under David Currie, called for a fresh look at the strategic plan. After appropriate consultations this was produced by the management team and discussed in a meeting of all staff in March 2003. Selected extracts from the strategic plan are useful in summarising the School's present achievements and its likely future development. 'The School is well positioned to break into the top league of world business schools, provided it can push through some fundamental changes in the way it operates internally and deals with its students, alumni, potential employers and media.' The plan pointed out that should it fail to make the necessary changes the School would continue as a middle ranking school, unable to generate the income needed to make it a rewarding place in which to work. Three objectives for the next five years were spelt out, and are reproduced in Box 6.1.

A SWOT (strengths, weaknesses, opportunities, threats) analysis indicated that the School's strengths were: its location, the undergraduate and MSc programmes, the Finance Faculty and the PhD programme (which had ESRC recognition). The School was aware that a number of areas needed to be improved, particularly: building the brand; the ranking of the MBA; Executive Development; research income; and the

Box 6.1 Three key objectives.

- *To be a top tier business school.* This relates to position in rankings, achieved entry standards, fee levels and cohort size, quality of research, a successful executive development business and media comment.
- *To be an intellectual hub of the City of London.* This means becoming firmly integrated into the City of London and used by City based and other financial services firms and umbrella organisations as their intellectual resource.
- *Profitability.* In the short term, this means achieving breakeven within two years, reinvesting any profits in the business. The School plans that Executive Development will breakeven within two years and thereafter generate profits equivalent to 10% of turnover. In the medium term the School would like to build a reserve equal to at least 10% of turnover.

number of academic stars. The new building and a strengthening of support staff (e.g. marketing and communications team) were generating major opportunities, as were the part-time markets for postgraduate courses. The launch of the China Executive MBA in January 2003, with its e-learning element, opened up an extensive overseas market. Bringing about intended developments all had financial implications. Hence the importance of the profitability criterion. The turnaround of Executive Development was a key factor. It was recognised that the product portfolio had to be managed so that priority of scarce resources in the new building went to the more profitable courses; the only exception to this would be the MBA where investment to build a world class degree had priority over its short-term profitability.

Some recent developments

In arriving at a historical perspective in the development of a business school, it is always difficult to cover events in the last few years. The difficulty here is that events selected to be discussed may not turn out to be the most critical in five or ten years' time. With this proviso in mind a number of observations can be made:

- The School has maintained its general competitive standing – for example, ranked 42 and 60 in the last two years in the *FT* world rankings of MBA programmes (see Chapter 13 for more details).
- While the intake quality on the MBA has improved (e.g. GMAT scores, years of managerial experience), so far this has been at the expense of numbers (as had been predicted over the short term).
- Increased opportunities in the new building have meant the launch of new degrees. Space shortages and the need to run high fee-earning degrees had given priority to finance related MScs while in the Barbican. The new MSc in Management (an idea that had been temporarily shelved in the mid-1990s) has proved a resounding success with annual intakes of over 80 good students in 2003 and 2004 – much larger than expected. The formation of The Centre for Charity Effectiveness (the outcome of a partnership between the School's VOLPROF and the Worshipful Company of Management Consultants) has added three charity-related MScs to the already highly successful MSc in Voluntary Sector Management. This makes the School the only one in Europe offering such a range of professional charity and not-for-profit courses.
- There have been noticeable advancements on the research front (see Chapter 11).

- The School's superb new building is increasingly being used as intended. A constant stream of functions (e.g. courses, conferences, seminars, workshops) create the feeling of a hive of intellectual activity – giving substance to the goal of being the intellectual hub of the City. Indeed, the building has already run out of spare capacity (some lecturers – and even a professor – having to share relatively small offices).
- The management structure has been strengthened and clarified to enable the School to be run more like a self-sufficient business than in the past.

An elaboration of last observation is important. As in the past the Dean has responsibility for the management of the School, and is answerable to the Vice-Chancellor of the University. The current part-time status of the Dean is compensated for by the close working relationship between the Dean (Currie), Deputy Dean (Haberman) and Chief Operating Officer (Royle), and their weekly meetings to deal with strategic issues. The Deputy Dean acts as head of the academic staff and works closely with the three heads of faculty; and the Chief Operating Officer as head of the professional staff works closely with the various functional managers (e.g. HR, Facilities, marketing and communications). The matrix structure of the School distinguishes between the School's products (e.g. MBA programme, research programme), and the inputs necessary for the successful delivery of these products (e.g. three academic faculties, marketing and communications, HR, budgetary control).

While the mission and strategies of the School have changed little under the last three Deans, the most notable changes under the current Deanship include: replacing departments with a faculty structure; the occupancy of the new building allowing an expansion of academic numbers, greater autonomy from the University with respect to a range of services, and an increase in professional personnel; more resources going into external relations, business development and marketing. There are now approximately 120 academics and 120 professional administrative staff. The Executive Development short courses arm of the School is now part of the responsibilities of an Associate Dean for External Relations and Business Development (currently Professor Chris Brady). Brady is Chairman of Cass Executive Education Ltd (formerly Management Development Centre Ltd), the wholly owned company that is the vehicle for delivering executive education and for launching new business initiatives. Scott Moeller, the chief executive of Cass

Executive Education Ltd, reports to Brady. Moeller joined in 2004, after having had extensive experience in the financial sector (including senior management positions with Deutsche Bank and Morgan Stanley), and part-time experience lecturing on the School's MBA programmes on mergers and acquisitions. The School's progress in the direction of self-sufficiency is illustrated by the appointment of Paola Barbarino in 2004/05 as Development Director, after the Vice-Chancellor agreed that the School could be responsible for its own fund raising (thus following American practice). Barbarino previously held related senior positions at the British Library and the Tate Gallery.

Conclusion to Part II

This Part has been mainly concerned with a chronological and descriptive account of the history of the School. These empirical findings now need to be analysed and interpreted in order to understand 'why' the School developed in the way it did. This is the task for Parts III and IV. The challenge involved is manageable with the help of concepts and frameworks drawn from organisation theory. The focus of Chapter 7 will be on the contextual factors or environmental forces to which the School has had to adapt in the course of its development. Exploring contextual issues is essential if one is to come close to answering the 'why' question (Pettigrew 1985). Chapters 8 to 12 in Part III will focus on the mission and strategies that the School adopted in the process of coping with its environment. Chapter 13 explores some of the quantitative and comparative measures that reflect the impact of these strategies.

Part III

Environmental Triggers and Competitive Responses

7
Institutional and Market Influences in the Development of Cass

Historical context

In order to understand the current profile and culture of Cass it is necessary to delve into the wider historical context. The history of management in the United Kingdom, and of management education, has been well documented by others (Brech 2002). Although there is a case for saying that some business schools such as Wharton in the United States and ESCP in France were founded in the nineteenth century, business schools are really a phenomenon of the twentieth century. As so often happens, the real impetus for their formation in the United Kingdom came about as a result of the strong convictions of a few individuals and their supporting networks. These individuals had direct experience of American companies (e.g. Col. Lydall Urwick of Urwick-Orr and Partners), American business schools (e.g. John Bolton, Chairman of various companies and a graduate of Harvard Business School), and some were in strong positions to influence government policy (e.g. Sir Keith Joseph, the then managing director of Bovis and a Conservative MP). Others such as James Platt (who had retired as managing director of Shell in 1957) also became more aware of the value of the theoretical basis of management when he attended the Administrative Staff College at Henley (founded in 1946 by a group of businessmen headed by Geoffrey Heyworth, the then Chairman of Unilever).

After the First World War syllabuses in industrial administration (as management studies was then known) began to be devised in technical institutions and colleges (including Northampton Polytechnic) to meet the needs of the professional engineering institutions. Immediately after the Second World War Urwick was appointed by the Ministry of

Education as chairman of a committee to advise on educational facilities required for managers. Their report was published in 1947 and was implemented in 1949 through the National Scheme of Management Studies to be provided in technical and commercial colleges. This was the scheme that was revised in 1952/53 as the Diploma in Management Studies. Both these qualifications were run under the auspices of the British Institute of Management (BIM); itself created in 1947 as a result of a Board of Trade enquiry (in the late 1950s and early 1960s the BIM failed to give an effective lead in the development of management education because of the ambivalent attitude they displayed toward management education in universities). In 1951 the government-sponsored Anglo-American Council on Productivity was advocating the establishment of university business schools. All these developments showed that governments were aware of the potential contribution of management education to productivity. The assumption driving these initiatives was that American superiority in terms of productivity was based on their superior management practices, and these in turn were based on their more advanced development in the area of management education.

Despite these developments there was still considerable antipathy among senior managers toward formal management education. These attitudes meant that 57 per cent of the funds, resulting from an appeal in 1960 to provide financial assistance for university level courses, came from John Bolton and six multinational companies (Wilson 1992, p. 8). The trust that was formed to manage the funds was called the Foundation for Management Education (FME). Sir Keith Murray, the Chairman of the UGC, indicated that the UGC was sympathetic to their aims and prepared to allocate some money toward postgraduate courses in management (it is worth noting that in their report for 1952/57 the UGC had queried the appropriateness of management studies as a subject for universities!). Accordingly the UGC set up a special panel to channel this money (Wilson 1992, p. 8), and 13 institutions applied for support. Thus by 1960 the FME had become a major influence in management education in the universities in the United Kingdom. In terms of individuals both John Bolton and Keith Joseph had been lead players, as was James Platt who became the first executive secretary of FME and its director in 1964. Thanks to the excellent memory and archives of Dr Edward Brech it is possible to throw more light on John Bolton's contributions. John Bolton maintained his links with Harvard by acting as a tutor when the Solartron case study was being used. He was the CEO of the Solartron Electronic Group Ltd. (coincidentally the company that financed the author at Birkbeck to do a PhD based on its highly innovative product the Solartron Automatic Keyboard Instructor). John Bolton wrote in 1957 an influential memorandum to Keith Joseph on the concept of a business school. This not only stimulated a visit to Harvard in 1957 by Keith Joseph himself, but also encouraged the Conservative Party to include in their 1959 Election Manifesto a commitment to found business schools in the United Kingdom.

In 1963 the FME gained two further allies for its cause. Sir Robert Shone, the first Director General of the NEDC, argued in his second report that there was a need for at least one high level school (along the lines of the top American schools), so that we would have better trained managers, better trained teachers of management for the technical colleges, and a centre for research into problems of management and education. In the same year Lord Robbins presented his report on Higher Education (Robbins 1963). From the point of view of the City University this was an important report since it was here that the recommendations were made for the Colleges of Advanced Technology to become universities. But the recommendation relevant to the present discussion was that two major postgraduate business schools should be built in addition to other developments already underway in universities and other institutions.

However, business was deeply divided as to the value of having management education in the hands of academics. One group led by FME was in favour of having any new schools attached to universities. A rival group led by two directors of the engineering firm GKN and the Chairman of English Electric, were in favour of having a high level school distinct from any university where the teaching staff would have management experience and be paid salaries outside the university structure. Since this group met at the Savoy Hotel they became known as the Savoy Group – a label given to them in the Financial Times of 17 June 1963 by Michael Shanks the industrial editor. Fortunately at the suggestion of Sir Robert Shone the main contenders (Director General of the Federation of British Industries; Chairman of BIM; Chairman of FME; Director General of NEDO; Chairman of Savoy Group) decided to ask Lord Franks to provide clear guidance on the development of management education in the United Kingdom. He was an inspired choice, given he had had impressive experience as an academic (Provost of Worcester College, Oxford), as a businessman (Chairman of Lloyds Bank) and as a civil servant (Permanent Secretary at the Ministry of Supply, and Ambassador in Washington).

Franks tackled his task with urgency, taking only four months to produce his report (Franks 1963). It was a masterly report. He recognised the importance of forging a partnership between universities and business. In the years that followed the majority of his recommendations were put into practice, the most notable of which was the formation of two schools in association with the Universities of London and Manchester. He pointed the way for the creation of school councils that would have representatives of both academics and businessmen; and insisted that both sectors should share the costs of founding the two schools and their operations. The acceptance of the report by the main protagonists led to the launch of an appeal in June 1964 sponsored by the Federation of British Industries, the BIM and the FME. The appeal was a success in terms of the sum accumulated. However as Wilson points out, of the 350 companies contributing, some were generous but others made no more than a pitiful gesture (Wilson 1992). The pioneers of management education still faced a business culture that was reluctant to invest in management education closely associated with universities. The impact of the report on the formation and governance of the two major schools subsequently established have been recorded in two scholarly studies (Barnes 1989; Wilson 1992).

How did these early developments of the business school movement in the United Kingdom affect the early beginnings of Cass? Its influence was felt in at least two ways. First, there were individuals on both the governing body of Northampton CAT (e.g. the Chairman was Oliver Thompson an ex-Shell person, and the London County Council representative was Sir Walter Puckey founding Chairman of Management Selection Ltd.) and on the Academic Advisory Committee overseeing its transformation to university status, who had an interest in management education and/or interacted with individuals in the relevant networks and pressure groups. The Academic Advisory Committee (dissolved in September 1972), with an external chairman, was a requirement spelt out in the Robbins Report for the CATs to approve the drafting of their charters and proposed courses. In addition to the Principal (James Tait) membership of the College committee included distinguished academics from University College, LSE and Imperial College, the Vice-Chancellor of Newcastle University and Sir David Watherstone of Tube Investments Ltd. (Sir David was to Chair the Business Liaison Committee of the MBS when it was formed in 1972 in response to the Owen Report).

Second, the management oriented staff in the Department of Management and Social Sciences absorbed the Franks Report (and the Robbins Report). They became even more committed to the development of management education within the university-to-be. Tait was already convinced of the need to develop management education at the College and this had led him to establish the Department of Social and Industrial Studies in 1961. His direct interest in this development is evidenced by his attendance with Alvyn Leyton (following Leyton's appointment to the Headship in July 1961) of a weekend conference at Ashridge in April 1962 on management studies. The conference had been organised by the Ministry of Education. This joint interest continued; for instance, they interviewed the author individually and together when he was recruited in June 1963 for a September start.

These two ground-breaking reports (Franks 1963; Robbins 1963) saw the official acceptance of the business school in the United Kingdom, and management studies increasingly became part of the university scene. As already discussed the groundwork had been prepared by others, particularly by the Foundation for Management Education (Nind 1985). However, many businessmen (and some academics) were still unhappy at the contribution that some business schools were making to management education. The next 25 years saw the publication of several opinion-forming reports. Some were critical of the scene; others adopted a more supportive stance and argued for an expansion of management qualifications such as the MBA. Among the latter was the Rose Report (Rose 1970), which was sponsored by the Management Education and Training Development sub-committee of the NEDC and the Council of Industry for Management Education (CIME had been formed by the CBI, BIM and FME to co-ordinate the views of industry and commerce on the provision of management education). This report highlighted the future need for full-time management teachers, and the urgency of taking steps to meet it. The John Constable and Roger McCormick report, which was commissioned by the BIM and the CBI, underlined the inferior education and training given to British managers compared to other advanced nations (Constable and McCormick 1987). Among their recommendations was the need to significantly increase the number of MBA students, and the greater use of distance learning techniques, part-time and consortium-type programmes (e.g. a business school together with a group of companies designing a programme that attempts to integrate the academic and work experience inputs). The relative paucity of management education and training was also hammered home by the Charles Handy report, sponsored by the Manpower Services Commission, National Economic Development Office (NEDO) and BIM (Handy *et al.* 1987).

In the early days of business schools in the United Kingdom the most critical evaluation study carried out became known as the Owen Report

(Owen 1970). The study was based on a 10 per cent sample of the *Times* list of 500 top companies. It was sponsored by CIME, and carried out by Trevor Owen of ICI with the help of David Casey from Reed International and Norman Huskisson from BP. The study aimed at determining the views of manufacturing industry concerning post-graduate and post-experience education in business schools – in reality this mainly meant LBS and MBS. It identified a gap between what business schools were offering and what industry needed. Thus as far as MBA programmes were concerned employers expected graduates to make an immediate contribution to management, and to lay the foundations for longer term development – in preparation for promotion to senior management positions. This was not a feature that sat comfortably with the course aims and design at LBS and MBS, where academic criteria tended to push out practical criteria. In contrast, it was exactly what the putative School at Northampton CAT set out to do when designing the MSc in Administrative Sciences in 1965/66, and hence the subsequent emphasis on 'specialisms' in the early and later versions of the School's MBA degree. Apart from these general aims the Owen report made a number of recommendations, including: achieving a higher standard of student and staff recruitment; establishing closer links between schools and industry; students should develop a better understanding of management as a system for getting things done in an imperfect world, with individuals of mixed ability; business schools should be prepared to experiment more in post-experience education. The latter recommendation was something that Alistair Mant was more concerned about in his study that was supported by the BIM and CIME (Mant 1969). He identified the problem that was being created as a large army of 'experienced managers' with relatively little management education and training reaching the top of the organisational pyramid.

The United Kingdom was not the only country where there was a difference of opinion as to what managers were wanting from business schools. In the United States this led to a major study being undertaken on existing MBA programmes. When Porter and McKibbin published their findings the main recommendation was that more attention needed to be paid to improving the interpersonal and leadership skills of students (Porter and McKibbin 1988), that is, the practical as opposed to the theoretical elements of the MBA. More recently in the United Kingdom similar emphasis is being put on the development of leadership skills. This emerges from the Council for Excellence in Management and Leadership Report (CEML 2002). The Council was set-up in 2000 under the Chairmanship of Sir Anthony Cleaver by the government to 'investigate the state of management and leadership in the UK and to draw up a strategy that would ensure that the UK had the managers and leaders of the future to match the best in the world'. After a very thorough investigation they arrived at 29 recommendations. The essence of those recommendations having a direct bearing on business schools may be summarised as follows: Business schools should be encouraged to incorporate practical skills combined with work placement in their first degrees in Business and Management studies, and to include in their MBAs the development of leadership skills; more needs to be done to improve the quantity and quality of management teachers; management research should be redirected to meet the needs of practising managers, knowledge transfer should be given a high priority, and practising managers should be active participants in the research process; more autonomy for business schools within the university sector should form the focus of a constructive dialogue between relevant parties.

Open systems theory

Open systems theory has become one of the most influential conceptualisations of organisations since Katz and Kahn promoted the approach in their book *The Social Psychology of Organisations* (Katz and Kahn 1966). Open systems theory draws our attention to the fact that organisations are dependent on their environment for their survival. Just as human organisms depend upon water, food and oxygen from the environment to keep alive, so a service or manufacturing organisation is dependent upon its financiers, its suppliers and its customers to survive. Others have developed these ideas further. Some (Pfeffer and Salancik 1978) view organisations as 'coalitions of interests' that can change the environmental constraints to which they are subjected. Others (Miles and Snow 1978) showed the importance of organisations striving for strategic fit with their market environment.

Building on these basic conceptualisations one can create a visual framework that reflects the highly complex situation in which the School has had to survive (see Figure 7.1). The framework is helpful in presenting simultaneously, and in a structured manner, those key elements in the environment that influence the School and the School can influence.

Institutional 'change agents'. Employer, government and foundation institutions have exerted a heavy influence on business schools because they

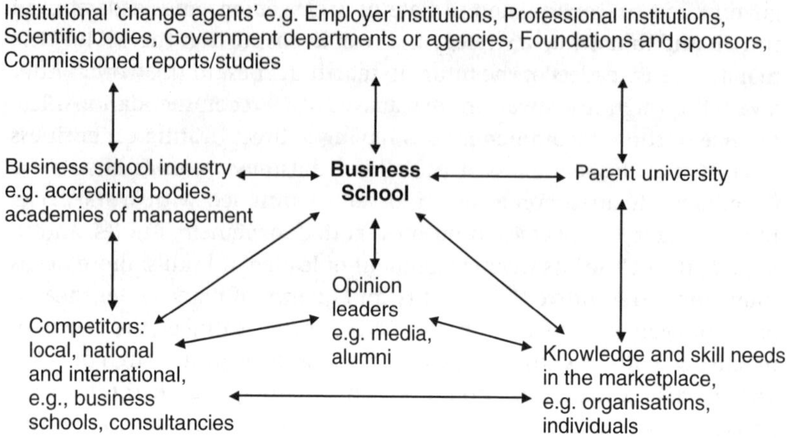

Figure 7.1 Environmental influences on the emergence and growth of a UK business school

have the financial muscle to steer schools in the direction that they consider to be in the best interest of their stakeholders. The continual reduction in state funding for universities (see Part II) meant that the School relied even more on the generosity of companies, charitable foundations and individuals for academic developments and for the housing of these developments. It is difficult to envisage the current standing of the School in the absence of those organisations and individuals who helped to finance the bursaries, fellowships and chairs reported in Part II and the Bunhill Row building described in Chapter 12. In relation to the latter it is fitting that the names of the major sponsors should be prominently displayed in the entrance to the new building (at 2004 they were: Sir John Cass Foundation, Cyril Kleinwort Trust, Worshipful Company of Saddlers, Wolfson Foundation; Christopher Reeves; Bagri Foundation; Corporation of London; Bloomberg LP; Credit Lyonnais; S.N. Roditi; Roger Brooke).

Professional institutions have less influence unless a school wants its students to have exemptions from particular professional examinations. It has long been the policy of the University and the School to introduce degrees that at the same time satisfy the criteria of professional bodies; they therefore can influence the range and depth of subject matter covered by a degree. The influence of the traditional scientific bodies is greater in single discipline departments, such as psychology and economics, than in the multi-discipline business school. Here influence comes via their individual members rather than as a result of their power as a scientific institution. Thus what was taught in modules relating to individual and organisational behaviour in the early days of the School depended on a lecturer's acquaintance with those aspects of scientific psychology that appeared to have relevance to those designing work environments and managing others. As this area of knowledge became more multi-disciplinary and standardised, so academic and professional bodies directly relevant to management and business emerged (e.g. British Academy of Management; the Chartered Institute for Personnel and Development).

Commissioned reports and studies have made considerable impact on business schools. Why is this? It is not because they have discovered anything new. The proposal for one or two top business schools for the United Kingdom had already been made before Lord Franks reported in 1963. The use of new methods of learning for experienced managers had already been applied before the Mant report. The value in these reports lies in their role as 'change agents' by bringing together already existing forces for change. This synergistic role comes about through a combination of several factors: when reports are sponsored by coalitions of powerful stakeholders, these stakeholders are more likely to support and to implement the recommendations made; they all involve the systematic gathering of information relating to the problem being investigated, and the packaging of this information for effective communication; the final report is effectively marketed and disseminated through press releases, publications, seminars and others. The combination of legitimate sponsors, a rationale for action and effective dissemination strategies, promotes and reinforces a particular way of viewing and solving the problem.

The School's parent-body: City University. Unlike some of its main European competitors (e.g. LBS in the United Kingdom, INSEAD in France and IMD in Switzerland) Cass is an integral part of a university and therefore subject to the higher educational policies of the State (initially through the UGC and then HEFCE). Through these State agencies the City University has had an enormous influence on the School. Contributions in the early days were critical in the process of giving birth to the School. But the routine, and sometimes traumatic (e.g. 1980 onwards), reduction in funding to universities by successive governments put severe constraints on the School's growth and on the quality of the premises that could be used to accommodate it. The initial idealism of a small team of academics, the long-term commitment and loyalty of staff, and the leadership shown by senior management at School and University levels all helped in coping with these financial constraints. The strategy of becoming financially more independent of the State has worked; indeed in recent years the City University has been in a more healthy financial condition than most UK universities.

This does not mean that the School/University relationships were always smooth. On the contrary, tension in the relationship has always been there and this may be inevitable. The University was, and is, run by two main committees: Council, on which there are mainly external representatives, is the governing body with ultimate responsibility for employees, finances and the estate; Senate consists solely of University members, and is the supreme body for academic matters. Both Council and Senate spawn a number of committees that conduct most of the work and prepare appropriate papers and recommendations for their approval.

This system of management by committees is common to UK universities, and enables different groups of staff to have a say on matters affecting their jobs, academic disciplines and the University. However, in this system individuals who are sufficiently keen and visible within the University are likely to volunteer and be elected to Senate and Council. Those parts of the University that closely identify themselves with it, or feel in a vulnerable position (such as the engineering departments in the last 30 years), are more likely to attempt to increase their power and influence on these committees. The School never really developed a culture of getting involved in University affairs; indeed for many years the dominant culture was one of distancing itself from University committee work. Most of the Deans were reluctant to participate in committees unless matters under discussion were directly affecting the interests of the School. In this system the leadership of the University Officers is paramount, particularly the Vice-Chancellor, the Academic Registrar and the University Secretary. They have to try and maintain a balance of power between different pressure groups while making the best use of individual talents in the interest of the University as a whole. While the School's Dean or Deputy Dean would normally be a member of several key committees, few other academics from the School became involved until the late 1980s (although there were normally at least one and sometimes two School members elected to Senate, and Gill Palmer as Chair of the Staff Association). Two committees where representation always occurred were the Higher Degrees Committee (ensuring good practice and maintenance of standards in MPhil/PhD programmes, and now called the Research Degrees Committee) and the Research Committee (to oversee the development of research in the University). In both of these committees the individuals heading these functions in the School became members of the appropriate committee. It was only in 1987 (when the author was asked by the Vice-Chancellor if he was prepared for his name to go forward for the post of Pro-Vice-Chancellor) that a path was created for the first in-depth involvement of a member of the School in University-wide affairs.

The degree of autonomy from the University has changed over the years; partly at the instigation of the School, partly forced on the University as it became too large to be closely managed from the centre and introduced a policy of devolved budgeting. As pointed out in Part II more financial control was gained following the 'UDI' initiative of Griffiths and Murray. On the academic side the approval for a new degree still had to undergo the rigorous examination of Senate's Courses Committee (now Quality and Academic Standards Committee). The expertise of this committee usually meant that modifications made would incorporate good practice before the proposals were recommended to Senate for approval. It would be rare for a proposal to be strongly discouraged – such an occasion was when an undergraduate degree in accountancy was turned down because of HEFCE constraints and scarce School resources. In the early 1990s the University was generating so many new degrees, and revising existing ones, that the committee had to operate as two committees in order to process the business within a reasonable time. The further need to relieve the pressure on the centre has resulted in the School being given more delegated authority to carry out some of the detailed work that Courses Committee had traditionally carried out.

Increased delegation has also been reflected in other areas. Thus, the School now manages its own appointments within the constraints of University policies. The inadequate standard of service provided by the centre with respect to IT, marketing and alumni has led the School to develop its own expertise in these areas. An implication of these changes is that a much stronger administrative infrastructure has had to be nurtured within the School. This in turn has created resentment in the School at having to contribute overheads for University central services that are being used to a decreasing extent.

Knowledge and skill needs in the market place. Individuals have knowledge and skill needs in the light of their careers and ambitions. The School tries to communicate that it can satisfy the needs of those individuals it is targeting through its promotional brochures and other public relations materials. The popularity and status of different business careers and professions in society fluctuate over time, and the School has to learn to be sensitive to these changes and to adapt accordingly. Its MBA programmes, and their revisions over time, illustrated this point. Similarly, individual organisations and whole sectors of the economy find that they develop knowledge and skill needs as they try to cope with new technologies (e.g. computerisation), new legislations (e.g. deregulation, equal opportunities, disclosure of information) and new forms of crime and terrorism (e.g. computer fraud, money laundering). The School also has to be cognisant of these changes and to respond appropriately; as happened when the Centre for Financial Regulation and Crime initiated a research programme under Dr Chizu Nakajima, and Executive Education ran a series of related short courses for the Metropolitan Police.

Opinion leaders. There are a number of groups and institutions in the School's environment that can have a disproportionate influence on the image created in the minds of potential students, clients and sponsors. These include: career counsellors in schools; HR managers in organisations; educational journalists in the media; prominent alumni of the School; and so on. The importance of influencing the thinking and maintaining good relationships with such opinion leaders is obvious, since they can influence the demand for the School's services and the attractions of being associated with the School.

Competitors: local, national and international. A major influence in the market place is of course competing business schools. In the 1960s and 1970s the MSc in Administrative Sciences faced a low level of competition. The competition with LBS was minimal, their two-year general programme appealed to a different market from the School's one-year specialist programme. The City location was an advantage over other former Colleges of Advanced Technology such as Surrey and Brunel which had moved to the outskirts of London. During the 1980s and beyond competition rose significantly as the number of business school multiplied at home and abroad (in 1986 there were 26 MBA courses in the United Kingdom, 10 years later there were 103, and now there are 117). Moreover, major consultancies were entering the executive development market, and some such as PA at Sundridge Park developed a strong brand image for quality courses. Henley and Ashridge had already established enviable reputations in the management development field.

The business school industry

Today there are several examples of institutions that represent the business and management education sector. They were created by individuals and groups who saw the need for the existence of pressure groups to:

- ensure that the interests of business schools were heard and responded to (both in their parent institution and in the wider context)
- improve the quality, and regulate the standards, of their products and services
- advance knowledge relating to business and management and to disseminate good practice.

Overlapping membership and common interests between the institutions ensured that there was a continual sharing of knowledge within the sector. Take for example the Association of Business Schools (ABS) – the 'trade body' for UK schools. The ABS was brought about by the merger of two bodies in October 1992: the Council of University Management Schools (CUMS) with its 30 plus corporate members, and the Association for Management and Business Education (AMBE) which represented the 85 major business and management units in polytechnics and colleges. This latter body was itself the result of a merger in 1987 between the Standing Committee on Business Schools and the Association of Management Education Centres. One of the factors that brought the bodies together was the 1992 legislation that ended the binary divide and brought the polytechnics within the university system. Another factor was the support of the Council for National Academic Awards (CNAA) – they provided the initial finance and accommodation for the merged ABS.

CUMS itself was formed in 1971. Its informal existence came into being in the mid-1960s when professors Kempner of Henley, Beresford-Dew of University of Manchester Institute of Science and Technology (UMIST) and Moore of LBS initiated the Conference of University Management Schools to provide a forum for discussing current issues relevant to business schools. The 12 schools represented at the first meeting agreed that a chairman would be appointed annually, that only directors or heads of departments would be invited, and that no formal secretariat would be established. Consequently there are no records of these early years, but these forums became so popular that when membership reached 27 records began to be kept. At the same time CUMS extended its influence in management education by negotiating a loan scheme with Midland Bank to assist postgraduates in management education. Working relationships were also established with EFMD, AMBA (under its initial name of Business Graduates Association), and ARMC (one of the two bodies later referred to as AMBE).

Within the context of the School, CUMS, ABS and BAM (British Academy of Management) there are several observations to make. First, the School was not one of the first 12 named as members in 1971, which were: Aston, Bath, Bradford, Cranfield, Durham, Henley, Leeds, LBS, MBS, MSM (UMIST), Salford, Scottish Business School. It was not until 1973 when the benefits became clearer that the School became a member, along with Imperial, Lancaster, Loughborough, Oxford, Warwick and others.

Second, during the CUMS era (i.e. 1973–92) most of our main competitors were involved as officers or executive committee members. Although Ivor Delafield was a member of the executive from 1980/81 to 1985/86, he was in fact based in other departments of the University for the best part of this period. This was indicative of the low priority the top management of the School attached to influencing the development of the business school industry. Chambers was the first Dean to be active in CUMS, being a member of the executive from 1988/89 to 1991/92. Indeed he and Georges Selim (sub-Dean at that time) contributed to a CUMS seminar on specialist masters degrees in management (a feature for which the School was becoming known). Minutes of its executive committee in the late 1980s show how active and successful the body was as a pressure group. Direct representations were made to the Permanent Secretary of the Department of Education and Science; individuals were briefed before the House of Lords debate on management education (16/3/88); the attention of various government departments and agencies (e.g. ESRC) was drawn to the lack of representation of the business schools on their committees; a submission was made to the UGC concerning the next Research Selectivity Exercise; executive lunches were held with key people able to influence government policy on management education (e.g. MPs such as Jack Straw and Timothy Raison; Lord Annan; Baronesses Blackstone and Seear). All these efforts bore fruit and a number of well-known names in the business school world soon found themselves on the targeted committees. These academics included: George Bain, John Constable, Leo Murray, Andrew Thomson, Andrew Pettigrew, Stephen Watson and John Burgoyne.

The promotion of business schools was also achieved through publications. For instance, in 1989/90 CUMS produced a brochure on 34 schools, including a full page on the School. There is no doubt that by enabling the major business schools in the United Kingdom to speak with one voice CUMS was able to influence relevant environmental factors. This influence increased as a result of the merger of CUMS and AMBE in October 1992. Jonathan Slack, the designated chief officer of the future ABS, wrote in the 11 September issue of the *Times* Higher Educational Supplement: 'ABS will develop policies that reflect its diverse membership and forge effective relationships with other national bodies within higher education and the world of business and management at large. Most importantly, ABS will need to demonstrate that it can achieve more than individual business schools can acting alone and, by listening and responding to members' needs, speak with authority on behalf of and to the benefit of the new business school sector.'

The third relevant observation to make is that both the BAM and CUMS/ABS have tried over the years to extract more money for management research out of ESRC. Management research has been grossly under-funded relative to other social science disciplines. The two main reasons appear to be: management research proposals were usually peer reviewed by economists and sociologists, applying frames of reference that were inappropriate for a good deal of multi-disciplinary management research; the relatively poor quality of proposals coming from management researchers. The perseverance of academics, particularly with their BAM hat on, has started to turn the tide. A key factor in this was the report of the Commission on Management Research under the Chairmanship of George Bain, the then Principal of LBS (ESRC 1994). The report lists its membership of 15, and the 91 organisations and the 49 individuals making a submission. Sadly, a scrutiny of these lists will show that the School's main competitors were well represented, but that there was neither a submission from the School nor from its individual academics. An early result of the report saw the ESRC devoting more money to the training of young academics in business schools (e.g. the Teaching Fellowship Scheme). More recently ESRC allocated a large sum of money to setting up a co-ordinating structure (Advanced Management Institute or AIM) and to create a series of fellowships that would allow outstanding management scholars to conduct research projects unencumbered by teaching and administrative duties. The School benefited from the Teaching Fellowship Scheme, but not from the initial selection of AIM Fellows. However, it has had more recent benefit from AIM funds such as the International Study Fellowship awarded to Chris Rowley in support of his research in South Korea.

A number of academics came together to create the BAM in 1986/87. The prime movers included Professors Andrew Thompson of the Open University, Cary Cooper of UMIST and Andrew Pettigrew of Warwick. BAM mirrors the very successful American Academy of Management by adopting similar objectives (see Box 7.1).

Box 7.1 Objectives of British Academy of Management.

- Encouraging the sharing and development of a research-knowledge base for all the management disciplines;
- acting as a forum for the various disciplines in management and to encourage the development of an integrated body of knowledge commensurate with management as a profession;
- encouraging and promoting interdisciplinary research and collaboration among the various management disciplines;
- furthering the professional development of those engaged in management education and development as a career.

The influence of BAM has increased over the years, and can claim membership of the majority of academics involved in management education. Before its formation the body that fulfilled a related need, but which focused primarily on course content and teaching methods and on bringing together academics and industrialists/consultants, was the Association for Teachers of Management. In the early years of management education in the 1960s and 1970s this body met a real need for exchanging theory and practice in relation to management education. This Association gradually haemorrhaged its academic membership as it catered more for consultants concerned with individual and organisation development, and was subsequently renamed the Association of Management Education and Development. The more research-based BAM was formed to fill the role that the Association had failed to meet.

The School has had a fairly low key involvement in the decision-making structures of these bodies. The author served in the 1990s on BAM Council, its Research Policy Committee, and its Fellowship Committee. Leslie Hannah was successfully persuaded to be a member of the executive committee of ABS, but soon after he was elected he moved to Ashridge. A similar picture emerges of low key involvement in the formal structures of international bodies such as the European Foundation for Management Development. However, the School has usually been well represented at conferences, meetings and accreditation panels arranged by these various bodies – thereby accessing important sources of information on academic developments, the new activities of competitors and examples of good practice.

From the discussion around the 'business school industry' it is fair to say that the School has benefited from the developments without having taken a leadership role. The value of Figure 7.1 is that it illustrates the concept of an 'open system' within the context of a business school, and identifies the potential factors/forces influencing growth or decline. The strength of these forces fluctuates overtime as new ones become dominant and old ones fade away. The most obvious new force is the entry of additional competitors such as the Said School in Oxford and the Judge Institute in Cambridge – both were latecomers to the business school scene and benefit enormously from the prestigious image of their parent institution. A force that has diminished over the years is that of the Foundation for Management Education; this has been counterbalanced by the new forces created by younger institutions such as BAM and ABS. The reciprocal arrows between the elements in Figure 7.1 are intended to emphasise the mutual influence they exert on one another, thereby continually changing the dynamics of the School's environment. For example the emergence of strong coalitions, as illustrated in the launch of EQUIS (the EFMD's quality assurance agency which was largely influenced by the thinking of ABS), will have profound implications for those schools wanting to achieve EQUIS accreditation since they will strive to satisfy its criteria. Reviewing the history of the School it is clear that some of these factors have exerted far greater weight in facilitating and/or holding back the School's progress. Government legislation and University policies are obvious examples.

Looking more into the future there is one trend in the business school world that is becoming more visible. This is the development of partnerships and strategic alliances between business schools, and between them and other non-academic organisations. Several top schools in the United Kingdom, Europe and beyond have been active in this area. It is a strategy that creates opportunities to enhance the internationalisation of a school, and to develop innovative programmes with the minimum of risk. For most of its history the School has developed such alliances, without it being a major plank in its strategy (see for instance references elsewhere to student exchange agreements, AMSEC, Consortium MBA, China MBA, SIMFONEC, Centre for Charity Effectiveness). The signs are that partnerships and alliances will become an even more explicit feature of the School's strategy in the future, and will mirror the trend highlighted in the Vice-Chancellor's introduction to the City University's Annual Report for 2002–03.

8
Mission and Vision

So far Part III has highlighted the contextual factors that have impinged, and continue to impinge, upon the School (see Figure 7.1). The following chapters identify and explore the School's strategies for coping and advancing in an increasingly competitive environment. These strategies generated planned and unplanned forces that had to be 'managed' over time. Potentially one of the most powerful internal forces in a business school is that generated by a shared mission or vision.

Cultural obstacles

In the days of the Department of Management and Social Sciences (i.e. before 1966) the small group of management-oriented staff shared a common vision of building one of the best centres for management education in the United Kingdom. They were supported in this by Sir James Tait, the Principal and first Vice-Chancellor. At that time an important aspect of the mission for the new department/School was to foster a mutually advantageous link between a technological university and the City of London with its dominant financial sector. The fulcrum of that link was to be management education. In 1966, and the years immediately before and after, there was no doubt that the School was a poor relation next to the two new prestigious schools of London and Manchester. The University had made the major decision of staying in central London, in contrast to Surrey and Brunel, and Tait and his advisors must have realised that the success of this decision would rest on the relationship with the City.

The process of building this relationship was much more difficult than many had thought, but with hindsight this is no surprise. The

University's early affinity to engineering and manufacturing industry created a culture that sat uncomfortably with finance and the City. The history of the School revealed its early culture to be heavily influenced by the University. Breaking out of this mould was a slow process, depending as it did on the snail pace of change in personnel and products that is characteristic of under-resourced academic institutions. Moreover, a change in culture depended upon the City recognising the relevance of the School for its needs. This was the greatest barrier to progress, since City institutions were reluctant to switch their allegiance from the officially sponsored LBS (to whom many had contributed financially) and the well established American schools such as Harvard, Wharton and Stanford.

Leadership in sharpening the mission

Through the cumulative efforts of successive Deans the School's mission became more focused and there was a greater sharing of the vision. Under the Deanships of Treasure, Griffiths and Chambers several Chairs were sponsored by financial institutions, and the City-cum-financial orientation became more pronounced. By November 1986 Andrew Chambers was able to report to the Business School Council the School's objectives as:

> In general terms the School is dedicated to the pursuit of excellence in business school education. We intend to be the leading UK business school and amongst the leaders worldwide. Being neither the first nor the best endowed business school in the UK, and in particular in the London area, our strategy has been to differentiate ourselves from our principle competitors in two ways: by setting out to be market leaders in serving the needs of the City of London; by setting out to be market leaders in undergraduate degree programmes ....

He went on to say that the School's strategy required it to be innovators in new programmes, and in view of its role as the City of London's business school 'a significant part of the development emphasis of the School should be directed towards achieving genuine internationalisation'.

When David Kaye was appointed Dean he adopted a management consultant's approach to the development of a formal mission statement. The whole of Kaye's career was as a consultant with Arthur Anderson, and therefore it was perhaps not surprising that he brought with him the toolbox of good practice that management consultants were selling to their clients. After extended discussions with senior staff in the School the agreed mission statement was: 'To be a top-rated business school serving industry and commerce across the world, and to be the business school of first resort for students and organisations focusing on activity associated with the City of London and the business professions.'

A brochure was printed in June 1994 entitled 'Mission Statement'. Preceding the actual statement was a preamble to explain the purpose of the statement, that is, to 'focus on what we do, giving it direction and drive ... (It) provides a framework of beliefs and aspirations to which business school staff can refer when making decisions, and against which those decisions will be judged'. Following the statement there were prescriptive guidelines relating to strategy, values, standards. Although this was the first time the School had undergone such a professional exercise, it encapsulated the essence of the main goals or objectives that had driven the senior members of the School since the days of David Glen (i.e. from 1968 onwards). However it incorporated a change of emphasis that had been evolving over many years – the mention of 'business professions' but no specific reference to 'management' or 'management education'.

Kaye's mission statement was explicitly adopted by Leslie Hannah and implicitly by David Currie, and both of them pushed even further the City of London focus. Thus, soon after taking up the Deanship Hannah said 'We'er aiming to be the bread and butter supplier to the City' to Della Bradshaw of the *FT* (20 October 1997). Lord Currie has repeated on many occasions, at staff meetings and to external audiences, that Cass aims to be 'the intellectual hub of the City of London'. As was pointed out in Chapter 7 an up-dated mission statement has recently been written by the School. This clarifies even more forcefully than before the aspirations of the School to be in the top 5 schools in the United Kingdom, and in the top 25 and eventually the top 10 in the World. The strategies to be followed, and the values and standards to be adopted, are consistent with those in the comprehensive mission statement prepared in the Kaye Deanship. However, there are subtle differences in the mission as stated by Kaye and the one now adopted under Currie: 'To be the business school of the City of London and its intellectual hub, serving the needs of financial institutions, professions and companies through business education, leading-edge research and stimulating debate on the key strategic issues and policy issues facing business'. The latest statement is more 'operational' and explicitly mentions the two core academic activities of education and research.

The School's mission and vision is compatible with that of the University as it should be. This has become even more apparent in recent years. The process of developing the most recent document was initiated by David Rhind, the current Vice-Chancellor, and approved by Senate and Council in 1999. The School's mission and strategies can readily be subsumed under those of the University as they appear on its website. From the point of view of the School an important turning point came when the University incorporated the words 'The University for business and the professions' in its publicity literature. This reinforced its changing profile in the eyes of the public, and recognised that the distinctive feature of the University was no longer engineering. Meeting the needs of the professions has been part of the University culture for a long time, and this has helped shape the School's culture and has affected the design and content of many of its degrees (the School has links with 14 professional bodies). Total or partial exemption from the examinations of professional bodies in the process of getting a degree is a strong incentive to potential students, as well as sealing a mutually beneficial relationship with a network of organisations critical to the employment of students. It is worth noting that the incorporation of the word 'business' in the University's slogan aroused a lively discussion at Senate when David Rhind successfully argued for its use. Symbolically this development was significant as it represented the dying throes of the old University culture, and the recognition of the new culture that had been emerging over the years.

Box 8.1 The School's broad and continuing strategies.

- Growth so as to strengthen the School's power base vis-à-vis the University and external competition.
- Differentiation from the University in order to establish and maintain a high rank among UK and international business schools.
- Catering for the professional market.
- Developing products and services for the City of London's financial institutions, and drawing on the practical expertise of these institutions in order to take full advantage of the School's location.
- Developing professionalism, that is, running the School as a business.
- Developing a quality research culture in order to meet one of the key criteria differentiating the top business schools from the rest.
- Occupying quality premises.
- Developing a quality teaching and learning culture in order to build and maintain the loyalty of students, their sponsors and employers.

Emergent strategies

Having a mission and a vision is one thing, realising it is quite different. The broad and continuing strategies followed by the School can be summarised as in Box 8.1.

These eight strategies are all consistent with each other. The last strategy is probably the only one common to all business schools, although even here the level of effort going into following this strategy can differ significantly. Given the historical evidence, how were these strategies realised? What proved helpful or unhelpful in the evolution and implementation of these strategies? These are some of the questions that will now be tackled under the four chapter headings: Growth through innovation and expansion; Differentiation and orientation; Development of a quality culture; Premises: the meandering pathway to a state-of-the-art building.

9

Growth Through Innovation and Expansion

In business schools sustainable growth comes via various pathways, including: new degrees to open up new markets; expanding student intake on existing degrees; increasing fees; expanding and innovating in the executive development market; increasing research income and associated research activity. This chapter will focus on growth generated through degrees since it was this pathway that contributed most to the School's resources.

An explicit strategy of growth has always been followed by those leading the School. This undoubtedly helped the University out of a succession of financial crises caused by a combination of a shrinking market for engineering courses and government policies involving financial cutbacks. The School was not the only part of the University able to innovate and expand, but it was the major player. The shift from engineering to business and management was highlighted in Raoul Franklin's review of the first 10 years of his office as Vice-Chancellor (see *CityPlus*, Number Two, Winter 1988–89, p. 4). In the review he pointed to the changes that had taken place in staffing. In 1976 the School had no undergraduates and Engineering had 49 per cent; by 1986 Engineering had 28 per cent of the University's undergraduates and the School 25 per cent. On the postgraduate side in 1976 the School had 41 per cent (101 students), and Engineering 27 per cent (66); by 1986 the School had 35 per cent (238) and Engineering 11 per cent (74). In both faculties during the period staff changes had been greater than 50 per cent, involving a significant fall in numbers among Engineering faculty and a slight rise among School faculty. The relevance of these observations is that they reflect, and precipitated, an organisational culture change from an engineering institution to a broader-based university in which 'business and management' was a major part. The School's growth strategy was given a particularly strong boost during the Deanship of Andrew Chambers, who saw it as a way of increasing the power of the School in negotiations with the University. Similar boosts occurred in subsequent years. Under Kaye, Hannah and Currie growth was a prerequisite to house the School in a quality building, and to build up the financial resources to maintain the successful occupancy of the building.

The forces at work that sustained this drive for growth are complex. They include: individual motivation of staff to experience intrinsic (e.g. a feeling of achievement) and extrinsic rewards (e.g. improved facilities); perceived market opportunities; approaches made by external bodies (e.g. professional institutions) to provide new courses or services; the need for some disciplines to build up critical mass thus giving individuals the opportunity to specialise; competition from other business schools; pressure from University Officers and Deans to increase student numbers (thus reflecting the political and financial reasons mentioned earlier). While these various factors were creating synergistic forces for innovative behaviours, each new degree had its own unique combination of factors. This is illustrated next.

MSc in Administrative Sciences

A highly motivated and cohesive team of seven full-time staff launched the degree in September 1966. Since there was no standard content for such a degree at that time, its design was very much a product of the team's experience and academic expertise. A year later the team expanded to 13 to cover all the functional areas of management. Three key principles influenced the structure, content and recruitment policy of the MSc: on graduating the students should be of immediate value to their employer in one of the functional areas of management; while students were given sufficient knowledge and skills for this aim to be achieved, it was critical that they should also be given sufficient knowledge of other functional areas so that they could appreciate their contributions within the overall organisational context; the first degree of students needed to be relevant to their chosen specialism. These principles were reflected in the nomenclature and specialisms available to the first intake (see Chapter 3). Choice of specialisms increased as new staff were recruited. Thus in 1968/69 'Investment Analysis and Management', and 'Financial Management' were added.

It is worth pointing out that the basic structure of this degree remained the same until the early 1990s. The promotion and marketing of the degree and the initial recruitment process were centralised, but potential students were required to prioritise their choice of specialism, and the interviewing and the acceptance/rejection of an applicant were made by the staff teaching that specialism. This arrangement reflected the structure that had emerged around disciplines and functions. The structure became more formalised over the years as specialisms or options became divisions, and then departments. Other changes that occurred reflected environmental forces: internal and external knowledge developments (e.g. occupational psychology changed to behavioural sciences and then to organisational behaviour); market declines (e.g. the closure of operations research); opening up of new markets (e.g. new specialisms in insurance; export management and international business); and changed employer needs (e.g. managerial work experience became more important than relevant first degree). An exception to the emphasis on managerial experience was in the area of finance where degree relevance remained the primary criterion. There were other ways in which the finance specialism was treated differently. Thus, finance students were awarded from 1976/77 to 1980/81 an MSc in Finance rather than an MSc Administrative Sciences (Finance). When the MSc title of the degree was changed to MBA in 1981, this differentiation between finance and the other specialisms disappeared. However, these early signs of finance faculty wanting to be seen, and being seen, as 'different' from the rest of the faculty evolved early in the School's culture and became self-reinforcing with the passing of time.

During the 1990s a combination of factors resulted in various attempts to re-structure the Day MBA: specialisms with falling student numbers were closed, external pressure to conform to the norm of presenting the MBA degree as a general management degree reduced the emphasis on the specialisms, recruitment was centralised under a single director in order to ensure a high quality intake across the board, an overall director for the different MBA programmes was appointed so as to maximise the use of potential synergies. These changes were initiated by management in an effort to confront increasing competition (Williams 1993).

MSc Information Science

This degree started off as a Postgraduate Diploma and an MSc version was introduced on achieving University status. The subject area's introduction into Northampton CAT was due to the foresight of Alvin Leyton (Head of Liberal Studies) and the entrepreneurial spirit of Jason Farradane.

As with many entrepreneurs and innovators Farradane was concerned in leading his own little group of enthusiasts, and would only become involved in departmental matters if they affected his degree. In 1973 the success of his course, and the absence of links with the rest of the School, resulted in the formation of an independent Information Science Department within the University. Its success has continued under a series of Heads to the present day.

PGDip/MSc Business Systems and Design

The business systems and design academics were another group of staff with entrepreneurial leanings. Here again they tended to operate as a separate sub-group; initiated no doubt by their original self-financing status and their professional orientation. However, they did become much more involved in the School as illustrated by Alwyn Jones being part of the management of the School as a member of the Triumvirate in 1976/77. This particular subject area developed in the School as a result of an approach made to Kenneth Shone by the Civil Service College in 1970. They wanted to establish joint courses in business systems analysis. As an experiment ten courses were run based on the National Computing Council syllabus. Their success led to the introduction of a Postgraduate Diploma in Systems Analysis in 1973, and to an MSc in 1977. In 1983 an Undergraduate Diploma in Business Data Processing was established to prepare students for the MSc as well as being a professional qualification in its own right. Also in 1983 a joint undergraduate degree in Business Computing Systems was launched with the Department of Computer Science. The steady expansion of courses offered in this area was accompanied by the recruitment of additional staff. In 1970 there were two academics (Owen Hanson and Alwyn Jones) and a secretary. By 1989 there were 11 academics and 5 administrators. As this area developed so the corresponding structure changed: the group of staff became a centre within the School in 1983, a department in 1988, and a fully independent department within the University in 1989.

Much of the growth in this area was due to the drive and determination of Owen Hanson. He came to the School with a degree in Natural Sciences from Cambridge, work experience in IBM and other companies, an MSc in Computer Science from Birkbeck, and a strong belief that what was being taught in his area of expertise in universities was not sufficiently business related. When it was not possible for the Barbican premises to house the whole School in 1981, the semi-autonomous nature of Hanson's group meant that Dean Treasure persuade them to be located in the main building of the University. This geographical separation, together with some disagreements over expansion that they subsequently had with Dean Chambers, generated the additional forces that led to their complete separation in 1989. However, the 'know how' most relevant to the School was preserved by one of his team (Ann Leeming) opting to remain in the School with the idea of introducing an IT stream in the full-time MBA. This duly came about in conjunction with Clive Holtham, who had taken up his appointment in 1988 to the Bull Chair in Information Technology.

BSc Business Studies and other undergraduate degrees

Intentions to develop an undergraduate degree had been incorporated into plans as far back as 1968. A few years later a tentative attempt to revive interest in an undergraduate degree was made by Basil Taylor, but he failed to get management support. Taylor had good contacts at LBS, and realised that it was going to be difficult to compete with LBS for good postgraduate students. He felt that the opportunity for the School to be the most attractive business school in London for undergraduates was there for the taking. However, it was not until Ivor Delafield provided the necessary energy and enthusiasm, and managed to gain the support of the Triumvirate and then John Treasure, that the degree was launched and the first graduates entered the market in 1982. While the early part of the degree covered the range of subject areas one would expect to find in the degree, the latter part divided the students into two streams of specialisation – finance and marketing. This reflected the City-orientation strategy and the interest of the marketing academics who were keen to be involved in the degree.

The second undergraduate degree that grew within the School was the BSc in Insurance and Investment. In 1990/91 this particular combination was probably unique in the United Kingdom. The degree grew out of the Centre for Insurance and Investment Studies. Initially this was an independent centre within the University focusing on research, under the direction of Professor Bernard Benjamin. When he retired Paddy Kennedy, a senior member of the insurance industry (former CEO of Eagle Star), headed the centre. He was keen to develop an undergraduate degree, being aware of its potential value to the insurance industry. In 1987 Gerry Dickinson, who had been a member of the School since 1973, joined the Centre to help develop the degree. Substantial donations over a ten-year period were made to the Centre by the Association of British Insurers. When Kennedy resigned in 1989 the Centre was integrated into the School with Gerry Dickinson at its head; and was relocated from the main site to the Barbican. Further undergraduate degrees were added to the School's portfolio as a result of absorbing centres or departments that had developed their own degrees elsewhere in the University. The BSc in Banking and International Finance was added when the centre with that name became part of the School soon after Griffiths was appointed Dean. The BSc in Property Valuation and Management came when the department of that name was incorporated into the School in 1992. The BSc in Management and Systems came when elements of the department by that name were dispersed to several parts of the University. The BSc in Actuarial Science came when that department became absorbed into the School in 2002 and Professor Haberman was appointed Deputy Dean. Prior to their absorption all these degrees had had various amounts of inputs from staff of the School, and this no doubt helped to smooth their transition.

A notable attraction introduced into the undergraduate programme in the latter half of the 1980s was the opportunity to graduate with both a BSc and a Master of European Business (MEB) if a fourth year of study was chosen. This involved studying at one of the School's partner institutions for six months before completing the course at the School by taking a selection of MSc programme electives and completing a dissertation. The fees for the MEB remained at the undergraduate level, and the course gave the student knowledge of European business, fluency in a second language, and experience of another culture. This combination made the MEB graduates attractive to employers. Apart from the MEB, undergraduates had the opportunity of spending their second or third year abroad at an approved institution. Thus the various alternatives the School provided enabled a selection of students to develop a firsthand international perspective.

Evening MBA (EMBA)

When this degree was introduced in 1983 it was the first postgraduate degree that had been designed from scratch for the School's hinterland. Given the success of part-time MBAs in American schools it was clear that the market for a two-year, two evenings a week, part-time MBA in London was wide open for institutions prepared to take the plunge. In the case of the School it was the entrepreneurial spirit of Professor Hugh Murray that played a large part in its introduction. He had already been responsible for introducing a new specialism in the Day MBA, that is, Export

Management and International Business. The successful launch of the EMBA, and its continued success, hid some of the problems that had to be overcome. Many staff who had been contributing to UGC approved courses (all scheduled for the daytime), were reluctant to contribute to this new 'self-financing' degree and even more reluctant to give up some of their evenings. Murray's business management background gave him a penchant for self-financing courses, and his boundless energy and determination overcame many of the difficulties he faced. Fortunately he also had the full support of Dean Griffiths and a core of full-time staff who volunteered to contribute to the teaching (these were mainly staff belonging to the Export Management and International Business division led by Murray). The University was also keen on expanding student numbers and in generating new income streams. The 'brushed under the carpet' problem of having two covert categories of staff – those financed out of UGC/HEFCE funds, and those recruited to teach primarily on self-financing courses – subsequently created difficulties for the management of the School until the dichotomy was firmly eradicated under David Kaye's Deanship. The University saw this as a problem of the School's own creation, referring the School back to the contract of employment for staff that gave management more power than they chose to exercise. However, for many staff this legally based contract was in conflict with their psychological contract, that is, the expectations they formed when they were first recruited (Schalk and Rousseau 2001).

MSc Shipping, Trade and Finance

This ground-breaking degree was even more the result of an individual effort when it was launched in 1984. Soon after Brian Griffiths became Dean in March 1982 he invited Costas Grammenos to lunch and suggested that he become a visiting professor at the School. Griffiths was already aware of the book that Grammenos had published in 1978 on finance and the shipping industry, the lecture he gave at the Harvard Business School in 1981, and the network he had started to build within the City of London. At the lunch Griffiths outlined his plans for drawing the School closer to the financial City, and persuaded Grammenos that there would be opportunities for him to extend his contacts in the financial and shipping sphere. As a visiting professor he offered two electives on the MBA specialism in export management and international finance: 'Shipping and shipping finance', and 'International banking'. In 1983 he started to work on a new MSc which he wanted to be part of a centre under his direction. He realised that this goal would only come about if he could raise enough money from the City. The degree (and informally the centre) was launched at the Baltic Exchange in May 1984 with Geoffrey Howe (the Foreign Secretary) as the guest speaker. An initial sum of £200,000 was quickly raised, and the Centre for Shipping, Trade and Finance was duly established within the School's Department of Business Studies. In its first year the MSc in Shipping, Trade and Finance had 23 part-time students. As numbers increased a full-time version was also introduced, as was a further MSc in Trade, Transport and Finance in 1997. These degrees have brought global praise and prestige to the School from the shipping industry.

Postgraduate Diploma/MSc Internal Auditing

This degree was a natural progression from the earlier pioneering efforts of Andrew Chambers. Chambers joined the School in 1971 as a Lecturer in Computing Applications and Accountancy. He soon developed short courses in computer auditing, and internal auditing became available as a specialism in 1975 in the MSc Administrative Sciences and in the MSc Finance. It had become clear to him and others that the academic development of internal auditing was in need of a more rigorous research base. Through a Senior Research Fellowship from the Leverhulme Trust he was able to focus on research over a four-year period from 1974. This research effort was distilled in a book *Internal Auditing – Theory and Practice* in 1981, and a steady stream of doctoral theses began to appear in internal auditing (one of the early theses being that of Georges Selim, a current professor who became Head of the Faculty of Management in 2004). In 1983 Chambers was promoted to a Chair in Internal Auditing, partly financed by BP. This was probably the first such Chair in Europe. The Postgraduate Diploma and MSc in Internal Auditing were introduced in 1987. Throughout all these developments Chambers, together with those he recruited to teach on the programme, worked closely with the relevant professional body – the Institute of Internal Auditors. Those successful in the School's examinations were able to get full exemption from the Institute's examinations. As one individual observed, internal auditing was something of a 'cinderella' subject in the School, and when student recruitment fell away the degree had to be revamped to incorporate more management in order to survive. In 2003 it became one of the streams on offer in the new MSc in Management (see later). Chambers has made the interesting observation that locating the early internal auditing teaching and research within a business school rather than an accounting department, has been a key to its successful development.

Consortium MBA (or Management MBA)

This degree was launched in 1987, and was yet another innovation of Hugh Murray's. The approach it adopted had taken on board the management learning philosophy of Reg Revans (Revans 1983). In this he was strongly supported by Ronnie Lessem, whose PhD thesis was in this area. Indeed Reg Revans was one of his external examiners, and the second was John Morris who promoted a similar learning method at MBS (and who incidentally lectured to the author in social and occupational psychology in the mid-1950s). Students learnt by carrying out live projects at their place of work, and by coming together as a learning group at regular intervals. Each student had an academic supervisor and a manager supervisor at their place of work. Projects had to be approved by both supervisors. There were no traditional written examinations. Students were given oral examinations on their projects by two external examiners. An even more radical element was the structure that was introduced to run the degree. It was seen as a joint partnership with a consortium of organisations, each company contributing toward the cost and having a say on the development of the scheme (always subject to the University's veto on academic matters). Moreover, the programme drew on a range of executive development courses available within the consortium companies to add to the tailor-made courses run by the School.

The innovative nature of the proposals meant that Murray had a struggle to get it through the School and the University. It was difficult to get already overstretched academic staff to become involved in the degree, and its success depended on external part-time lecturers/supervisors even more than the Evening MBA. The degree brought favourable publicity to the School, and was used by Henry Mintzberg as an example of innovative thinking in management education in the United Kingdom. Ronnie Lessem took over as director of the programme once it was established, and adapted it to accord with his ideas without prejudicing the action learning philosophy. During the Deanship of David Kaye the decision was taken to close the programme; the School's management felt that its financial performance was poor and that the difficulties involved in monitoring the quality of the programme were too great (this particularly related to that part of the programme that was being run jointly with a partner consultancy firm in the Middle East). Also competing business schools (e.g. Warwick) had been quick to develop similar programmes that catered more successfully for the same market.

MScs in Property Valuation and Finance

A clutch of three postgraduate degrees and an undergraduate degree came to the School in 1992 as a result of the Property and Finance Department being merged into the School. As an independent department its future had been looking bleak, and the University was keen that small departments should be absorbed by the most relevant school. There was certainly an overlap in expertise, although the immediate advantages of the merger were rather skewed against the interests of the School with respect to finance (they brought a deficit with them as the School subsequently discovered!), and to a lesser extent with respect to research and quality systems.

MScs in Insurance, Investment, Mathematical Trading

A Centre for Insurance and Investment had brought together the relevant research and teaching elements within the School. In the mid-1990s three postgraduate degrees were added to its BSc: MScs in Insurance and Investment (subsequently changed to Insurance and Risk Management); Investment Management; Mathematical Trading and Finance. These degrees were introduced earlier than anticipated in the School's strategic plan. Forces at work here undoubtedly included: market opportunities; external support (City Corporation); Elias Dinenis' entrepreneurial spirit and focused drive (including ambition for promotion to a Chair); and Dean Kaye's strong management hand in pursuing the School's strategies (e.g. City orientation, building-up the financial reserves), and his own background in mathematics.

The development of the Mathematical Trading and Finance degree is an interesting story. The degree, and the Centre of that name, was sponsored by the Corporation of London. Within two days of the press release publicising the launch of the degree the news had penetrated all relevant institutions in the City. The official launch at Merchant Taylor's Livery Hall in 1996 took place with the first intake present. The quality of the intake was such, that every one of the students had become an attractive commodity in the City when they were only a few weeks into the course!

MScs relating to Finance

In the last five years of the MSc in Administrative Sciences (i.e. 1976–81), students who opted to specialise in finance did in fact receive an MSc in Finance. Apart from the finance element in the MBA programmes, the Shipping Trade and Finance MSc, and a putative attempt to launch an MSc by Mike Beenstock in the early 1980s, no new Masters in the finance area were introduced until the mid- to-late 1990s. The restructuring of the School during Kaye's Deanship was accompanied by a crop of MScs. This development was facilitated by a number of factors in addition to a market need, including:

- a working party (consisting of the three MBA directors and chaired by the author) reporting in 1994, indicated the need for new MScs to compensate for the likely saturation of the MBA market;
- the competitive tensions (internal market?) created by the new departmental structure (e.g. particularly between the heads of 'Accounting and Finance', and 'Investment, Risk Management and Insurance');
- the need to increase the income of the School so as to strengthen its position when negotiating over new premises with the University;
- the need for the Department of Banking and Finance to use its spare teaching capacity to generate income for the School.

On their own these factors were insufficient; they had to be combined with the efforts of an individual prepared to take the lead, and a supportive management pushing for results. The outcomes were the three MScs already referred to earlier; an MSc in Finance led by Professor Mario Levis; an MSc in Banking and International Finance led by Professor Roy Batchelor; and an MSc in Finance, Economics and Econometrics led by Professor Mark Salmon.

Postgraduate Diploma/MSc in Voluntary Sector Management, and related MScs

This is yet another example of an innovative programme that came into existence along a novel route. Ian Bruce, the Director General of the Royal National Institute for the Blind since 1983, had developed expertise in marketing and strategic planning as a result of working in commercial and voluntary organisations. He had identified a need for management development at the senior level of the voluntary sector, and together with nine leading charities he designed an advanced management programme. The nine were: RNIB, Help the Aged, Age Concern, RELATE, British Red Cross, WWF, Family Welfare Association, YMCA and Guide Dogs for the Blind. He persuaded the School to host the programme, and from 1994 those participants who wished to register for the Diploma and duly satisfied the examiners were awarded a postgraduate diploma. An MSc was introduced in 2000 to meet the demand from students who wished to take their studies even further. The arrangement with the School was that as a Visiting Professor he would be the Honorary Director of the Centre for Voluntary Sector and Not-for-profit Management. The Centre was self-financing and since all classes were held outside the School, minimal demands were made on the School (this amounted to desk space for a part-time course manager, and an occasional part-time lecturer). Academics contributing to the courses have all been part-timers. This arrangement has meant that the fees charged have been considerably less than for other programmes at the School, and this has been managed without affecting the quality of the programme. In 2001 the Quality Assessment Agency (QAA) singled out the programme for special commendation. Although the programme is aimed at individuals, it closely involves sponsoring organisations. The design elements include: five taught course modules of two to three days each; learning sets with programme colleagues; coaching and mentoring by senior charity managers, involving the student's line manager, as well as a senior executive, possibly from another organisation; shadowing a senior manager who is expert in an area unfamiliar to the student; three work-based assignments; a project.

The inevitable drawback of this arrangement for VOLPROF was that its research contribution to the School was limited, and despite its teaching reputation this was a threat under the prevalent RAE climate to its longer term membership of the School. In 2001 a window of opportunity arose for yet another creative solution. The Guild of Management Consultants which was formed in 1993 (now the 105th livery company as the Worshipful Company of Management Consultants) was seeking to establish a mutually beneficial relationship with the School (Fraser 2004). As part of its charitable aims the Guild was keen to contribute to the education of those likely to enter the consultancy profession, to improve the management of charities through pro bono consultancy and the mentoring of their CEOs, and to sponsor related research. The Company began to explore the possibility of creating a centre in the School around which it could base the work it was doing to enhance the effective management of charities. The School was a natural choice for several reasons: several members of the Company had already helped by opening doors to consultancies for a School research project into the consultancy process (Williams and Woodward 1994); two members had also contributed to electives on the School's MBA programmes (i.e. Calvert Markham and Barry Curnow); the Company awarded the Urwick Cup and a cash prize annually to the most meritorious student on the MBA programme (the cup commemorated Col. Lyndal Urwick's pioneering contributions to the development of management education and consultancy in the United Kingdom); there was a strong link with the Company through its Court of Assistants (the author being a Founder Member in 1993, and a Founder Liveryman in 2004). It made sense to explore the mutual advantages of linking the Company's new initiative to the already established activities of VOLPROF. A proposal for a centre to be jointly run by the two institutions was approved by Lord Currie and his executive committee, on the understanding that the necessary funds would be obtained from external sponsors. In the process of fund raising it became clear that potential sponsors were reluctant to contribute toward a centre that was indistinguishable from the School. This led to the formation in 2003 of the City Centre for Charity Effectiveness Trust Limited – jointly owned by Cass and the Company.

A further boost to the School's activities in the voluntary and charities sector came when Professor Paul Palmer negotiated for his team and MSc programmes to be transferred from the South Bank University to join the newly formed Centre for Charity Effectiveness (officially launched in December 2004). Under the leadership particularly of Professor Ian Bruce (for Cass) and John McLean Fox (for the Company) the Centre has brought together an array of expertise in the voluntary and charities sector that has no serious rival in Europe. It provides academic research, postgraduate degrees, practical short courses, as well as specialist mentoring and consultancy services (www.centreforcharity effectiveness.org). The latter services are provided on a pro bono basis for those charities that would not otherwise be able to benefit from them. To date most of the corporate sponsors have been appropriately City based – Barclays Bank, Baring Foundation, Bridge House Trust, Esmee Fairbairn Foundation, HSBC, Gatsby Charitable Fund, Pears Foundation, Shirley Foundation, Worshipful Company of Haberdashers, Lloyds TSB Foundation. These developments mean that the School now has, in addition to the Postgraduate Diploma/MSc in Voluntary Sector Management, MScs in Charity Accounting and Financial Management, Charity Marketing and Fundraising, and Grant Making Management. The importance of this sector to the British Economy is evident when one realises that it accounts for as much as 9 per cent of gross domestic product, and employs some 500,000 paid workers in the United Kingdom and several million volunteers.

Other new degrees

Further undergraduate and postgraduate degrees were added to the School's portfolio with the incorporation of Actuarial Science and Statistics from the School of Mathematics (i.e. a BSc and a Dip/MSc in Actuarial Science, and a Dip/MSc in Actuarial Management). Reference has already been made to the new MSc in Management that was introduced in 2003 with an initial intake of over 80 well qualified students. This degree is designed to cater for those who want a qualification in management before meeting the experience criteria required to join an MBA programme; at the same time this degree caters for those students who previously took the Internal Auditing and Management MSc. Reference has also been made in Chapter 6 to the China MBA launched in 2003. The final degree that should be mentioned is the MSc in Science Entrepreneurship. This was launched in the autumn of 2004, and is the result of the collaborative effort between four of London's universities, led by Cass. It is a unique degree designed to equip those with a science/technology background with the business skills needed to progress their entrepreneurial ideas. SIMFONEC is the centre in which the degree is based (Science Ideas to Market Focussed on Enterprise and Commercialisation).

10
Differentiation and Orientation

Striving for a separate identity

A strategy to differentiate management (and thus the School) from the rest of the University was apparent from the earliest days. Before becoming a university, 'liberal studies' was intended as a means of broadening the education of engineers and scientists, and was not associated with academic endeavour. Tait, Leyton, the Advisory Body and the early pioneers of management education at the Northampton College were determined that 'management' should be taught at the highest academic standard. Creating an independent department and a separate Board of Studies were the start of this process of differentiation. Several subsequent developments already mentioned accentuated this process, including: the formation of Advisory Panels in the 1970s (see Appendix 3); the Griffiths and Murray paper floating the idea of privatising business schools which resulted in the establishment of the Business School Council and the Finance Sub-Committee; the geographical separation from the University and the corresponding physical proximity to the City. Also the move into the bespoke building in Bunhill Row allowed the School to manage many of its own services. For example, in 2002 Pam Smethhurst was appointed facilities manager responsible for such things as reception, portering and maintenance; the School became wholly responsible for its IT and marketing services; and Richard Farmer, a professional human resource manager with City experience, was appointed in 2003 so that the School could manage its own human resources within the policies set down by the University. Using the name 'Cass Business School' rather than 'City University Business School' accentuated the differentiation in the eyes of others.

City-oriented products and services

From the profile of degrees the City orientation is there for all to see (see Chapter 13). This may not have been so apparent in the early years, given the composition of academic staff at that time. But the GBC's location in Gresham College, the short courses introduced by Sir Robert Shone for the City, and the efforts of John Bruce Lockhart, John Bell and Oliver Vesey-Holt in gearing the Post Experience Unit to the needs of the City, and Basil Taylor's finance specialism in the MSc in Administrative Sciences, all contributed toward building an organisational culture that was City oriented. In the early days the Post Experience Unit formed both City and Industrial Advisory Panels; the latter was dropped when the Insurance Advisory Panel came into being. Eventually these panels were replaced by the Business School Council and its successors (i.e. the Board of Overseers and since 2003 the International Advisory Board).

One of the early examples of tailor-made executive development courses for a City institution was introduced in 1972. It grew out of a lunch organised by Bruce Lockhart at Gresham College, hosted by the City Advisory Panel with Jack Davies (a director of the Bank of England at the time) in the Chair. The purpose of the lunch was to introduce Sid Kessler and the author to an invited audience of some 15 senior managers/ directors, so that they were made aware of the School's strengths in the human resource area. Prior to this the focus of the Post Experience Unit had been mainly in finance, economics and law. One bank that felt that the School had something of value to offer outside these disciplines was Barclays – a Vice-Chairman had attended the lunch and the Head of Personnel was subsequently asked to follow-up the lunch initiative. At that time it was a challenge to persuade senior managers in financial institutions that experts in industrial relations and the behavioural sciences had anything useful to tell them! The result was a series of two-week residential courses spread over two years aimed at sensitising those who were responsible for personnel (i.e. directors, assistant district managers, staff assistants) to the changes occurring in the bank's environment, introducing them to the professional HR skills that they now needed, and stimulating appropriate changes to bank policies and procedures. This programme was highly successful, and served as a model for a number of their competitors. Similar courses were subsequently run by Barclays themselves when they set-up their own management centre. It was an example of how a close partnership between a business school and a commercial organisation could work effectively to the mutual advantage of both (Kessler and Williams 1978; Williams 1980).

As an aside it is interesting to note the subsequent careers of at least three alumni of these courses – all three having worked their way up from Assistant District Manager or equivalent. Bill Gordon became an Executive Director of the Barclays Board in 1995. Peter Ellwood became the Chief Executive of the Lloyds TSB Group in 1997. David Turner has contributed significantly to the success of the University and the School through the expertise he acquired in heading the property function at Barclays. For several years he was the University Council's representative who chaired its Estates Committee (thus overseeing the Bunhill Row building among other things); more recently he was Pro-Chancellor of the University.

Developments in later years reinforced this emerging culture. Mike Beenstock was recruited to the Esmee Fairbairn Chair in Finance and Investment by Dean Treasure in April 1981. He came with a strong academic reputation from LBS. As was the practice at the University his selection panel included a Head of Department/Centre from another part of the University; on this occasion it was Brian Griffiths. Beenstock became more excited about the vacancy when Griffiths intimated that there was a possibility of his Centre for Banking and International Finance coming into the School. The 'psychological contract' he perceived was that he would be expected to re-vitalise the financial teaching and research and lead the finance faculty of the School to new academic heights. He made significant contributions in this direction before he resigned in 1987 to take up a position in Israel. He brought more publicity to the School in the national press than any other previous academic. Indeed he was even 'hauled over the coals' for one article he wrote for the *FT* criticising pension schemes that did not allow transfer when moving jobs (these were the days before one could). He subsequently discovered that the reason for this response on the part of the University was that it might have prejudiced the successful launch of the Diploma in Actuarial Science under Steven Haberman (a development sponsored by insurance companies with the full support of the Association of British Insurers). This little anecdote is worth recounting now that Actuarial Science is an integral part of the School and that Steven Haberman is the Deputy Dean.

Another strong boost to the developing culture came when Brian Griffiths was made Dean of the School in 1982 on the resignation of Treasure. He was a strong supporter of Costas Grammenos' endeavours in the Shipping Industry; and within a year of becoming Dean he had persuaded his former colleagues in the Centre for Banking and International Finance that it should be integrated into the School as a department. Developments under subsequent Deans continued to reinforce the City-oriented culture. For example: the incorporation of the Property Valuation and Finance Department (1995), and the Actuarial Science and Statistics Department into the School (2002); and of course the growing number of MSc degrees in the broad finance area.

A mutually beneficial relationship with the City gradually emerged, although the benefits to the School were perhaps more visible. The School took advantage of its location not only to build a customer base, but also to draw on the prestige and expertise of City-based individuals. The external bodies advising the School over the years, starting with the City Advisory Panel, are one example. Leslie Hannah's innovation of introducing Executives in Residence is a second example – the first two were Michael Teacher (a venture capitalist) and David Essex (a former finance director). Both these individuals were alumni with very successful careers. A third example must be the special lectures delivered by distinguished individuals. The most prestigious series is undoubtedly the 'Mais Lectures' (see Appendix 4), named after the University Chancellor and Lord Mayor who led the Appeal for funding the Centre for Banking and International Finance. When the Centre became part of the School, these lectures continued to be organised by Professor Geoffrey Wood. The standing of the speakers ensure good publicity in the national media, and are normally published (Capie and Wood 2001). The Henry Thornton Lectures have also attracted distinguished speakers and are published (Capie and Wood 1996).

Further evidence of the City orientation can be found in the School's 1988 submission to the UGC's Business and Management Sub-Committee. For example:

- The annual City/Whitehall and City/Industry seminars to which ten senior representatives from each side are invited to discuss under Chatham House rules major policy issues of mutual interest. Sir Peter Carey (Chairman of Morgan Grenfell), and Sir Austen Pearce (ex-Chairman of British Aerospace) were the respective chairmen of the early series of seminars.
- The Price Waterhouse Symposia were addressed by leading directors in the City such as Kenneth Berrill, Sir Peter Carey, Sir Nicholas Goodison and Sir John Nott.
- The Big Bang conference held in 1987 was addressed by Professor Gower, Rodney Galpin (Chairman of Standard Chartered Bank), Dr Andreas Prindl (CEO of Normura, London), and others.
- Funding for research came from several City institutions to support the work of the School's Centre for the Study of Financial Institutions, the

Centre for Insurance and Investment (mainly from the Association of British Insurers), and the Centre for Personnel Research and Enterprise Development (Company of Information Technologists, Prudential, National Westminster, Abbey National, British Telecom).

- Seven out of ten outside sponsored professorships were funded by City-based institutions.
- 75 per cent of participants attending executive development courses were from City institutions, as were 56 per cent of those attending the Evening MBA. City institutions employed the largest proportion of the School's graduates – as high as 90 per cent in the case of the BSc in Banking and International Finance.

City networks have always been very important to the School. Reference has already been made to the contributions of John Bruce Lockhart as an Adviser to the Post Experience Unit, to Deans, to academics and of course to a succession of advisory bodies. The value of the external members of these bodies can be gauged from their standing in financial institutions and the City (see Appendix 3 and Boxes 4.1 and 10.1).

Box 10.1 Chairmen of the School's advisory bodies.

1971 Sir Cyril Kleinwort, Chairman, Kleinwort Benson, and Chairman Committee on Invisible Exports (Advisory Panel)
1974 Malcolm Wilcox, Director and Chief General Manager Midland Bank (City Advisory Panel)
1974 B.H. Wilson, Town Clerk & Chief Executive, London Borough of Camden (Industrial Advisory Panel)
1977 D.P. Wratton, Senior Director, Post Office Telecommunications (Insurance Advisory Panel)
1978 A.R.N. Ratcliff, Chief General Manager, Eagle Star Insurance (Insurance Advisory Panel)
1978 Sir Peter Graham, Managing Director, Standard Chartered Bank (City Advisory Panel)
1986 Sir Peter Graham, Chairman, Standard Chartered Bank (Business School Council)
1986 Sir Brandon Gough, Senior Partner, Coopers & Lybrand (City Advisory Panel)
1991 Sir Brandon Gough, Senior Partner, Coopers & Lybrand (Business School Council)
1993 Robin Fox, Vice-Chairman, Kleinwort Benson (Business School Council)
1999 Robin Fox CBE, Chairman, Dresdner Kleinwort Benson (International Board of Overseers)
2003 Lord Currie, Dean, Cass Business School (International Advisory Board)

In keeping with 'mature' world class business schools, when Dean Hannah formed the International Board of Overseers in 2000 he was able to invite an impressive array of School alumni to join the Board. There is no question that City links have mushroomed as a result of such initiatives, together with the large number of financial specialists educated at the School.

11
Development of a Quality Culture

A 'quality culture' can cover a range of issues. In this chapter the term will be used to discuss the evolution of the School's research culture, teaching and learning culture, and professional management culture.

Development of a quality research culture

While this was always part of the spoken strategy, the forces at work in the early years ensured that the evolution to a research culture (let alone a quality one) would be a slow process. In 1964 there were 20 academic staff in the Department of Management and Social Sciences, but only 3 had a PhD – a philosopher, a social anthropologist cum social psychologist, and the author with a PhD in occupational psychology. When the Department of Management was formed only one member had a doctorate until Peter Grinyer completed his PhD. Over a period of several years while the School was based at Gresham College the proportion of staff with doctorates remained at around 12 per cent. This statistic does not mean that the majority of staff were inactive researchers, but it is indicative of the research culture at that time.

In an attempt to meet the needs of the early research students for basic formal training in research, the author was encouraged to design and run a two-week non-residential course in research methods. The first course ran in October 1967. The printed flyer advertising the course served to open the course up to attract research workers attached to Industrial Training Boards. The first week of the course covered such topics as: the scientific method; the nature of measurement; the generation of ideas; research planning; the use of models in research; the use of existing knowledge; the research proposal; statistics and experimental design; methods of data collection; the control of research; the research report. Most of the second week was spent on an individual mini project that required participants to draw on the knowledge that they had been introduced to during the first week. Seven of the contributors came from within the Management Department, three (including Ludwig Finkelstein on the nature of measurement) from other parts of the University, and three from outside (the National Economic Development Office; the Ministry of Labour; and an industrial consultant). For the 1960s this formal course to supplement the traditional informal tutorials was sufficiently unusual to deserve a mention here. Many more years passed before the ESRC increased the pressure on universities to incorporate formal courses as standard practice in the training of research students.

The restructuring that took place when Glen was made Dean in 1968 specified two individuals responsible for research: Manning was Director of Formal Courses and Research Programmes (and Deputy Dean), and Peter Grinyer Co-ordinator of Research Programmes. The former was an administrator and not a researcher, the latter was an active researcher. Seniority and 'politics' dictated this arrangement. The research co-ordinator was mainly concerned with overseeing the recruitment and supervision of research students. During the Deanship of Glen there were relatively few incentives for academics to invest time and effort into research. The management systems in operation failed to recognise that those carrying out research involving fieldwork necessitated an adjustment to be made to their teaching and administrative loads. Indeed, some of those inactive in research tended to believe that research-oriented staff were lucky to find the time to do research, and assumed that they must have a lighter teaching load than themselves. The absence of a transparent system for allocating workload meant that the main incentives motivating research-oriented individuals were: (a) the expectation of promotion and /or career advancement, and (b) academic standing among immediate peer groups, and among extended peer groups in scientific and professional bodies. In a context where colleagues were supportive, but this supportiveness was not translated into management systems, meant that the active researcher either worked excessive hours or shunned all voluntary/avoidable activities (thus devaluing good citizenship behaviours). Over the years several schemes were introduced to monitor workloads and to facilitate the development of a research culture. The first was developed by Jock Scholefield during Glen's Deanship, but the most successful (in terms of its impact) came into being under Kaye's Deanship thanks mainly to the efforts of Donal Walsh, the Director of Administration recruited by Kaye.

Returning to structure, as co-ordinator for research from 1968 to 1979 (nowadays we would use the title of director or associate dean) Peter Grinyer chaired a research committee to help in the development and implementation of a research policy. In October 1970 he circulated a paper on a 'Research Plan for the Graduate Business Centre', prepared by the research committee. It is worth quoting the key paragraph in this paper:

> It has been generally agreed that the objective of research at the Centre should be to contribute to greater knowledge of, and progress in, British Industry, Commerce and Finance. By so doing, the Graduate Business Centre should fulfil its academic function of advancing knowledge in its fields of study, should contribute to current and extended teaching programmes at postgraduate level, and is likely to enhance its reputation in government, industry and the City of London. The committee believe that these objectives will be achieved by adoption of a policy of promoting research particularly in the fields of Finance, Insurance, Banking, Portfolio Management, and on issues of strategic rather than tactical importance in the Administrative Sciences. Strategy may be defined for our present purposes as relating to the development, acquisition and disposition of human, financial, and material resources to permit effective interaction of an enterprise with its dynamic environment. The committee feel that this policy will permit full exploitation of the strength inherent in its links with the City of London, the Centre's geographical position, its membership of a technological University, the research already being done by it, and its team of academic staff.

The remainder of the paper summarised actual and planned research under each Division, allowing for the interests of members of the academic staff and those of the School as a whole.

Committee initiatives included the introduction of a successful working paper series in 1977, research seminars given by staff and research students, and administrative support for the implementation of research policy. When Grinyer resigned in 1979 to take up a headship at St Andrews, Dr Gerry Dickinson filled the gap for a few months before John Treasure appointed the author to head research; and he continued as director of research under Brian Griffiths until 1984 when he had a sabbatical year. Thus the two most active researchers of the early academics at the School were given the main responsibility for leading the research effort from 1968 to 1984. An important development during

John Treasure's Deanship was his willingness to be an active member of the research committee, thus visibly providing support from the very top. This strong support continued under subsequent Deans, and was reflected in the recruitment of active researchers and in the strengthening of the research infrastructure. The RAEs became the critical force in the 1990s for the serious investment of resources into the research effort.

A document produced in the early 1980s conveniently indicates some of the achievements that had taken place in the research culture since 1968. This was a booklet that had been printed listing staff publications from 1968 to 1980. 15 books (excluding edited books) were published during this period. The three most influential ones were: *The Rise and Decline of Small Firms* (Boswell 1973); *Turnaround: the Fall and Rise of the Newton Chambers Group* (Grinyer and Spender 1979); and *Motor Insurance and the Consumer* (Dickinson and Cockerell 1980). A critical review of the 113 refereed papers published by 23 staff over these 12 years would have to conclude that only some of these were in the better quality journals such as: *Journal of Business Policy, Bulletin of Economic Research, Long Range Planning, Journal of the Royal Statistical Society, Operational Research Quarterly, Journal of Management Studies, Industrial Relations Journal, Journal of Occupational Psychology*. The many other publications may not have guaranteed quality but they did serve their purpose in disseminating knowledge generated by the School.

By current RAE standards this performance was disappointing. The turnaround came in the late 1970s and early 1980s. A number of things happened during this period that gave a boost to the research culture and subsequent performance. First, in the financial crises that faced the universities (due to the severe funding reductions associated with the Thatcher Government), it became necessary for the City University to invite older staff to consider taking early retirement. The School had several volunteers, and most of these were from the original team that formed the Department of Management Studies and who carried moderate publication records. Second, several younger staff were becoming more productive on the research front. These included: Robert Grant, Gordon Gemmill, Andrew Chambers, Richard Taffler, Axel Johne, and Gill Palmer. It is interesting to note that all these are currently holding Chairs at home or abroad and have made very successful careers for themselves. Moreover, five of these completed their PhDs while at the School. Third, a working party of the University Senate had been given the task in 1977 of coming up with recommendations for improving the research performance of the University. The main recommendation of the working party was that the University should invite proposals for the setting up of research units to be headed by individuals with a track record in research, and that pump-priming finance should be made available to these units. On the basis of the proposals received the University created three initial units in 1978. One never got off the ground because the proposed director moved to Australia, but two did and one of these was based in the School. This was the Personnel Research Unit (subsequently re-labelled the Centre for Personnel Research & Enterprise Development or CPRED) with the author as director.

The idea behind CPRED was to carry out research projects that would increase one's insight into the factors and processes effecting the utilisation of behavioural science knowledge by organisations. Action research was the main method adopted. A wide range of projects were intentionally conducted: some were initiated by the researchers (e.g. proposals submitted to grant awarding bodies), some were arrived at by approaching organisations experiencing problems that could be tackled by behavioural science methods, and some were the result of approaches made by 'client' organisations. Since the centre was interested in both utilisation and the publication of findings to peer groups, many projects had to be both client and academically oriented (Williams 1998). This dual approach enabled it to be self-financing from 1978 for nearly 20 years, and to achieve a moderate record of publications. From the point of view of the School its main contributions lay in the research income it generated in carrying out over 60 research projects, in the mutually beneficial relationships it developed with City of London institutions (e.g. banks, insurance companies, the Stock Exchange, Company of Information Technologists) and professional bodies (e.g. Institute of Chartered Accountants for England and Wales, Institute of Personnel and Development, Institute of Management Consultants), and in the contribution it made toward the development of a research culture for the School (e.g. during its initial years its five full-time research fellows/officers were the largest research group in the School; it also provided the first 'model' for team research in the School).

The appointment of Michael Beenstock (1981–87) led to the establishment of another highly successful centre in 1981 – CIFER. It had three main research interests: the development of a medium-term economic model of the UK economy, an analysis of social security and pension arrangements and a study of domestic and international financial markets. CIFER was funded by several banks, the Institute of Economic Affairs and the ESRC. It was also responsible for the publication of the School's *Economic Review* – a vehicle that generated considerable publicity for the School in the media. At one time it employed as many as seven research officers. Unlike CPRED this centre adopted the more traditional academic strategy for funding research. Roy Batchelor took over responsibility for CIFER on the resignation of Beenstock; but it soon became moribund when the research money ran out and with it went the *Economic Review*.

The same approach to funding research was adopted by the Centre for Research in Monetary History. This had its beginnings in 1980 in the Centre for Banking and International Finance before it became part of the School, and was financed by the SSRC/ESRC. It was jointly directed by Forrest Capie and Geoffrey Wood, and aimed to write the definitive monetary history of the United Kingdom 1870–1980. It laid the foundations for major monetary studies by producing a better research base than had hitherto been available. It also aimed to bring together much of the secondary literature and to employ recently developed econometric techniques to explore the relationship between money, prices, output and exchange rates in the institutional and historical context of the British economy over this period.

The Centre for the Study of Financial Institutions (CSFI) was the brainchild of Shiv Mathur. Its aims included: to undertake research that leads to a better understanding of the problems that confront general managers in financial institutions; to communicate the results of the research to those who shape financial institutions and policy toward them; to create a forum in the City where senior management of financial institutions can share experience or raise issues of common concern; and to develop teaching material (e.g. case studies), to be used for the education of those seeking careers in financial institutions. The funds for the centre came from an appeal in 1987 by Dean Chambers to City institutions to support three centres in the School (CPRED, CIFER and CSFI). Barclays, Eagle Star, Citibank, Lloyds Bank, Standard Chartered, and Esmee Fairbairn Trust, contributed a little under £100,000 over three years. Stipulations made by three of the donors meant that 66 per cent of the fund was earmarked for CSFI. Although the centre did not develop sufficiently to fulfil all its aims, and to generate significant research income from City organisations, a book that was largely based on its case studies made an important contribution to the business strategy literature. Indeed, the book won a prize for the best business book of the year (Mathur and Kenyon 1997).

These four research centres were subsequently followed by others, gaining formal university recognition if they satisfied certain criteria (i.e. minimum amount of research income, steering committee to include a member of Senate research committee, submission of an annual report to Senate research committee). One of the initial advantages of a University recognised research centre was that a proportion of overheads from the University were returned to the director for reinvesting in the centre, and support was more likely to be given for pump-priming purposes or for bridging gaps between grants thus enabling the retention of skilled researchers. As the School's research activities grew and it became managerially more independent, the advantages of having University recognition for a research centre or unit disappeared. Some research groups in the School just continued as research groups or obtained the 'local' approval of the Board of Studies to be called a centre or unit. An example was the Innovation Research Unit headed by Axel Johne.

Research centres or groups are essentially built around individuals, and new ones are established as old ones disappear. Current centres, many of which emerged in the 1990s are listed in Box 11.1. The number and titles are indicative of the academic entrepreneurialism, City orientation and School climate that are characteristic of the evolved research culture.

Further evidence of the positive development of the School's research culture comes from other sources. In the 1980s, during the Deanship of

Box 11.1 School's Research Centres in 2004/05.

- Centre for Financial Regulation and Crime (directed by Dr Chizu Nakajima)
- Emerging Markets Group (Professor Kate Phylaktis)
- Centre for Econometric Analysis (Professor Giovanni Urga)
- Private Equity and Venture Capital Research Centre (Professor Robert Cressy)
- The Actuarial Research Centre (Professor Richard Verrall)
- Risk Institute (Professor Les Mayhew)
- Centre for Research on European Financial Markets and Institutions (Professor Alistair Milne)
- International Centre for Shipping, Trade & Finance (Professor Costas Grammenos)
- Research Centre for Real Estate Finance (Professor Tony Key)
- Alternative Investments Research Centre (Professor Harry Kat)
- Pensions Institute (Professor David Blake)
- Centre for New Technologies, Innovation and Entrepreneurship (Professor Chris Hendry)
- Centre for Charity Effectiveness (Professor Ian Bruce)
- Centre for Research in Corporate Governance (Professor Georges Selim)
- Centre for Leadership, Learning and Change (Professor David Sims)

Andrew Chambers, there was a significant jump in the number of staff achieving personal Chairs (see Chapter 12). Promotion to personal chairs is a rigorous process. First the candidate has to convince an internal committee that they have a strong enough cv. Second, two external academics are consulted by the Academic Registrar to establish that there is a prima facie case. Third, a positive response from externals leads to the establishment of a promotion committee, normally chaired by the Vice-Chancellor, and consisting of two external assessors, the Dean, a member of staff who is an expert in the relevant area, a Senate representative and the Academic Registrar. Research performance (as revealed in publications, research income and successful PhD students) has been the most important criterion until recently. Now other criteria of academic leadership (e.g. course design, teaching, contributions to the development of a profession) are recognised as legitimate criteria. In effect a dual pathway to Chairs has become formal University policy – the more traditional research and publications route and the more general academic leadership route (the criteria applied here are those that have been applied for many years in relation to promotion to senior lecturer).

When one adds to the above the formal recognition of the School's PhD programme by the ESRC, and the external rankings of the School that are influenced by research performance, evidence of a strong research culture emerges. The *FT* survey of MBA schools has ranked the doctoral programme in the top 20 worldwide for several recent years. A global review of finance research published in Financial Management (the review studied research productivity in 16 core Finance journals from 1990 to 2001, ranking the top 100 academic institutions) ranked the School 42 overall, 2 in the United Kingdom and in Europe after LBS (Chan *et al.* 2002). The RAE ratings, which are based largely on publications in quality journals, show a steady progress from predominantly national to a predominantly international level of performance (see Chapter 12).

Developing a quality teaching and learning culture

Until recently this has been one of the most difficult strategies to implement. There are many reasons for this. First, while developing a quality teaching and learning culture was always a strategy it did not attract serious attention until the University itself began to invest more resources into the area. The regulatory activities of the QAA had a profound effect in forcing universities to critically examine their structures and procedures to ensure that students experienced a quality education. Second, the very concept of 'a learning culture' still does not have a shared meaning among all academics beyond the narrow and traditional sense of enabling students to acquire knowledge and to pass examinations. Third, while higher education culture accepted that feedback from peers (i.e. external examiners) was necessary for the setting and maintenance of academic standards, feedback from students was regarded as an optional 'good practice'. Fourth, the development of an effective learning culture (e.g. in terms of QAA criteria) depends on the existence of appropriate management systems, many of which were not functioning routinely until the late 1980s. Fifth, only when the new building in Bunhill Row became operational were premises and facilities contributing positively to the support of a quality learning culture.

In other words, the early learning culture of the School was influenced by the beliefs that were prevalent at that time within higher education generally. Namely: students are there to be taught, to listen, and to provide evidence that they had acquired prescribed knowledge; individual academics, as experts in their subjects, know best how to transfer their specialist knowledge to students. In the 1980s and 1990s this attitude became less and less appropriate. The School, along with its main competitors, became more aware that postgraduate students were customers who were expecting a quality service for the financial investment they were making to advance their career prospects. The forces generated by competition for students, the QAA, and the advancement and dissemination of knowledge about adult learning, have combined to bring about a general cultural transformation. Most business schools in the United Kingdom now share the belief that a learning culture needs to be managed so that all the contributing elements (e.g. participants, technology, management systems, premises) contribute toward the achievement of educational goals. The laissez-faire learning culture is all but obsolete. In order to give substance to these generalisations the following observations on 'management systems' are relevant. Chapter 12 will deal with premises.

Developing a professional management culture

In the early days the School was very much subject to the management systems in operation in the University. Along with most academic institutions in the 1960s these systems were relatively 'unprofessional' by today's standards – in the sense of not being sufficiently business-like, systematic and based on what we now accept as good practice. In the last 30 years or so successive governments, and external representatives on university councils, have put increasing pressure on universities to improve their management. While the School has benefited from these developments as an integral part of the University, it has sometimes found that the systems at the centre have failed to meet its special needs. The appointment of individuals in the School with business experience (as deans and/or senior administrators) has speeded up the process whereby the School has acquired more autonomy in the design and operation of its management systems. An example of how things have changed is illustrated by the in-house training courses now being run by the School on 'customer care' – the aim is to develop a culture where customer care is practiced and not just taught in the School!

Scheme for allocating teaching loads

One of the most challenging managerial tasks in a business school is to enable academics to cope with the inherent conflicts in their roles to the satisfaction of the individual and the school. These conflicts arise because of the competing demands made on them as teachers, researchers, consultants and administrators. A few skilfully juggle all four roles; some devote their energies to one and neglect the others; and so on. Persuading individual academics to spread their efforts according to School objectives is a frustrating experience unless there are supporting management and reward systems in place. Individual academics no longer have the degree of autonomy that they once had, but the little that they retain is jealously guarded. All this means that an acceptable system for allocating teaching loads can be critical. In the days when staff numbers were small, and cohesion was strong, peer pressure was thought to be a sufficient means for maintaining a fair workload across the School. As the School became larger and the need arose to enhance research as well teaching performance, so the weaknesses of the informal management systems became more pronounced. The first such scheme was implemented in 1970/71. An examination of the scheme will show that it was compatible with the culture of the time in that the only acknowledgement to research activity was in the supervision of research students. The demise of the scheme after a few years was partly due to this, but was also due to the scepticism attached to the validity of the data on which it was based (e.g. individuals could make exorbitant claims for their administrative loads). Lack of confidence in the data led to its underutilisation and eventual demise in decision making.

When no generally accepted scheme operated, teaching loads were very much determined by the persuasive ability of individual academics either as subordinates or as superiors. A transparent scheme was badly needed not only to ensure a degree of fairness in the allocation of workloads, but to provide reliable information for manpower planning purposes (e.g. priority areas for recruitment) and for improving research performance. Such a scheme was introduced in David Kaye's reign with the explicit strategic goal of achieving a '5' or '5*' rating in the 2001 and subsequent RAEs. This was facilitated by a number of factors that were inadequately represented in earlier years:

- an additional person was appointed to the administration team, and at a more senior level than before (i.e. Donal Walsh);
- a stronger executive team combined with a more authoritarian and management-oriented Dean;
- the scheme that was introduced took into account lessons learnt from competitors' schemes;
- the information fed into the scheme was more rigorously obtained and the application of the scheme was more effectively managed.

A key element of the scheme was the research rating given to each academic; this was arrived at by the School's research committee following the RAE criteria as far as possible. The scheme was designed so that individuals with high research ratings would be expected to have fewer teaching contact hours than those with lower ratings – the difference was quite marked with the highest being allocated less than half the contact hours of the lowest. In addition all were expected to supervise ten student projects (MBA or MSc) and two research students. An allocation of contact hours was agreed for those with special administrative responsibilities such as the Director of the MBA programme. The scheme incorporated some flexibility so that in allocating teaching loads a head of department could take into account class sizes, new or repeat syllabuses and development needs. Heads of department had to feed the 'raw data' into the administrator's office. This was processed and checked for inconsistencies, and then used as a basis for a discussion between the Director of Administration, the administrator, the Deputy Dean, and the Head of Department, to agree the workloads of individuals and to discuss solutions to any anomalies uncovered. This core teaching commitment (CTC) scheme was first discussed in November 1995, and introduced in 1997/98. In the light of experience a revision was introduced in 2004.

An important by-product of the scheme for allocating teaching loads was that it gave the School an indication of the numbers of staff falling under each of the six rating categories used by the RAE. This provided a baseline against which individual development, recruitment and early retirement 'initiatives' could be assessed. In other words, the School was better informed as to whether it was winning the battle of shifting the median rating toward the desirable end of the scale.

Performance appraisal schemes

The first attempt to introduce an appraisal scheme in the School was in the late 1960s when the 'two Davids' (Glen and Manning) asked the author to design a scheme that would be acceptable to academics. After appropriate consultation a scheme was introduced with the primary purpose of helping individual academics to assess their own competence in relation to various key aspects of their job (e.g. teaching, research, administration), to identify those areas where further development was needed and where further support from the School would be helpful, and to arrive at a joint undertaking with their line manager for concrete follow-up action. At that time appraisal schemes were recognised as being most useful for developmental purposes (Rowe 1964), and this was reflected in the School's scheme. As with many appraisal schemes this one worked for a few years and then gradually fell by the wayside as other priorities took precedence with increasing work pressures.

The next serious initiative for an appraisal scheme came from the University 20 years later in 1988. The pressure to implement appraisal schemes in universities was initiated by the Secretary of State Kenneth Baker in 1987 when he announced the provision of government money to fund a pay award; in return he made it clear that he expected to see evidence of progress in the introduction of improved promotion, career development and staff appraisal procedures. At this time there was considerable opposition from the Association of University Teachers (AUT) to the introduction of appraisals. The Vice-Chancellor Raoul Franklin and the Personnel Officer Robin Dunn used an open and consultative approach to its introduction. Thus, Professor Gerry Randell who was well known as a speaker on appraisals from the Bradford School of Management, gave an invited lecture to staff on the value of appraisals, and there was ample opportunity for individuals to voice their concerns. In the next phase the author was asked to design and run two one-day courses for all senior administrators and academics on the skills involved in the appraisal interview (role playing exercises were included in the programme). The Vice-Chancellor showed the way by participating in the first course. The AUT were prepared to tolerate appraisal schemes so long as they focused on the development theme, and this was the orientation adopted by the University.

A standard University appraisal scheme was introduced and managed by the Personnel Department. Since this was an added burden on already over-burdened staff at the School considerable pressure was needed to bring about an acceptable completion rate. When David Kaye became Dean he re-oriented the scheme to emphasise the monitoring and controlling aspects rather than the developmental ones. By this time student feedback was a practice that had become routine on the MBA programmes (but not the MSc degrees), and it was made clear that this information had to be discussed at the appraisal interview and that follow-up decisions had to be recorded. When Leslie Hannah became Dean the scheme reverted back to the spirit of the University model. Currently, under David Currie, staff submit themselves to two appraisal interviews per year. One focuses on development and the setting of targets, and the other on the assessment of performance for the purpose of the performance related pay scheme introduced by the School in 2003. Separating out the two aims of appraisal in this way reflects what is generally regarded as 'good practice'.

Training and learning Committees

The same environmental events (i.e. government pressures) that had resulted in the introduction of staff appraisal also stimulated the development of staff training in the late 1980s. The University already had appointed a training officer (Amanda Johnson), and an academic-led structure was created to monitor and initiate training activities and make regular reports to Senate. A training committee was established as a sub-committee of Senate Courses Committee, and shared the same Chairman (this happened to be one of the author's roles as Pro-Vice Chancellor at that time). This new structure identified some obvious training needs among staff: conducting appraisal interviews, participating in selection procedures, and chairing committees. A survey was carried out to discover the extent to which sabbaticals were being used as a career development tool by different parts of the University. The School was one of those that had been under-utilising sabbaticals. This was partly due to the thinly spread expertise in many areas, making it difficult for colleagues to cover for those on sabbatical. On the rare occasion that a sabbatical was taken, a part-time lecturer had to be brought in from outside. One of the recommendations to Senate was that greater use should be made of this tool for developmental purposes, and an appropriate procedure was put in place for approving, financing and monitoring the scheme. Sabbaticals have now become part of the culture of the School, and have proved rewarding for the individual and the School in terms of publications and teaching skills.

Following these developments at the University level, Boards of Studies were encouraged to set-up their own parallel committees with particular emphasis on teaching and learning. The School's main thrust in this area was to identify good teaching and learning practices, to spread these more widely within the School through seminars, workshops and a Learning Laboratory, and to introduce the incentive of cash prizes for those who excelled in their jobs whether as teachers or in a supporting role. The individuals responsible for such activities have gradually been given more status as reflected in the titles associated with their roles – initially Chair, then Director, now Associate Dean – emphasising the weight the School now attaches to this aspect of the learning culture.

Marketing and communications function

In the competitive environment in which the School operates, 'brand image' or reputation is of critical importance. For a quality culture to impact potential and existing stakeholders requires quality performance across a range of criteria (such as those used by EQUIS and the *FT*) as well as effective marketing of products, services and people. The School's performance in this area has been mixed in the past. As the School grew in size and achievements its corresponding impact on City institutions and the national/international media failed to keep pace. Even in the 1990s people were still 'discovering the School', claiming that it was 'the best kept secret in the City', or confusing it with LBS. Poor premises, and the lack of a frontage while in the Barbican, undoubtedly had a part to play in this. All Deans recognised the importance of marketing, but some were more prepared to pump effort and resources into this function. It was only in the latter half of the 1980s that the School began to employ marketing professionals, and to hire public relations consultants, to supplement the expertise provided by the University. It is interesting to note that one of the suggestions made by the EQUIS accreditation panel in 2001 was that the School should manage its marketing efforts more from within and become less dependent upon the University for this purpose. This is now the case, and the function is headed by Gemma Lines as Director of Marketing and Communications.

The School and University have always been good at creating opportunities to be associated with 'quality' individuals and organisations. The various mechanisms through which this was done included: bestowing honorary doctorates on distinguished individuals associated with the City of London; establishing prestigious annual lectures such as the Mais Lectures; appointing outstanding individuals to the School's advisory bodies. Given the 40-year history of the School, many alumni have now reached the pinnacle of their careers. Alumni who achieve powerful and prestigious positions are valuable ambassadors for the School, particularly when the link is made by the media. The School's website continually up-dates the list of alumni in the news. The individual who gains more than his fair share of publicity is Stelios Haji-Ioannou, the founder and Chairman of EasyGroup. He graduated on the MSc in Shipping Trade and Finance in 1988. But there are others such as Michael Cassidy, an alumni of the 1985 Evening MBA, who chaired the powerful City Corporation Policy and Resources Committee for a number of years; Derek Sach, an alumni of the 1972 MSc/MBA, who became a managing director at the Royal Bank of Scotland; Carole Sergeant, an alumni of the 1979 Day MBA, who was Director of the Banks and Building Societies at the Financial Services Authority, Deputy Chair of the Building Societies Commission, and now Chief Risk Director of Lloyds TSB Group; Liu Mingkang, an alumni of the 1988 Evening MBA, former President of the Bank of China and now Chairman of the Chinese Banking Regulatory Commission.

From time to time attempts have been made to produce regular 'quality' publications aimed at enhancing the reputation of the School and keeping its stakeholders informed of developments and achievements. The first such publication was the sister publication to the University's '*Quest*', and was appropriately entitled '*Business Quest*'. It was intended as an annual publication and aimed at practising managers and students of management, and was financed from Post Experience funds as the group most likely to benefit from this venture. The first issue appeared in November 1974 with a picture of the Guildhall on the front cover and included the following five articles: 'The impact of prices and incomes policies' (Douglas Vaughan); 'Efficient business reading: a guide for the professional manager' (Gerry Smith, School Librarian); 'Ecole des Affairs de Paris' (Oliver Vesey-Holt); 'The selection and follow-up of 272 business school students' (Allan Williams and Ken Gardner); 'Employee participation and the theory of enterprise' (Clive Schmitthoff). *Business Quest* had a limited life, as did other comparable subsequent publications. The current equivalent publication is '*InBusiness*' (2004). This is very much more of an image-building publication, and includes articles by prominent journalists as well as academic staff. The contrast between these two publications, some 30 years apart, can hardly be greater. *InBusiness* reflects the world-class standing of a School that has 'arrived', whereas *Business Quest* reflects an aspiring School's attempts to communicate its academic legitimacy to its market.

Building and maintaining relationships with alumni have had a chequered history. In the late 1960s and early 1970s there was quite a flourishing alumni-led society that had the Gresham grasshopper as its emblem – hence known as the Gresham Grasshoppers. In order to inject new life into the alumni, and to extend membership beyond the MSc in Administrative Sciences to include the future BSc alumni, the name was changed in May 1979 to 'The City University Business School Graduates Association', automatic membership was given on graduation, and the annual subscription was abolished. While the association continued to be run by an elected alumni committee plus one representative from the School, the School took over the responsibility for financing the association and provided basic administrative support. As time passed alumni matters seemed to be put on the back burner, the active groups centred around specific degrees (e.g. the MSc in Shipping, Trade and Finance). Because the majority of alumni identified with the School and not the University, few became active in the latter's alumni events. Efforts to revive alumni structures and activities were initiated by different Deans, and reached a peak under Leslie Hannah as part of the process of 'building friends' for the University Development Appeal to help finance the new School building. Currently administrative structures and data bases are being improved to ensure that alumni see themselves as legitimate stakeholders in the School and in its future (they formed the majority on the School's International Advisory Board in 2000 – see Appendix 3).

Reference has already been made in Chapter 6 to the new structural arrangements now operating in the School. It is appropriate to add here more information about Professor Chris Brady's role as Associate Dean, External Relations and Business Development. The School is very aware of the importance of its brand image or reputation, and one of the responsibilities of this new role is to help build and promote an image that is consistent with the School's mission and strategies. As part of this process effort is being made to develop joint undertakings with strategic partners in the commercial and educational world. A stronger brand, combined with the additional resources of partners, can open up new opportunities. This is particularly true in the context of executive education – an area in which the School has under-performed relative to other high-ranking schools in the United Kingdom and Europe. Examples of the development of such partnerships are now increasingly seeing the light of day, including: professional institutions (e.g. Chartered Institute of Insurance), banks (e.g. Bank of China), the local community (e.g. Metropolitan Police), and academic institutions (e.g. Shanghai University of Finance and Economics).

It is interesting to note that executive education fulfilled a similar function in the 1970s as it does today in providing opportunities for networking, and through these promoting and marketing the School. The most obvious example was in connection with the *FT*/City courses (see Box 11.2), one of the mainstays of the Post Experience Unit over many years. In the Lyons Suite at Gresham College luncheons were held for up to 20 guests prior to the Thursday afternoon sessions. The guests included the two speakers, senior managers from City institutions, a senior academic from the University or another university, and those School academics who had a special interest in meeting one or more of the guests. These social gatherings were a resounding success even though they sometimes aroused the gastronomic envy in other parts of the University! In order to assuage this envy academic staff were charged 30p when attending a lunch, settling their pantry accounts at the end of the month. During those parts of the year when the *FT*/City courses

Box 11.2 Speakers for the *FT*/City course in session 1973/74.

- Opening address: Sir James Tait, Vice-Chancellor
  'Europe, the City and the British Economy' (Dick Taverne QC, MP, former Financial Secretary to the Treasury; Director, Equity and Law Life Assurance Society)
  'The City's Economy Today' (Prof. John Dunning, University of Reading)
- 'London as an International Banking Centre' (M. Harper, Director, Keyser Ullman Ltd)
  'The Physical Environment of the City' (E. Chandler, City Architect)
- 'The City as the Monetary Centre of the Economy' (Dr F. Lomax, Manager, Economic Analysis, NatWest; and A. Coleby, Deputy Chief Cashier, Bank of England)
- 'The Merchant Banks and other Financial Institutions' (David Bucks, Director, Samuel Montague; Patrick Coldstream, Director, Charles Fulton)
- 'The City and International Finance' (J. Spurdle, Jr. Vice President, Morgan Guarantee Trust; E. Porter, Senior Foreign Exchange Manager, NatWest)
- 'The City and the British Economy' (William Rodgers, MP, Minister of State at the Treasury; Professor T. Rybczynski, Director, Lazard Securities)
- 'Institutional Investors and Insurance' (Hugh Cockerell, OBE, Senior Research Fellow, GBC; A. Higgins, Member of Lloyds)
- 'The Stock Exchange' (B. Cottrell, Partner, Phillips and Drew; J. Hollis, Head of Public Relations, The Stock Exchange)
- 'The City as a Trading Centre' (F. Bolton, MC, Chairman, Bolton Steamshipping, President, The British Shipping Federation; T. Dumas, Senior Partner, Messrs. E.D. and F. ManSugar Brokers; P. Tudball, Idwal Williams & Co., Director, The Craig Shipping Co.)
- 'The City: A Debate' (C. Johnson, Managing Director, The *FT*; C. Gordon Tether, 'Lombard', The *FT*; Peter Tapsell, MP)

were not running, the luncheons continued to be held under the title of 'Dean's Luncheon'. Another series of annual courses that proved highly successful were aimed at introducing younger bankers from overseas financial institutions to the banking and financial activities of the City of London; in the fifth series (1974) the Lord Mayor invited the participants to a private reception at the Mansion House.

One of the problems that beset all growing organisations is that of internal communications. Relying on formal committee structures and informal interactions to keep everyone informed of School objectives, developments and achievements, has its failings. This has meant that various attempts have been made by management to produce 'news sheets' which would be circulated to all staff. Thus in an effort to improve internal communications in 1973, Dean Glen gave an academic (Jock Scholefield) the responsibility for 'co-ordinating internal communications and maintaining the effectiveness of the Centre's internal information system'. One result was a news sheet which was edited and produced by one of the School's secretaries (initially Ann Newport then Chrissie Bowers who is still employed at the School!) on a regular weekly basis from June 1973 to June 1981. Subsequently the news sheet or its equivalent appeared infrequently. In recent years internal communications have used the internet, but its limitations have been revealed in the 2004 Mori attitude survey referred to next. More systematic and comprehensive information is now being introduced to all staff via the internet under the label of 'Cass news'.

Recent developments (2004/05)

Two activities in the human resource management area are worth highlighting to illustrate further the professionalism that is becoming part of the School's culture. They both coincide with the senior HR appointment of Richard Farmer. First, the School subjected itself to the 'Investors in People' process in 2004 and it is now allowed to use the accolade in its literature. The scheme is a useful diagnostic process for judging the effectiveness of developmental activities and policies, and in identifying areas for improvement. Although the University encourages its schools to submit themselves to the scheme, so far only the Business School has taken the plunge. Second, the School carried out a Mori attitude survey to monitor staff motivation and commitment. While there are areas for improvement (and these have stimulated follow-up activities), the overall results have been very satisfying in the light of the norms that have been developed by Mori over many years. The survey was solely an initiative of the School, and it carried the cost; whereas the 'Investors in People' was paid for by the University.

12

Premises: the Meandering Pathway to a State-of-the-art Building

The history of the successive premises occupied by the School could have been included in the previous chapter relating to the development of a quality culture. But the topic has played such a dominant role in the history of the School that it deserves a chapter on its own. More premises have been occupied than the School has had Deans! (See Box 12.1). Wigton House was a commercial block of six floors, mainly used as a warehouse (the site has now been re-developed but it was just south of the Walmsley building and shared a similar appearance). The Department of Education and Science authorised the College to lease the first floor of this building for five years from May 1964. This was the first home of the 'management group'. Plain breezeblocks were used to divide up the space into offices, classrooms and a psychological laboratory and workshop. While part-time management students in 1964 were somewhat taken aback by the premises, the staff accepted them in their stride. It was after all an improvement on the Nissen-type hut where some of the undergraduate teaching took place. In contrast Gresham

Box 12.1 Main premises occupied by the School.

1964	Wigton House (St. John Street)
1966	Gresham College (Basinghall Street) & Wigton House
1971	Lionel Denny House (Goswell Road) & Gresham College
1979	Lionel Denny House, Charterhouse building & Gresham College
1981	Frobisher Crescent & Main Building
1992	Frobisher Crescent & Parkes Building
1993	Frobisher Crescent, Parkes Building & 24 Chiswell Street
1997	Frobisher Crescent, Parkes, Chiswell & Walmsley Building
2002	Bunhill Row & Parkes Building

College was a palace despite the cramped space. Gresham Hall in particular had a touch of luxury and history about it, and this compensated for its poor lighting and the architect's total lack of foresight for modern learning needs! The School had use of the hall and two upper floors. One of the rooms was called the 'library' because of its floor to ceiling bookcases; it matched the hall in its historic luxury and proved ideal for small receptions and staff meetings. With the approval of the Mercers (the livery company who were the landlords), and generous funding from the catering company Joe Lyons, part of one of the floors was converted into two high quality inter-connecting rooms with an adjoining kitchen. This 'Lyons Suite' enabled the School to entertain in the fashion that was acceptable to City institutions on its doorstep, as well as providing the quality accommodation expected by executives attending the short courses run by the Post Experience Unit.

Gresham College was far too small before the School had even moved into it, and so the University rented the whole of another building in Goswell Road (i.e. apart from a showroom displaying the wares of the Japanese company Noritake on the ground floor). The plan was to retain Gresham College for the Post Experience Unit, and for all the other activities of the School to be located in the newly converted building that was named 'Lionel Denny House' after the University's first Chancellor. While this property was more 'up-market' than Wigton House, it had the failings associated with a converted warehouse. Indeed, John Treasure accepted the position of Dean before seeing the inside of Lionel Denny House – he claims he would have turned it down if he had! The contrast between the premises of an advertising agency and Lionel Denny House was so great that the culture shock had to be experienced to be believed. John Treasure recounts how he was so appalled when he first arrived at Lionel Denny – dust everywhere, lift out of order, cheap furniture, dripping taps in the toilets – that within three days he went to the Vice-Chancellor and threatened to resign unless £10,000 (worth substantially more in 1978) was made immediately available to make minimal improvements. The University quickly agreed for an emergency fund to be available. Being an advertising man Treasure did his best to make Lionel Denny House as cheerful as possible by having all the doors painted red, arranging for flowers to be displayed in the entrance hall, and so on. But there was a limit to what could be done, and so he did all the entertaining of visitors at Gresham College. One exception was when he entertained Professor Andrew Thomson (Director of the Open University Business School at the time) in his office at Lionel Denny; Thomson recalls Treasure apologizing for the lack of light but that he was not allowed to replace the bulb, having to wait for someone from the University main site to come and do it! Three years ago the late John Treasure took pleasure in recounting an observation he made in 1980: when one came out of Lionel Denny one had the choice of turning left and going toward the University, passing a rather run down area with leanings toward the Labour Party; or turning right and going toward the City, rich and predominantly Conservative where many Oxbridge graduates worked. For him there was no hesitancy in saying that the School should turn right! Hence his enthusiasm and drive to ensure that the School moved to the Barbican.

Space in Lionel Denny House was very quickly in short supply, and when the CPRED took on more research staff it had to move to the Charterhouse building about 50 yards to the north. The University rented a floor in this building to accommodate CPRED and the administrative staff running the MBA programme. The premises in the Barbican were preceded by five years of negotiations. In 1975 the UGC gave its provisional approval for the University to acquire a long-term lease of part of the 'horseshoe' building in the Barbican – the construction of which was about to start. The City Corporation was keen on the School moving into the three top floors of Frobisher Crescent, and was prepared to come to some arrangement whereby part of the payments would in effect be like a mortgage. However, when the UGC was approached to see if they would cover the cost they said that this would not be possible because it would be like a capital investment. Eventually the UGC did agree to subsidise the rent on the understanding that another part of the University also moved into the premises because they thought it too large for the School. This was agreed by the University Officers, and thus the Department of Arts Policy and Management and subsequently the Centre for Banking and International Finance moved into Frobisher. Lord Alport (the University's Pro-Chancellor and Chairman of its Council) had been given to understand at an early stage of negotiations with the Corporation that full commercial rates would not be levied for the rent; unfortunately this did not occur and it is unclear as to where the blame for the misunderstanding lay. The cost of the new premises, and the Mercers desire to generate more income from the Gresham College premises, forced the University to relinquish the use of that valuable foothold in the centre of the City.

The limited space in the Barbican meant (once more) that parts of the School had to be housed elsewhere. The downsizing Civil Engineering Department vacated five offices for the use of the School's CPRED in the main building of the University. Gradually more and more additional accommodation had to be found as the School expanded. In 1992 Parkes Building (named after the second Vice-Chancellor Sir Edward Parkes) housed the administrative staff for all the undergraduate programmes. This building was shared with the Property Valuation and Finance Department, and the Department remained there when it merged into the School in 1992. When the Department of Systems and Management was dissolved in 1997 those elements that came to the School were incorporated into the Department of Information Technology Management. The majority of that department were then housed in part of Walmsley Building. Executive Education was the next unit to be moved out of the Barbican; they went to occupy newly furbished premises on the first floor of 24 Chiswell Street. They were soon joined by full-time researchers and those PhD students who had been accommodated in the Parkes Building. In summary, the School managed its expansion by acquiring another half floor in the Barbican (to add to the three floors it already occupied), and by spilling over into additional properties.

The School faced unfavourable physical constraints in all moves that were made to cope with the accommodation shortage, except for the last move in 2002. Raked lecture theatres were not possible, and lifts did not cater for the movement of large numbers of students. Flexibility was confined to moving tables and chairs in the classrooms, but the most common group size meant that the tables had to be placed in traditional rows facing the lecturer rather than alternative arrangements that encourage student interaction. Staff and students will recall the frustration associated with the lifts in buildings not designed for heavy use (i.e. Lionel Denny and Frobisher). This frustration is typically conveyed in an extract from the '*CUBS News*' of 1 November 1978: 'You may have wondered as you toiled up and down the stairs in Lionel Denny House over the past few weeks why the lift wasn't in good working order for the beginning of the new academic year, and why, on the few occasions it has operated recently, it has broken down again almost immediately, and taken days to repair'. While that extract applied to Lionel Denny House, it could equally have applied to the early days in Frobisher Crescent. Moreover, there was little scope for modifying social areas to encourage interactions between staff, between students, and between staff and students. The first opportunity came to consider these factors seriously when the School and University were in discussion with the City Corporation over the occupation of Bastion House (next to London Museum). The possibility of Bastion House triggered the preparation of a detailed specification of the accommodation needs for the School.

Bastion House had to be turned down because it could not cater for the provision of tiered lecture theatres. This 'disappointment' started a train of events that resulted in the present purpose-built accommodation in Bunhill Row.

It is worth going into the Bunhill Row story in some detail because this building will undoubtedly prove to be one of the most critical elements that enables the School to achieve its mission and vision of being a top-rated business school in the world rankings. The first purpose-built proposal for the School had been back in 1970 when negotiations took place for a hall of residence and a business school on a site by the Tower of London. All the other premises used, or considered for housing the whole School, were existing buildings in need of major modifications before they could be put to educational use, for example, Wigton, Gresham College, Old Stock Exchange, Lionel Denny, Frobisher, Bastion. There are four key sources of information for recounting the Bunhill Row story: Minutes of the University Council (including those of the School Council); notes prepared by Michael O'Hara, the University Secretary and the lead person for the University in all the negotiations; a review article written by an architect for their main professional magazine (Pidwill 2003); and interviews with some of the main 'thought leaders' who had an influence on the design of the new building.

Four guiding principles dominated negotiations. First, the School and the University were determined that the new building should be designed to take into account relevant knowledge from the building experiences of other leading business schools, both United Kingdom and worldwide, especially the United States. Second, the design should incorporate the developing School philosophy relating to progressive adult learning methods (e.g. opportunities for social interaction; small group project assignments; plenary case study assignments; advanced technological facilities). Third, everything about the building and its furnishings should reflect a feeling of quality. Fourth, it would be short-sighted to go for a smaller building on financial grounds, that is, a basement plus five floors instead of the permissible basement plus six floors. The first two points were readily accepted by the University. The third one required some persuasion, and the fourth one required the School to produce rigorous evidence that it could generate the extra income required to service an increased mortgage. Approval for a seventh floor (including basement) was eventually given by the University Council on the basis of a ten-year plan prepared by Donal Walsh and approved by the Executive Committee and the Board of Overseers, the persuasive arguments put forward by Leslie Hannah on the Bunhill Row committee, and the firm support of David Rhind the Vice-Chancellor. Those project-minded readers, who are interested in the 'managerial' and 'legal' sequence of events leading up to the opening of the new building, will want to peruse Appendix 5. This is an edited version of Michael O'Hara's notes on the unfolding story of the building, and provides a chronological list of the complex train of events that can characterise a major project of this nature. But even this account is not the full story, since it makes no mention of the influences and negotiations that took place within the University Council's Estates Committee, the Chiswell Street and Bunhill Row committees, and all the other interactions between interested parties.

The architectural article gives a good idea of some of the basic beliefs underlying the building's design (Pidwill 2003). Pidwill points out that the School conceived the new building as an experiment to test out beliefs about how physical space affects the way people learn, and to get maximum benefit from both human contact and technology.

> The clients are experts in knowledge management, and they know that knowledge creation comes not just from flashes of inspiration but also through social interaction. It must suit different personalities and happen at different speeds, ranging from gradual incremental change to shocking innovation, and therefore a diversity of subtly different environments is important. Clive Holtham, professor of information technology at Cass and one of the principal movers in the project, identified the medieval monastery as the most useful metaphor: a building dedicated to the creation and extension of knowledge which could accommodate travellers whose work was not rooted in one place. The library, chapter house and cloister are seen as the most relevant spaces – respectively, the 'temple of knowledge', meeting room and communication conduit. The cloister in particular is multi-functional, offering private study (the carrel), private contemplation (walking alone), conversation (walking together), accidental contact and small group discussion. Bennetts have sought to realise the potential for such prized chance encounters throughout this building. The fire staircase on the front corner manages a glass wall and 'monastic benches' at each landing, so spontaneous conversations can last a little longer, and every pocket of interstitial space in the building is available for informal conversation, meeting or study. Deep benches are provided throughout, although so far these seem to be the least well-used of all the props, perhaps because they do not

encourage face-to-face contact. The café, the 'pump-primer' of new relationships, was originally intended for the second floor but was relocated to the ground floor so that one is greeted on entry with activity and a sense of a buzzing intellectual hub.

A good rapport between Bennetts and the School ensured that adjustments could be made in the interest of user requirements. Extensive consultations took place with groups of staff, both academic and administrative. One consequence was to reverse an initial proposal not to have cellular offices. The two atriums, open break-out spaces, and window-fronted syndicate rooms and offices (with partly obscured glazing so as to provide an element of privacy), all contribute to the experience of light and spaciousness. The building provides a significant investment (£36m excluding land) and in order for it to retain its commercial value it was a requirement of the University that it was designed to allow ready conversion into commercial offices. This flexibility can also cater for any changes that may be required by the School itself at some future date. The current design caters for 1750 students and 250 staff, and includes a 180-seat auditorium, 11 lecture theatres (six on the Harvard U-shaped layout), 16 syndicate rooms, break-out lounges, a learning resource centre (incorporating the library), café, restaurant and office accommodation. There are three computer rooms with a total of about 150 seats in addition to the computing facilities in the library and a Bloomberg sponsored dealing room. Computer access is also available in every lecture room. What appeared to be fairly generous space facilities in 2001 are now very tight following the merger of Actuarial Science into the School.

The Cyril Kleinwort Learning Resource Centre (i.e. the library) is tailor-made to the School's needs. It includes some 25,000 books, 400 periodicals with a further 400 periodicals online. The School has invested heavily in electronic information with subscriptions to more than 20 specialist databases. As a specialist library these resources compare very favourably with other UK schools. The School first established its own specialist library as a sub-section of the main University library when it was based in Gresham College. By 1970/71 the library was in Lionel Denny House with the full-time librarian Gerry Smith in charge. Apart from a gap of 13 years (1983–96) the present Head of the School's library services, Leslie Baldwin, has managed the development of the library since 1978. While space has always been a problem, a marked improvement in facilities and furnishings took place under the Kaye Deanship thanks to the efforts of Donal Walsh and the generous donation of the Cyril Kleinwort Foundation. The new building has provided further opportunities to ensure that the School's library fulfils the needs of staff and students. There are now over 100 study places and a suite of PC workstations.

Occupying the Bunhill Row building was the first time that the School was not made to shoe-horn itself into premises that fell far short of requirements – 37 years is a long time to wait for a key strategy to be realised (particularly when compared to some of the School's main competitors). It was the first time that premises were designed for the School that both encapsulated its learning philosophy and symbolised the 'brand image' it sought to create. Hence the relevance of the premises story to the topic that was discussed in Chapter 11 – the development of a quality culture. When Figures 12.1–12.7 are combined with the relevant text in this chapter a better 'feel' can be created for the progressive development of the School.

Figure 12.1 Walmsley House, St. John Street

Figure 12.2 Gresham College Building, Basinghall Street

Figure 12.3 Lionel Denny House, Goswell Road

Figure 12.4 Frobisher Crescent, Barbican

Figure 12.5 Bunhill Row Building

Figure 12.6 A traditional learning layout in Gresham Hall

Figure 12.7 A modern learning layout in the Bunhill Row Building

13
Impact of Strategies

Evaluating the success of strategies is difficult in the context of a single business school. However, comparative data is available to indicate the relative standing of Cass in the business school world. The Quality Assessment Agency and RAE results indicate how the School stands up to UK competition with respect to various quality criteria. Media generated rankings indicate the relative standing of the School and selected programmes. Accrediting bodies ensure that acceptable standards are maintained by only recognising those schools that satisfy their criteria; they include the UK's Association of MBAs, the European Foundation for Management Development, and the American AACSB International. In terms of the history of the School all these measures are of recent origin. More historic data of a quantitative nature is needed in order to gain a fuller picture of the School's academic progress across time. Hence the additional measures presented next: degrees offered since the School's birth; number of students graduating; number of professors in post. For practical and interpretative reasons only recent financial information is mentioned. As has already been pointed out until the late eighties it was difficult to reliably separate out the School's accounts from those of the University as a whole. Financial and other criteria (e.g. research income, publications) have of course influenced the outcome of the more recent conglomerate measures referred to earlier.

Degrees introduced under each Deanship

The basic framework adopted for presenting these data trends is the Deanship, thus maintaining the framework already used in Figure 1.1. For practical reasons Lord Currie's Deanship is treated as incorporating the six-month 'cabinet period' chaired by Professor Grammenos. For the

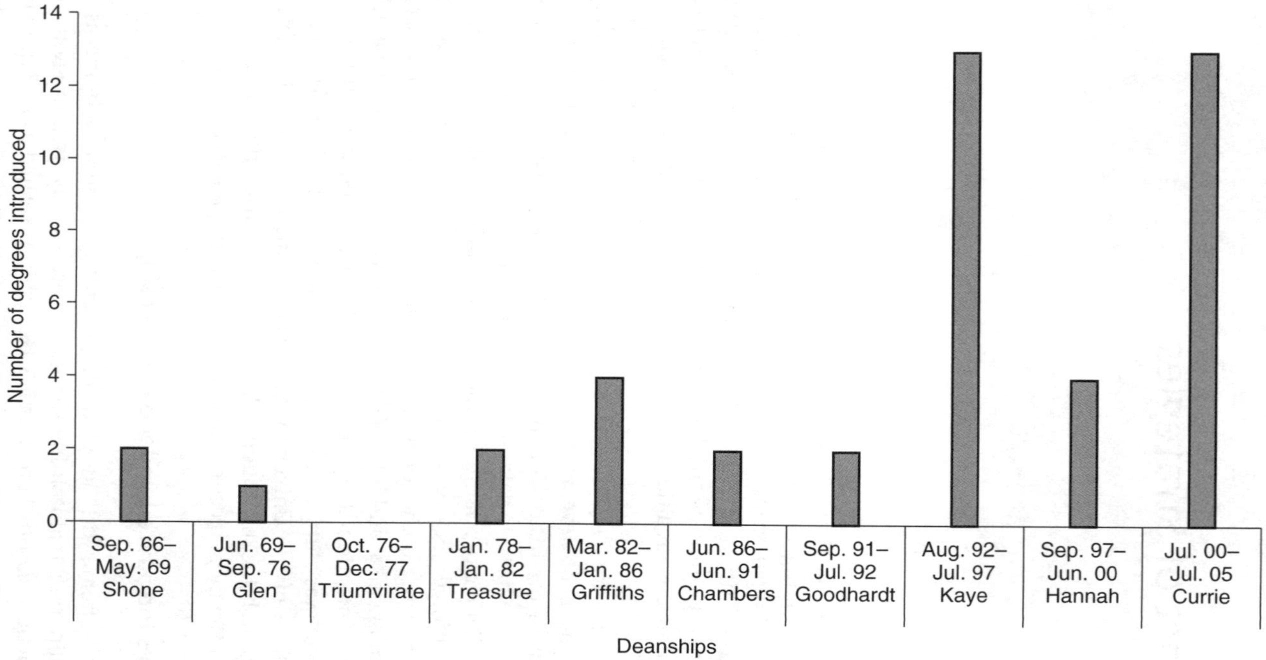

Figure 13.1 Number of degrees introduced during each Deanship

purpose of the study this Deanship is taken up to July 2005 although it continues into the future. The histogram in Figure 13.1 summarises the number of degrees introduced under each of the ten Deanships. The marked increase in the Kaye Deanship has already been commented upon in previous chapters. The other significant period of increase occurs in the Currie Deanship, reflecting Actuarial Science merging into the School and the opportunity provided by the new building for introducing new degrees.

The strategy for growth is amply demonstrated by these data. In the University's first year (1966/67) the School ran two Masters and two research degrees. In the year 2004/05 the School was running three MBA degrees, two research degrees, twenty-three MSc/MAs, and seven BScs.

Number of students graduating

In order to explore further the changing profile of the School the numbers of students qualifying for the different degrees were collected. The degrees were sorted into the broad categories of MBA, MSc Finance, MSc non-Finance, MPhil/PhD, BSc Finance and BSc non-Finance. To enable some comparison across Deanships, and to draw out the shift from the MBA toward the specialist Masters, the annual average post-graduate awards in each category were calculated for each Deanship. Thus the average annual MBA awards during the 3 years of Kenneth Shone's Deanship was 18; while the average for the first five years of David Currie's was 178. The latest data included in the calculations are those for the May 2005 graduation ceremony. The trends are shown in Figure 13.2. The trends are consistent with the historical observations made in earlier chapters about the School's strategies and the mergers and demerges that took place. If the average undergraduate awards for each Deanship had been presented in Figure 13.2, they would have shown a steady rise from an annual average of 52 in the Griffith Deanship to 177 in the Currie Deanship; and the finance/non-finance differences would have been less marked than in the postgraduate data.

Alumni profile

It is only in recent years that UK universities and their business schools have devoted sufficient resources to developing and maintaining an effective alumni database. This has become more important as these institutions have recognised the value of alumni in promoting and development their institutions, particularly in the context of increased

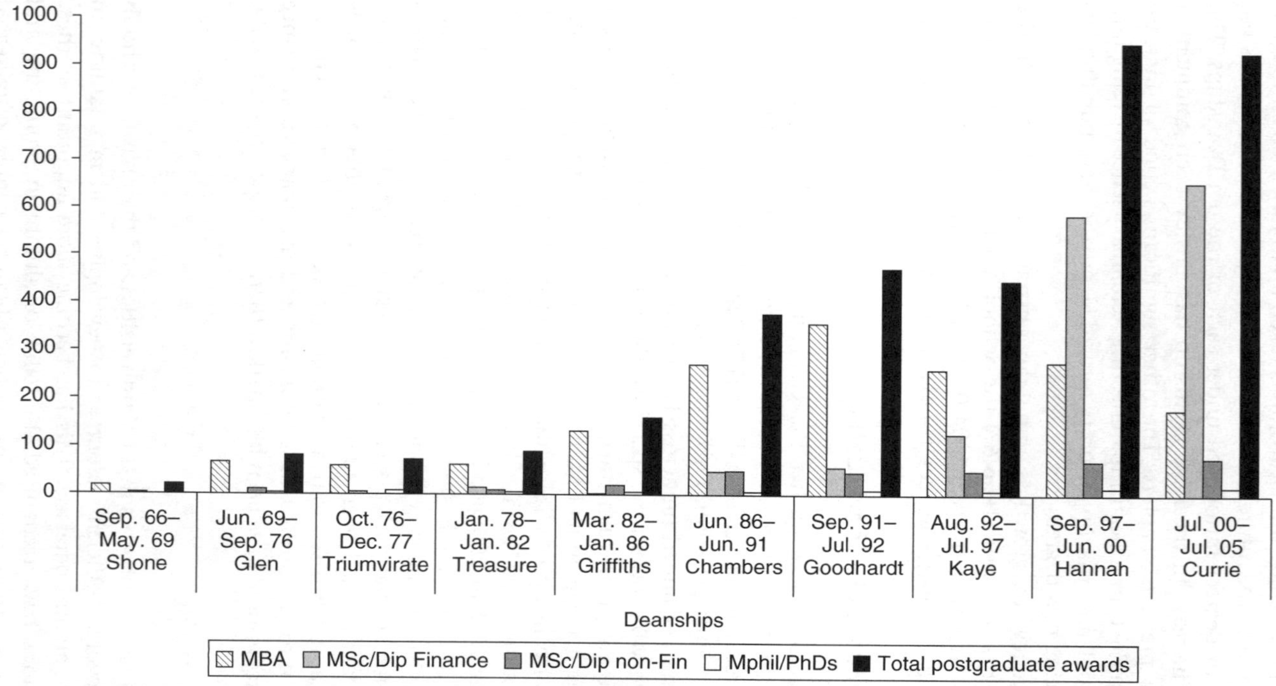

Figure 13.2 Annual average number of students awarded postgraduate degrees during each Deanship

competition and reduced State funding. Early alumni records are too incomplete to attempt to produce their changing profile across the history of the School. However, the profile of alumni in April 2005 has been analysed to gauge the extent that graduates are (a) known to be employed in a financial or non-financial function, (b) based in the United Kingdom or abroad, (c) graduated from the School with an MBA, MSc or BSc.

The analysis of the current alumni database revealed:

- Of the 17,108 alumni on the database 32 per cent had an MBA, 39 per cent an MSc and 29 per cent a BSc. From this database it was possible to classify 74 per cent as operating in either a financial or a non-financial job.
- Of the 1697 alumni (for whom relevant information was available) from the MBA programmes, 41 per cent (n = 698) had finance-related job titles, 64 per cent (n = 446) of this 'finance subgroup' were based in the United Kingdom and 36 per cent (n = 252) abroad.
- Of the 1309 alumni (for whom relevant information was available) from the School's MSc programmes, 45 per cent (n = 585) had finance-related job titles, 43 per cent (n = 252) of this 'finance subgroup' were based in the United Kingdom and 57 per cent (n = 333) abroad.
- Of the 1016 alumni (for whom relevant information was available) from the BSc programmes, 48 per cent (n = 489) had finance-related job titles, 80 per cent (n = 392) of this 'finance subgroup' were based in the United Kingdom and 20 per cent (n = 97) abroad.

These findings hold no surprises despite the gaps in the information available. They reinforce the School's strength in finance, the international nature of the MBA/MSc alumni network, and the predominance of postgraduates over undergraduates. The limitations of the current database restrict what further generalisations can be made.

Professors in post at the end of each Deanship

It can be argued that the number of full-time professors in post at any one time is an indication of the academic standing of a business school. This was certainly true when the University operated the rigorous process described in Chapter 11. In more recent years, while the process remains rigorous the criteria have been broadened. In effect there are now two routes to a professorship: the traditional route where the quality of publications is paramount; and the more professional route where academic leadership in a subject area (e.g. in the development of the discipline and related degrees), outstanding performance as a teacher and significant contributions to the development of a professional institution, are all relevant criteria that help to compensate for shortfalls in publications.

Figure 13.3 shows the number of full-time professors in post in the final year of each Deanship. The data differentiates between external and internal appointments; this split gives an indication of the success with which the School encourages academic staff development. Also presented are the total number of full-time academics (i.e. teaching staff), and the percentage of academic staff of professorial standing. In the first ten years of the School the maximum number of professors in post was three. Although this doubled to six in the next eight years, the majority represented external appointments. It was not until the period 1986–91 that there was a sizeable professoriate, and that internal promotions outstripped external appointments. This pattern continued for subsequent years.

During the 1986–91 Deanship the increased number of internal appointments was facilitated by the fact that the Dean (Andrew Chambers), the Vice-Chancellor (Raoul Franklin) and the Academic Registrar (Adrian Seville) were all keen to give staff the opportunity of promotion to a Chair if they had a good chance of meeting the traditional academic criteria. The financial implications for the University were negligible since these staff were almost certainly at the top of the senior lecturer scale, and on promotion would normally only be given one incremental increase in salary with no commitment to future increments. The effect of this policy was that eight internal staff were promoted to Chairs during this Deanship. Over the same time period five external appointments were made to sponsored Chairs.

The first three departments absorbed by the School had little effect on the number of Chairs at the time of the mergers. The Centre for Banking and International Finance brought one (Brian Griffith); Property Valuation and Management one (Piers Venmore-Rowland); Systems and Management none. The fourth merger with Actuarial Science in 2002 brought in four new professors (Steve Haberman, Richard Verrall, Celia Glass, Les Mayhew).

There has been a significant rise in academic staff in the current Currie Deanship; indeed numbers have virtually doubled since the proliferation of specialist MScs in the last ten years. The percentage of academic staff of professorial status has been remarkably consistent across the last

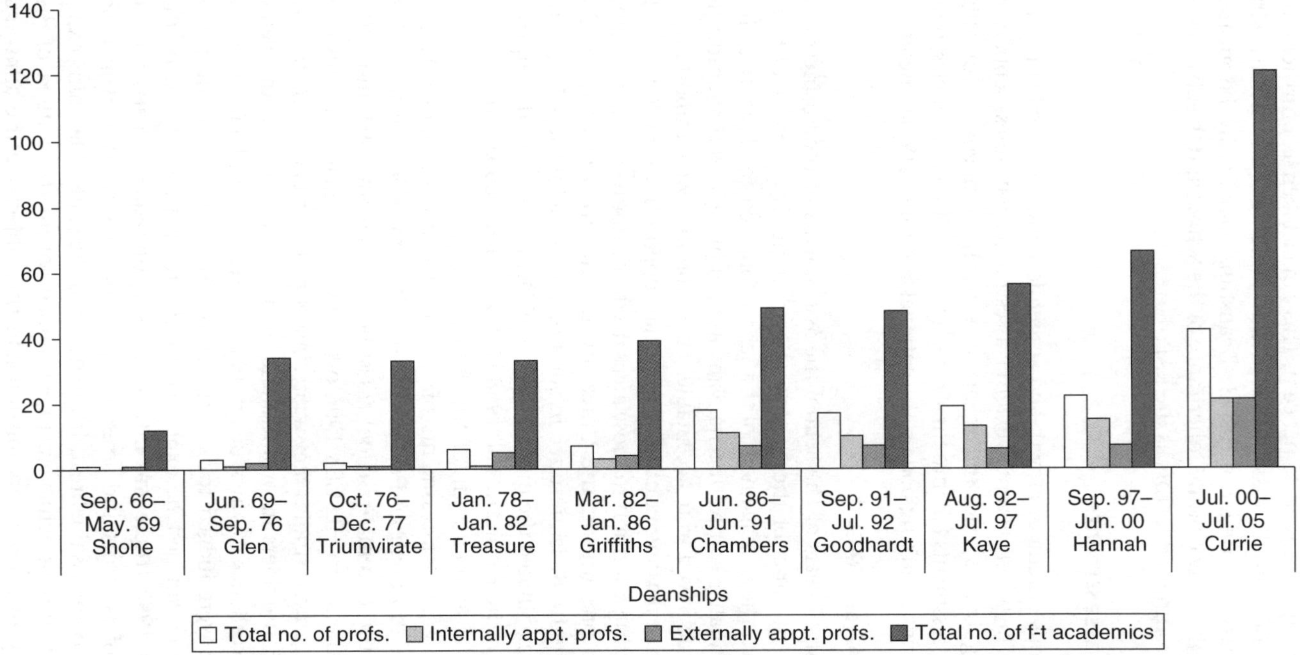

Figure 13.3 Number of professors (promotions within School + external appointments) and total number of academics in the final year of each Deanship

four Deanships – around 35 per cent. This can be taken as a further indication of the School's sustained academic standing. The contrast with the 11 years covering the first 3 'Deanships' can hardly be greater, reflecting the early cultural inheritance of the School and the absence of such environmental factors as the RAE.

External assessments

The previous criteria of growth and academic standing lacked comparative data. The widely accepted external assessments of business schools by accrediting bodies and the media can partly compensate for this. External assessments fall into three categories: government agencies, non-government accrediting bodies, the national and international media.

HEFCE: QAA and RAE

In the first 25 years of the School the assessments of the business and management panel of the UGC were important. The panel had to be assured that the management of the School followed good practice, that adequate quality control mechanisms were in place, and that academic standards achieved were acceptable. Their opinions were important for at least three reasons: continued financial support from the State; feedback directing attention to those areas needing improvement; providing additional pressure on the University to cater for the needs of the School. The 1968 visit resulted in additional finance for the School. The 1981 visit facilitated the move from Lionel Denny House to the superior premises in the Barbican. The 1988 visit provided feedback (e.g. loss of MBA market share) for stimulating future change.

The subsequent assessments of HEFCE's Quality Assurance Agency were more thorough and systematic but the aims were the same. The results of the two main School assessments so far (in 1994 and 2002) were 'excellent'. In HEFCE's 1994 overview report relating to business and management studies they wrote: 'Assessment visits were made to 47 of the 105 providers in business and management studies. An overall grade of excellence was awarded to 19 institutions, and all but one of the remainder were judged to be satisfactory'. The meaning of an 'excellence' rating can best be explained by the template produced by the Agency in 1993 (there was little change in subsequent years) for the guidance of assessors and assessees: 'The Council's assessment method seeks to encompass the breadth and depth of the student learning experience and student achievement, examined within the context of the particularly institution, its mission and the subject-specific aims and objectives'. The headings of the six sections in the template (together with their guiding criteria) are shown in Box 13.1.

The RAE was introduced by HEFCE in 1992 as a method of distributing money for research. The governing principle was to give more money to those universities able to demonstrate that their research output was of a high quality. The original rating scale to indicate research quality has remained basically the same across the different exercises. The School's rating of '4' achieved in 1996 (a repeat of the 1992 rating) was well above the median rating of around '2' for the business and management studies distribution of scores across institutions. The '5' achieved in 2002 was also well above the median of around '3a'. In the latest exercise the School's national excellence in research, with some sub-areas of international excellence, are recognised. The gradual upward drift in ratings over the years has been interpreted as a genuine improvement in the quality of research in the business and management area generally (Bessant 2003). However, the ratings achieved by the School have been bettered by some of our main competitors such as LBS, Warwick and Lancaster. The pockets of research excellence in the

Box 13.1 Criteria used by the QAA in assessing 'excellence'.

- Aims and curricula ('Discussion of the institution's mission; its approach to quality; the subject aims and objectives; curricula and syllabuses; meeting the needs of students').
- Students: nature of intake, support systems and progression ('Entry profile and student progression in the light of aims and objectives; existence and impact of academic and personal support services').
- The quality of teaching and students' achievements and progression ('Discussion of the quality of teaching; relationships between scholarship/research and teaching; evidence of student achievement and progress in light of aims and objectives; range and effectiveness of assessment methods; external opinion – external examiners, professional bodies, subject associations – and its impact; internal annual reviews and impact; employer opinion and graduate/diplomate employability; student satisfaction').
- Staff and staff development ('Quantity and quality of staff – well-qualified, up-to-date, well-matched to the curriculum; institutional and subject support for staff development; relationship of staff development to aims and objectives; staffing issues').
- Resources ('The quality of the learning support facilities available e.g. library, student access to IT; the quality of the physical resources available e.g. teaching and learning accommodation, equipment').
- Academic management and quality control ('Subject level impact of internal quality control mechanisms; subject level impact of any academic audit report; plans and priorities for the future').

School have been dragged down by a tail of research inactive staff. This was partly corrected by the time of the last RAE. The constantly shrinking tail of research inactive staff should lead to an even better result in the next exercise in 2007/08.

Accreditations: AMBA, IPD, EQUIS

The AMBA is the national accrediting body for MBA programmes. The history of AMBA as recounted by Peter Calladine of AMBA in an email in 2003 to the author is worth reproducing:

> We were established in 1967 by British graduates of MBA programmes in the USA and as such we actually preceded the MBA in this country. City University's MBA has been on our list of accredited schools since its inception. In the early days (in the 70s) 'accreditation' in the UK did not exist as such. The Association, then the Business Graduates Association or BGA, merely had a list of schools from which it would accept members. We talked then in terms of 'member schools' but even then we did have an 'accredited list of schools'. This was arrived at with basic knowledge of the market and included UK schools, all the top American and continental schools plus leading schools elsewhere. Given that by 1985 there was still only 26 providers in the UK 'quality' wasn't an issue. However, between 1985 and 1990 the number of providers in the UK grew to 76 and 'quality' did become a real issue. We ceased to accept members from new schools in around 1985 and created our first accreditation criteria in, I think, 1987/88 so as to monitor quality. At more or less the same time we changed our name to the Association of MBAs. We then reviewed the programmes at all of the old schools and deleted about four of the 26 original UK providers on the 1985 list because they did not meet our criteria. The assessment criteria have been revised on a regular basis since then and are now under the bailiwick of our International Accreditation Advisory Board.

The School's full-time Day MBA, the part-time Evening or Executive MBA, and the Engineering MBA programmes were all accredited. The areas explored by the accrediting panel include: the mission, and supporting strategies and values; finances and relationship with parent institution; faculty – their qualifications, teaching and research competences, involvement in consultancy; management structures; students – quality of intake, recruitment literature, alumni services; curriculum structure and content; relevance and supervision of student projects; assessment and examination procedures; facilities – library, computing, teaching rooms. Although it is the MBA programmes rather than the School that are being assessed, inevitably a good deal about the School has to be examined.

The Institute of Personnel and Development is one of the largest professional bodies in the United Kingdom with over 100,000 members, and received its Charter in 2000. It covered much the same ground as AMBA, but focused its attention on those students who were taking the appropriate combination of modules on the Day MBA in order to obtain exemption from the Institute's professional examinations. Re-accreditation, and the right to use the title of 'centre of excellence' (which applied to the School since it was introduced), was not sought in the late 1990s when this particular group of students were too small to justify the continuation of this specialist stream in the MBA programme.

EQUIS accreditation was sought toward the end of Leslie Hannah's Deanship (1997–2000) and awarded in January 2001. Equis stands for European Quality Improvement System, and is managed by the European Foundation for Management Development. It is concerned with accrediting the whole School. Accreditation involves a panel who supplement the study of a self-assessment report with a three-day visit. Similar features of the School are critically examined as applied to other accreditations such as quality of degrees and assurance mechanisms, research and teaching, resources and so on. The main differences are that the panel looks more thoroughly at executive development performance, relationships with the University and the corporate world, and the School's international characteristics. These criteria reflect the international corporate world's involvement in the European Foundation for Management Education. The School was successfully accredited, obtaining flying colours on all criteria except for two. The exceptions were: the learning environment for students (the School was still in the Barbican when the visit took place); and the performance of executive education (at that time, neither the size of the undertaking nor the profitability achieved ranked alongside the achievements of competitors such as LBS and Cranfield).

Taken together the outcomes of these 'involuntary' government schemes, and the 'voluntary' non-government accreditation schemes, are relatively objective evidence of the overall quality of the School and of its potential for even greater success in the future.

Media rankings: *FT*, *EIU* and *Guardian*

At the end of the day a school's reputation is going to be influenced by its comparative standing within the national and international business school sector. Hence the importance of the widely consulted league tables. League tables have dominated the American scene for many years. In 1999 a new international assessment of MBA degrees appeared in the *FT*, and apart from some minor changes in criteria has continued ever since. Their rankings have gathered sufficient status to influence the standing of schools in the eyes of students, staff, employers and sponsors. 20 criteria are used in arriving at the rankings. Eight criteria are based on responses given by course participants. These reflect the performance of the MBA programme and career progression, and salary data is the largest component. 55 per cent of the total weighting is given to this group of criteria. The next nine criteria are based on a business school survey and measure the diversity of students, faculty and board members (i.e. gender, nationality). These are worth 25 per cent of the total weight. The last group of 3 criteria measure research performance, and carry 20 per cent of the total weight (see *FT* for 26 January 2004 or 24 January 2005 for further details on methodology). In the first published findings in 1999 Cass was ranked 44 in the world. Since then the rankings based on the full-time MBA have fluctuated somewhat (81 in 2002, 68 in 2003, 42 in 2004 and 60 in 2005). The equivalent *FT* rankings in the context of European and UK schools have shown less fluctuations: between 12 in 1999 and 17 in 2005 in Europe; and between 6 in 1999 and 9 in 2005 in the United Kingdom.

Two further international assessments have been introduced by the *FT*: executive MBAs and executive open/tailored short courses. The School's Executive or Evening MBA programme was as high as 10 in the world, 4 in Europe and 2 in the United Kingdom in 2001. Performance has deteriorated slightly since then (15 in the world, 5 in Europe, 3 in United Kingdom in 2002; 22 in the world, 5 in Europe, 3 in the United Kingdom in 2003; 13 in the world, 4 in Europe, 3 in the United Kingdom in 2004). Unfortunately Cass' open executive and custom executive education programmes are too small to take part in the *FT*'s top 50 business schools in this category. The UK schools that are ranked in the latest *FT* rankings (16 May 2005) are those that have an established reputation in this area: LBS, Cranfield, Ashridge, Henley, Warwick and MBS. It is significant that these are schools that have not suffered from the lack of adequate premises, including residential accommodation!

Care must be taken in interpreting the trends in media rankings. For instance data derived from the *FT* surveys reflect the views of alumni having graduated three years before. Also, the composition of the business schools included in the exercise has changed over the years. Both of these factors help to explain the apparent fall in the School's rank for the full-time MBA from 1999 to 2002. A school's position can fluctuate considerably from one year to the next if it falls outside the top 25 or so schools – hence the importance of making this top group. It is encouraging to see that the School's MBA programmes within the UK context are consistently within the top ten (normally including of Cass, Cranfield, Judge, Lancaster, LBS, MBS, Said, Tanaka, and Warwick).

The 'lottery' element in rankings is illustrated by the *Economist Intelligence Unit*'s 2004 rankings of full-time MBA programmes. Their 16th edition of 'Which MBA' (http://mba.eiu.com) spells out the criteria they use. It is worth noting that their criteria reflects ranking over the last three years, only measures research criteria through a measure of percentage of faculty with PhDs, emphasises 'Open new career opportunities' (35 per cent weighting) and 'Personal development/educational experience' (35 per cent weighting), and includes a 'Potential to network' alumni-related criterion (10 per cent weighting). Given that these criteria do not reflect the strengths of the School it is not surprising to find that the Cass full-time MBA is ranked 91 out of the 100 worldwide schools evaluated, 35 in Europe and 17 in the United Kingdom. Within the United Kingdom, Birmingham Business School, Henley, Cranfield and Warwick are all ranked above LBS! These observations, and the discrepancies between different media rankings, underline the importance of understanding the criteria being applied.

In terms of its undergraduate degrees the School has done well: for example, the Guardian league tables for business and management have ranked the School in the top four in the United Kingdom for three years (2002–04) and in the top ten for one year (2005). Again further words of caution are needed. The criteria used across the media are not standardised. The *Guardian* ranking of undergraduate degrees ignores research criteria because it is thought to be less important to undergraduates, but it takes into account criteria relating to teaching, money spent per student, student/staff ratio, employment, value added (e.g. whether those with low qualifications on entry get good degrees), entry qualifications, inclusiveness (proportion of under represented groups). The interpretations of fluctuations in rankings across the years can get complex, as when the *Guardian* changes the weighting given to different criteria. For instance, the fall in rankings in 2005 was mainly due to dropping the Teaching Quality Assessment scores in favour of a measure of full-time academic teaching seniority and qualifications.

It is also worth pointing out that the publications used in judging research performance by the *FT* is heavily influenced by American journals. Unfortunately, the *FT* rankings do not adequately recognise one of the main strengths of Cass – its excellent reputation in the broad finance area. In recent years various finance journals have judged the School's insurance and risk management research to be ranked second in the World, and its finance research second in Europe (Chan *et al.* 2002).

Finance

It is difficult to show financial trends relating to the School for the whole period of its history. The point has already been made that until the late 1980s the School's accounts were integrated with those of the University. The introduction of devolved budgeting changed this, but the turnover of School accountants and the introduction of a new accounting system by the University in 1998 mean that only from that date are records comparable and readily obtainable.

A number of observations are worth making in relation to the School's accounts from 1997/98 to 2003/04 when the turnover increased from £15 to £30 million. First, the proportion of State funding to total income reduced from 19 to 12 per cent over this period. From the history in Part II it is clear that State funding played a diminishing role in the success of the School as more self-financing degrees were introduced and fees charged were market-led. Second, since moving into the new building and becoming more self-sufficient there has been a slight decrease in central overheads charged by the University (they amounted to 19 per cent of the School's income in 2001/02 while in the Barbican, to 16 per cent in 2003/04 which was the first full year of occupying the new building). Third, the non-voluntary contribution to University funds of around 3 per cent of the School's income has continued throughout the period, even when the School was having to draw on its reserves and, since 2001/02, was repaying the loan on the new building. Helping to finance the deficit of other parts of the University is only of concern when the School is competing against other business schools which are neither 'taxed' in this way nor having to service a loan for their building! However, it is only fair to point out that without the sale of City Technology Ltd the University would probably not have been in a position to commit itself with respect to the Bunhill Row building, and the School would not be occupying its present state-of-the-art building. The University realised about £20 million from the sale of the wholly owned City Technology Ltd in 1993/94. Fourth, the fluctuating fortunes of the School's executive education activities in recent years are in marked contrast to its profitability in the early history of the School. Fortunately, the policy initiated by Dean Kaye in building-up the reserves (a cumulative balance of 15 per cent of total income in 1997/98) helped the School to cope with the erratic performance of executive education.

Conclusion to Part III

Chapters 7–12 have attempted to understand and explain the descriptive history of the School. The theoretical approach adopted has on the one hand emphasised the context in which the School has developed and, on the other hand, highlighted the strategies that the School followed in pursuit of its mission and vision. This approach is consistent with conventional managerial thinking. Chapter 13 attempted to evaluate the School's achievements, in spite of the difficulties encountered in researching a single case. Taken as a whole, the data discussed add up to a convincing case that the School is one of the major schools in the United Kingdom, in Europe and worldwide. How can one account even further for this success in a way which is communicable and useful to others interested in the management of business schools in a competitive environment? This is the challenge for Part IV. Strategic leadership, within a framework of organisational culture and change, is the theoretical framework selected for carrying out this task.

Part IV

Strategic Leadership in a Business School

14
An Open Systems Model of Key Organisational Elements

In terms of the criteria applied to business schools Cass stakeholders can be proud of their achievements. A closely knit team of less than 10 'unproven' academics had, with the support of superiors and advisers, launched a venture that has grown to over a 100 'proven' academics. It took nearly 40 years for these achievements to be realised. What practical insights can be gained from the historical development of Cass Business School? Although any insights emerging may not be novel, their reinstatement and reinforcement in the context of business schools may be useful to those who are concerned with their development. Insights in this chapter will be framed around the open systems concept. Those in Chapter 15 will focus around the concept of leadership within the context of change.

An open systems model of organisational elements

There are three key aspects of systems thinking relevant to understanding this case study. The first is the dependence of an organisation upon the environment for its growth and survival. This means that academic institutions constantly have to adapt to changes in their environment. These changes may relate to government policy, the entry of new competitors in the market for students and staff, the availability of new technology to facilitate new methods of learning, and so on. The second is the interdependence of organisational elements and processes. Basing a departmental structure in a business school upon disciplines will have repercussions for the level of co-operation across these disciplines. Appointing a business person rather than an academic as Dean of a school will affect the climate as well as the strategy and culture of that institution. The third aspect is the concept of organisation/environment fit. Underlying the concept of fit is the assumption that management can always improve upon the effectiveness of their organisation by introducing changes that re-define relationships with a dynamic environment.

These basic ideas have been around for a long time (Katz and Kahn 1966) and have contributed to the emergence of new disciplines (e.g. business strategy, organisational development), and to the enormous growth of the consultancy industry (i.e. external interventions for bringing about 'better fits'). Academics and consultants have developed frameworks for highlighting those organisational characteristics that are of strategic significance, and therefore the natural targets for change (Leavitt 1965; Peters and Waterman 1982). Figure 14.1 presents a model that builds on earlier ones, and reflects the findings of the present case study. The meanings underlying elements in the model are outlined next; their significance is self-evident.

Mission and strategies. This refers to the goals the School is striving to achieve and the methods being used to achieve them. To be one of the top business schools in the world is an over-arching goal. In the 1990s this meant for the School a place in the top 25 on the *FT* rankings of the top 100 business schools world-wide. The strategies that were followed

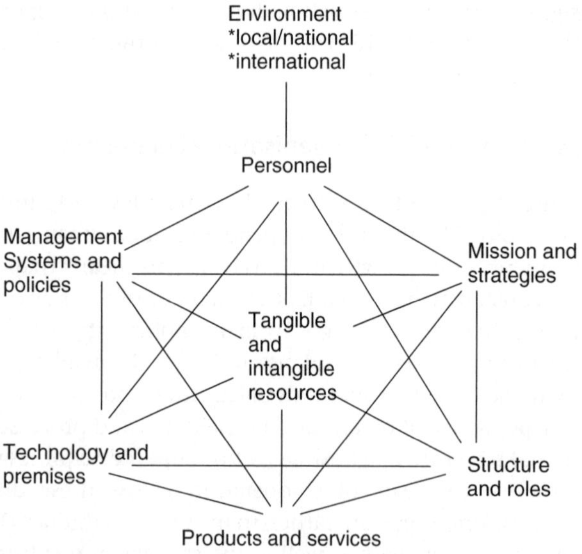

Figure 14.1 An open systems model of key organisational elements

have already been outlined; they include recruiting staff with international academic reputations and the occupation of state-of-the-art premises with the latest learning technologies. One of the problems in using *FT* rankings as the most important criterion is that it fails to recognise another important objective of the School, that is, its City orientation. Meeting the needs of the City, and the needs of management education both nationally and internationally, were stated goals when the School was formed in the 1960s. These were re-emphasised in David Kaye's formal mission statement for the School in 1994: 'To be a top-rated business school serving industry and commerce across the world, and to be the business school of first resort for students and organisations focusing on activity associated with the City of London and the business professions.' More recently Lord Currie's goal for Cass to be the 'intellectual hub of the City' highlights that aspect of the School's purpose that most differentiates it from competition.

Over its 40-year history the formal purpose of the School has remained much the same, although the ways of expressing it have changed. The key strategies have hardly changed, but the extent to which they have focused down on the essentials have changed. In contrast, major changes have occurred in all the other variables in Figure 14.1; one of the most marked being the profile of degrees being offered (i.e. 'products and services'). These observations (i.e. the stability of the mission relative to other variables) are not surprising given that the School has remained part of the City University, which in turn has remained part of the higher education system in the United Kingdom. Also the geographical location of the School in or adjacent to the City of London has had a profound and steadying influence.

Structure and roles. This refers to the way in which roles are allocated to individuals within the organisation, and determines the extent to which individuals and groups can exert influence over decisions affecting their interests in the organisation. The structures of business schools are difficult to design and manage because the conventional superior–subordinate relationship found in commercial organisations do not exist. The little that is left of the once sacrosanct 'academic freedom' can still create problems for senior academics trying to influence teaching content and methods, research and publications. But it is less difficult than it was, thanks to the various rewards/sanctions available and quality control mechanisms in operation.

One of the most difficult problems facing Deans is determining the most appropriate structure for their school in the light of mission, strategies and environmental factors. Just as physical premises inhibit interaction between individuals and groups, so do the psychological barriers created by organisational structures. Departments that feel that they 'own' degrees will be highly motivated to ensure their success; the BSc in Banking and International Finance undoubtedly benefited from this situation over many years. However, this strength became a management problem when greater co-ordination was needed to increase the efficiency and effectiveness of the undergraduate programme as a whole and of the multi-disciplinary MBA degree. On the other hand, a degree of internal competition can be beneficial. There is no doubt that the multi-departmental structure at the School in the 1990s created forces that resulted in a crop of new degrees in at least three departments – all in the finance area. While structure created forces pushing for this, it may not have been sufficient if the School's need to generate more surplus income in pursuance of new premises did not dominate management thinking.

In the early history of the School the numbers of staff were sufficiently small for individuals to feel that they had opportunities to influence decisions affecting themselves and the School. The introduction of split sites (i.e. Gresham College and Lionel Denny House), the numerical growth of the School, the increased diversification of interest with the introduction of new degrees, growing external competition, reduced State funding, all generated strains on the formal structures operating in the different departments/schools of the University – Boards of Studies, Departmental/School Boards. Different Deans had to adapt to these changing scenes by modifying the role of the formal committees or by introducing additional management structures. These additional structures were advisory to the Dean, and usually referred to as the 'executive committee' or more informally as the 'management team'. On paper Departmental/School Boards were intended to act as a constraint on the power of the Dean and to give some influence to the individual academic, in practice they could be circumvented by executive committees in the interest of 'effective management'. While Departmental/School Boards still met infrequently, their role became one of consultation and communication rather than decision making. Dean Glen introduced the first executive committee and it met weekly under his chairmanship, and the six individuals who had been allocated key responsibilities in the School were invited to be members. This developing management structure highlighted the need for more effective internal communications, and this in turn brought about the weekly 'GBC News' which would include matters discussed at the last executive meeting. This pattern was repeated by subsequent Deans, although pressure to increase the membership of the executive committee led to monthly meetings and the emergence of a much smaller 'management team' with frequent meetings. Governance changes at the University level in 2005 now enable the School to be managed in a way that has in effect evolved over time: the Departmental/School Board disappears; the School Management Committee (similar to the executive committee in earlier days) is retained in an advisory role to the Dean; the Executive consists of the Dean, supported by the Deputy Dean and Chief Operating Officer.

A structural anomaly that arose as a result of the need to reduce dependence on State funding was the two-category status of academic staff. Staff who were originally recruited to lecture on UGC-approved courses, such as the Day MBA and the BSc in Business Studies, were treated as one group. A second group of staff were those recruited to lecture on the self-financing courses, such as the Evening MBA. This situation created a managerial headache because of the difficulties of getting co-operation across the divide; the only way of getting some staff to contribute across this divide was to fall back on financial rewards. The additional factor contributing to this problem was that many staff recruited before the introduction of the Evening MBA, saw evening lecturing as outside their contractual obligations and therefore requiring additional compensation. Deans had to negotiate through these minefields without alienating staff and without prejudicing the effective delivery of courses, despite the Academic Registrar assuring Deans that the form of the contract was no barrier to greater flexibility (the University could set contractual obligations for each member of staff, subject only to 'reasonableness of duties'). Gradually a culture of flexibility as to when and where one lectured did come about, and became legitimised with the introduction of the formal system for distributing workload in the 1990s.

The self-imposed barriers created by 'structure' combined with 'custom and practice' (or culture) are nowhere more evident than in the treatment of executive education at the School. In the late 1960s this aspect of the School's products was brought together in the Post Experience Unit and it was headed by an academic Sub-dean (Oliver Vesey-Holt). At this time and during the 1970s academic staff contributed to the design and delivery of courses because it was in the interest of the School to educate the City about the relevance of its expertise to their needs. The small faculty size meant that cohesiveness was sufficiently high to generate co-operation without additional financial compensation (rewards came via support for research assistants and travel expenses for attending conferences). As the School got larger, a distancing occurred between executive education and the rest of the School. This distancing was physically and psychologically reinforced when executive education occupied separate premises (i.e. Gresham College building and later 24 Chiswell Street), and when it was formed into a legal company for financial reasons.

Products and services. These attempt to satisfy the markets in which the School operates, and include all degrees, executive development courses, consultancy and research as detailed in Part III.

Technology and premises. This is a term used to cover all those tools, devices and physical premises that facilitate the creation and delivery of products and services necessary to achieve given goals. In the business school setting this includes library and computer technology (hardware and software) with its vast potential for learning, communication and the removal of geographical barriers. These technologies are means of accessing, recording and distributing information relevant to learning, research and administration. 'Premises' is not normally mentioned as a significant organisational characteristic in models similar to that in Figure 14.1. This may be because its importance is taken for granted. In the educational environment premises can yield significant competitive advantage, since they are an integral part of the learning experience 'bought' by customers as well as contributing to a school's reputation or image. They affect the 'quality of life' experiences of employees, and can facilitate or inhibit mutually beneficial social interactions (e.g. between academic staff and research students).

The importance of premises is highlighted in the School's history. Sir James Tait (the Principal of Northampton CAT) and Oliver Thomson (Chairman of the Board of Governors) had the vision of linking the new university to the City of London, and hence came about the battle with London University to use the title of 'The City University'. This confrontation has been elaborated elsewhere (Teague 1980). The objections of London University were twofold: confusion with its long established name; several of its schools were located within the City boundaries unlike Northampton CAT. The latter objection was no doubt due to a felt threat to its own connections with the City of London. Fortunately, Tait and Thomson gained the support of the Lord Mayor and his recent predecessors; they were enthusiastic with the idea that Lord Mayors would be invited to become Chancellors of the new university. In order to give the City link more substance Tait tried to create a foothold within the City boundaries that would house the management education activities of the new university. The first opportunity came when part of the premises of Gresham College in Basinghall Street became vacant, and the Mercers and the Corporation agreed that it should house the GBC. Although the GBC was formally still the Department of Management, this name change was thought to be more effective in spearheading the School's entry into the City. It proved to be so.

As already explained the move to the Barbican had its problems which were eventually resolved as a result of the efforts of Edward Parkes and Raoul Franklin (Vice-Chancellors) and Dean Treasure. The move was important because it enabled executive development to be housed with the rest of the School, was an improvement on the previous shabby building (Lionel Denny House), and was within the City boundaries. The expense involved in the Barbican premises meant that the Gresham College premises had to be relinquished. The UGC insisted that the Barbican premises were too large for the School, and the University agreed to move the Centre for Banking and International Finance into the Barbican thus paving the way for its incorporation into the School. This latter development had a significant impact on the reputation of the School's strength in finance.

Although the move to Bunhill Row was only recently brought about, the size, facilities and quality of these premises are such that it has already facilitated significant changes (e.g. new products, incorporation of Actuarial Science). The aspiration of 'being the intellectual hub of the City' is now a realistic goal, given the number of activities being organised throughout the day and evening involving City institutions, professional bodies, livery companies, international conferences and workshops (see *www.cass.city.ac.uk* for a regular up-date of activities).

Management systems and policies. These cover many things, particularly systems and processes for managing staff (e.g. selecting, consulting, appraising and developing, rewarding), students (e.g. student selection, welfare, careers advice and placement), alumni, employers and of course finance. It is these systems that will determine the effectiveness with which appropriate staff are recruited and managed for implementing the School's strategies. It is also these systems that will be closely reviewed by government agencies and accreditation bodies in their efforts to spread what is currently regarded as 'good practice' and 'quality systems' in the operations of business schools.

Many of these systems are derived from, and have to be compatible with, the corresponding University systems. This is most apparent in relation to the School's financial system. Annual budgets and accounts have to be integrated with those of the University, and the University's Finance Director has responsibility for overseeing the whole picture. Negotiations over financial matters are a constant source of friction, particularly with respect to the 'general tax' imposed on the School for the support of other parts of the University. It was only in the 1980s that the need for more financial decentralisation was recognised. This opened the door for a number of developments since the School was allowed to keep and to determine how it spent its surplus income. One of the outcomes of these developments was for the School to start to employ its own specialist staff in those areas where the service provided by the University was perceived as inadequate (e.g. computer services). Nowadays, given the growth of the School and the University, there is more delegation from the centre, but this is always within the boundaries of the University's management systems and procedures. This has required the School to employ more senior professional personnel to develop and manage appropriate management systems relating to finance, personnel, computing, facilities, and so on.

Over the years HR systems have become more systematic and better managed through the employment of professionals. One of the implications of maintaining HR systems in line with the rest of the University has had some advantages (e.g. taking the need for training and development seriously), and some disadvantages. An example of the latter were the national salary scales at which appointments could be made, with the result that for many years academic salaries were well below those at LBS who had taken an independent approach to determining salaries. International business schools with high aspirations must be in a position to pay salaries determined by the international market, which usually means the American market. A strategy that has enabled the School/University to partially resolve this problem is by paying special responsibility allowances to those academics taking on additional managerial roles (e.g. Head of the Management Faculty; Associate Dean for Research), by introducing performance related pay, and by making appointments to suitable candidates at the professorial level. The greater autonomy the School now has means that competitive salaries can be offered in the recruitment of 'academic stars'.

Personnel. They design, run and change organisations. Through the different roles that they play inside and outside a business school, individuals import new ideas and resources and are instrumental in exporting the ensuing products and services. Exploring the nature of leadership within the context of a business school is relevant because of the differences that exist between educational institutions and other sectors of the economy. Deans are not the only ones well placed for providing leadership in the sense of influencing the thinking and activities of others. While they and their top team are expected to provide corporate leadership by clarifying the mission and aligning strategies, many others are expected to provide academic leadership. Individuals fulfilling the latter role lead in the development of degrees and courses, and initiate research projects that contribute to the generation and application of knowledge.

Individuals who see themselves primarily as academics are not motivated or trained to fulfil the increasingly complex administrative roles that emerge in an expanding business school. In the early history of the School a non-academic administrative post was created with a title such as executive officer or administrator. One of the longest serving individuals in this role was Geoff Moulton. He and others such as Michael Ambler played a key role in the smooth running of the School. Two early attempts to appoint a School Secretary at a senior level to mirror the corresponding University post, failed to meet expectations. After a gap of some years the idea of making a senior administrative appointment was revived in the early part of David Kaye's Deanship. This led to the appointment of Donal Walsh as Director of Administration in 1993, and on his resignation to the appointment of Henrietta Royle as Chief Operations Officer in 2002. Both these individuals became part of the senior management team and thus involved in strategy development as well as implementation. One of their main responsibilities meant taking the lead in the development and implementation of management systems, and in taking an active part in negotiations with the University on matters relating to finance, premises and services.

The positioning of the 'personnel' element in Figure 14.1 is intentional to emphasise its twin role of 'ambassador' and 'conduit'. In the former role individuals represent the School to the outside world; in the latter role they are part of a complex communication network through which ideas are imported and exported into the environment. The critical influence of these twin roles can best be illustrated through the development of the School's orientation and reputation in economics and finance. Sir Robert Shone, as a Visiting Professor, initiated the first executive development courses in this area. The first research assistant he recruited was Basil Taylor, who subsequently was appointed Reader in Investment Analysis and he took the lead in the development of finance as a main stream on the MSc in Administrative Sciences. Taylor was the first person to be appointed in the School to a full-time academic post from a City institution (Midland Bank). The next key appointment in the finance field was that of Michael Beenstock from LBS. It was intended that he should provide academic leadership in the area, bringing teaching syllabuses up-to-date and developing cutting-edge research that would attract the attention of both academics and practitioners. His task was made somewhat easier with the retirement of several 'old hands' such as Douglas Vaughan and Basil Taylor, and the arrival of Brian Griffiths as Dean. Michael Beenstock developed a research and publication programme (including an academic journal) that gave the School considerable exposure in the media. Brian Griffiths' appointment as Dean in 1982 brought further publicity to the School through his appointment to the Court of the Bank of England, his publication with Hugh Murray arguing for the privatisation of business schools, and his secondment to head Margaret Thatcher's Policy Unit at 10 Downing Street. He was the first 'academic' to fill the top leadership role in the School. Brian Griffiths (now Lord Griffiths) brought with him the University's Centre for Banking and International Finance, together with two academics with established reputations for researching monetary history – Geoffrey Wood and Forrest Capie. He was also instrumental in bringing on board Professor Costas Grammenos with his expertise in shipping finance and his strong connections with that industry. From the 1980s onwards there have been a long line of economic/financial experts in the School, including: Shelagh Heffernan in 1982 (author of the highly successful book *Modern Banking in Theory and Practice*), Alec Chrystal in 1988 (co-author of the famous textbook now in its 10th edition *Principles of Economics*), and many others referred to in Parts II and III. The cumulative strategic implications of these City-oriented appointments are self-evident.

Tangible and intangible resources – finance, culture, reputation. These are resources that can strengthen or weaken the capacity of an organisation to survive in a competitive world. They affect and are affected by the other elements in Figure 14.1. *'Finance'* is the most basic and versatile resource since it provides the means of acquiring the other resources that enable an organisation to function in a physical environment – personnel, technology and premises. The City University has been more successful than most in remaining in credit over the last 20 years or so. This has come about mainly by enlarging its stable of postgraduate courses, attracting more students from overseas, and delaying the capital expenditure involved in new premises. Such a strategy has had the effect of reducing dependence on State finance, and therefore better able to cope with the recurring reduction in State (i.e. HEFCE) funding. The University's Annual Report for 2003/04 shows its low reliance on State funding: only £26 million out of a total income of £118 million.

A new building for the School was the main project in the 1968 University Appeal, but this failed to be realised for various reasons (see Part II). The quite different set of circumstances present toward the end of the last century has resulted in a new building. A gap of nearly 35 years is a long wait! The University has had to be persuaded that the financial risks involved were minimal, and the School had to demonstrate it was capable of bringing in sufficient income to service a mortgage in addition to its normal running expenses. Historically and culturally the School had shown its long-term viability and commitment to success. Indeed one of its outstanding achievements has been its ability to generate resources despite the cut-backs in State funding (in 2003/04 State funding only accounted for £3.6 million of its turnover of £30 million). Sponsored posts, the endeavours of entrepreneurial academics, and the increasing professional management of the School have all contributed to this success.

An additional factor that undoubtedly enabled the University to take concrete steps toward a new building for the School was the £20 million 'windfall' it orchestrated when it sold City Technology Ltd in 1993. The School owes much to the inventiveness and entrepreneurial skills of those who designed and produced the company's main product (i.e. gas sensors), and to the business acumen of those University personnel who aided its development and sale.

Discussing *'culture'* as a resource may surprise some readers, not least because of the difficulties of defining the concept. One of the potential weaknesses of a neat framework such as Figure 14.1 is that it may give the impression that organisations can be managed on a rational basis and, like a puppet show, all that needs to be done is to manipulate the puppets in order to bring about the desired result. Those who have tried to bring about change in an organisation will know that changing the formal system (e.g. structure, management systems, etc.) is only half the story. Social interactions within an organisation, and between an organisation and its environment, generate their own 'informal systems'. The norms, values and beliefs that come to characterise an informal system may support or oppose change. This phenomenon has been recognised since the days of the classic Hawthorne Studies (Roethlisberger and Dickson 1939), but managing it is a tortuous task.

Organisational culture is a holistic concept that derives from, and reflects, the collective learning that takes place as an organisation interacts with its environment. This organisational learning process results in routine or familiar ways of dealing with situations. Much of this knowledge becomes tacit or taken for granted. Culture's very covert nature often means that it exerts more influence on organisational behaviour than is generally recognised. This is both a strength and a weakness. Through the routinisation process (compare the habitual behaviour of individuals) culture enables a lot to be done with the minimum expenditure of effort. But routinisation can inhibit change because the unfamiliar is less comfortable, predictable and controllable than the familiar.

Despite the difficulties of measuring organisational culture, the concept has demonstrated its practical usefulness when examining the slowness of implementing change and the difficulties in realising the benefits of merging units within or between organisations. Thus there were a number of problems that arose when the department of Property Management and Finance merged into the School. Their routine methods of dealing with quality assurance matters were not as rigorous as those developed in the rest of the School (e.g. with respect to the formal follow-up of comments made by external examiners). An unfortunate consequence of this occurred when a QAA visit took place in 1997 before the department could be effectively absorbed into the culture of the School. The failure of the department to obtain the 'excellent' rating that by now the School had come to expect, was a disappointment. The merger of a major part of the Department of Systems Science and Management into the School demonstrated similar cultural differences – different ways had developed in dealing with such things as the processing of examinations and the supervision of research students. All these differences were eventually ironed out, but it takes time before interpersonal and intergroup processes bring about collective learning and shared perceptions.

While there are many definitions of organisational culture in the management literature a common theme is the reference to shared values and beliefs (Schein 1992; Williams *et al.* 1993). These in turn give rise to the shared perceptions, or interpretations of the world, that will have a bearing on the behaviour of individuals or groups within the organisation. Non-members looking at the organisation from the outside also tend to have shared perceptions. These form the *'reputation'* or brand image that the market place has of the School relative to competing schools. The power of reputation to influence people's behaviour is well known. Thus the strong financial reputation that has emerged may benefit the School's MScs for financial specialists, but may do little for the general management MBA. Reputation is partly why the strategy of differentiating the School from its parent university in the eyes of the market is important, as is the need to develop a quality image with respect to both learning and research. The University is usually ranked in the 40s in the top 100 UK universities (i.e. near the tail of the 'old universities'), whereas the School ranks in the top 10 in the United Kingdom. Leaving LBS aside (which has its own charter) the four UK schools whose full-time MBAs were ranked above Cass in both the 2004 and 2005 *FT* rankings were Oxford's Said, Warwick Business School, Cambridge's Judge and Manchester Business School (*FT*, 26.1.2004; *FT*, 24.1.2005). The fact that the universities to which these schools belong are among the very best in the United Kingdom, and indeed in the world (THES, 4.2.2005), is an indication of both the strength of competition facing Cass and its outstanding competitiveness to date.

Throughout the book the concept of 'culture' has been used to help explain several outcomes. In the early years of the School's history there is no doubt that the culture and reputation of the University influenced developments. The University was a College of Advanced Technology until 1966, and it had an international reputation for its engineering and its ophthalmic optics courses. Its undergraduate sandwich courses had established excellent contacts with manufacturing industry. This cultural orientation affected the orientation of the School's founding members. The bulk of their work experience had been gained outside the City, for example: the Army, the National Coal Board, the Miners' Union, the Civil Service, manufacturing industry, market research. The majority were more concerned with management education generally rather than with academic research and the City of London. The CAT mentality of the senior members of the new university, combined with resource constraints, affected the level at which appointments were made. Tradition and academic respectability demanded that heads of department should have the title of professor. Since the Department of Management and Social Sciences had minimal track record in research there was no one meriting the title of professor, and two outsiders had to be brought in to head the two departments that were created from it in 1966. Apart from the one professor, the Department of Management Studies had two senior lecturers and the rest were lecturers in late 1966. This contrasted markedly from the situation relating to LBS and MBS where their munificent resource bases meant that they could appoint professors with established academic records to take the lead in establishing the development of each main discipline underlying management. It is interesting to note that the early development of LBS took place with the minimum of the cultural trappings of London University, whereas MBS was more closely integrated into Manchester University. In terms of world rankings the former is currently the only one that comes close to holding its own against the top American business schools.

Right up to the 1980s opportunities for research were regarded as a right that belonged to academic appointments. Those who had academic ambitions, and the necessary research skills, made good use of the time available for research. The development of a research culture (where strong norms exist for attracting research income, conducting research and publishing) in a business school is a slow process, particularly one with the early history of the School. Many staff gave priority to other aspects of their role. The lack of critical mass in selected areas meant that the opportunity for team research was limited unless one could generate income to recruit one's own team (this was the model initiated by the CPRED in 1978). Research was always encouraged by Deans, and a rudimentary structure to support research (e.g. a director of research and a committee) always existed. In the late 1970s the University provided the incentive of returning 40 per cent of overheads charged to formally recognised units and centres (the School is now in control of this policy). But it was only in the latter part of the School's history that adequate resources were invested in the research effort. Nowadays not only does the University have a Pro-Vice-Chancellor for research, but the School has an associate dean for research, a director of the PhD programme, an administrator for research, a research development officer, individuals responsible for organising weekly research seminars for staff and research students in the different faculties, a research budget, a teaching allocation scheme that gives lower teaching loads to highly rated researchers, and a recruitment and retention policy that favours research oriented staff and self-investment in research. The recruitment and development of staff are probably the most critical elements that have helped in establishing the current research culture. If anything near this level of support had been available in the first half of the School's history, the effects could have been quite dramatic.

The variable 'finance' differs from 'culture' and 'reputation' in that it can be more directly monitored and controlled. This has enabled formal systems to be developed for the purpose of managing the resource. Culture and reputation are more difficult to manage because of their 'intangibility', and the lengthy time lag that normally occurs between managerial action to change them and the visible outcomes of these changes. The term 'normally' is used because it is a known phenomenon that reputation can take years to develop but days to be destroyed, as

Ratner discovered to his cost when as CEO to the UK's biggest jeweller in 1991 quipped at the Institute of Directors' annual conference that a 'sherry decanter and glasses set' sold by his stores was 'total crap'. The joke wiped £500 million off Ratners' stock market valuation and led to his departure from the company.

Conclusions

This chapter set out to describe an open system model incorporating those elements of a business school that are interdependent upon each other and have strategic significance. Each group of elements has been described and illustrated with material from the School's history. *Competitive advantage comes with the coherent management of these elements in a changing environment.* This means two things. First, each group of elements must be compatible (i.e. at least neutral if not positively reinforcing) with other elements. Second, the cumulative effect of management actions on resources (e.g. finance, culture, reputation) must be supportive of the business school's mission and vision. Exploring the role of 'leadership' in this process is the challenge tackled in Chapter 15.

15
Leadership in Change

Tackling the leadership theme is not for the soft-hearted given the difficulties in its definition and conceptualisation. A working definition that is compatible with the strategic orientation used in analysing the School's case history would be: *Leadership in a business school setting is a dynamic process whereby one or more individuals initiate/support those changes that are conducive to the achievement of the school's mission and objectives*. This is not intended to be an all encompassing definition of leadership, but to reflect what appears to be the main function of leadership in the development of a business school across time. The 'dynamic process' mirrors the complex open system model described in the Chapter 14; 'one or more individuals' recognises that it is a process that is not confined to the top person; and 'initiate/support those changes' emphasises the critical proactive and reinforcing function of leadership in improving the school/environment fit in a continually changing world. This conceptualisation of leadership puts the management of change at its core.

Transactional and transformational leadership

Current literature on leadership within the context of organisational change identifies two types of leadership: transactional leadership (typically concerned with doing things right and reinforcing compatible behaviours of others); transformational leadership (typically concerned with doing the right things and inspiring others to share common goals) (Bass 1998). Transactional leaders are more concerned in showing the way, and to introduce incremental improvements to existing structures, management systems, technologies, products and services. Transformational leaders are more likely to focus on radical change to structures, to products, and so on. Attempts to argue for the superiority of one type of leader (e.g. transformational) over another (e.g. transactional) ignores the importance of context. A contingency approach to leadership, where both approaches are needed depending upon the situation, is the one favoured by current reviews of the literature (Yukl 2001) and is also supported by the School's case history. For example, during the Deanship of David Glen, when the School was operating in a relatively favourable competitive environment, a predominantly transactional leadership approach on the part of the Dean was sufficient. However in the post 1980s, when competition was significantly greater and State funding to academic institutions continued to decline, a more pronounced transformational leadership approach was needed and adopted by David Kaye in the 1990s.

Academics as leaders

As already pointed out a distinctive characteristic of academic institutions is that strategic leadership comes from individual academics as well as Deans and their executive teams. In Part III it was clear that the strategy for growth encouraged innovation. In the Cass context the innovations that had significant impact on the School/Environmental fit were new degrees that opened up new markets, such as the part-time evening MBA or the full-time MSc in Shipping Trade and Finance. Academics are unlikely to innovate unless they feel that the goal they have in their sight is attractive and achievable. This means that they anticipate the experience of reward, and perceive the context to be sufficiently supportive, or feel that they have the ability and power to make it more supportive. These basic conditions were originally spelt out in Porter and Lawler's expectancy theory of motivation (Porter and Lawler 1968). Situational supportiveness comes in two ways: a number of factors just happen to come together without the conscious intervention of the innovator ('the time was ripe' syndrome); the innovator uses his or her change management skills to intervene in the balance of forces so that the probability of success is increased (Lewin 1951).

Within a business school, where the diversity of interest is exacerbated by different disciplines and there exist weak authority structures, consensus in decision making is difficult to achieve and support not guaranteed. This was only too apparent in executive committee and Board of Studies meetings under successive Deans. Innovators as leaders deal with this problem in a number of ways, but they are all concerned with their perceived power to influence change through a mix of

Box 15.1 Creating and negotiating support for innovation.

- Sharing a vision and winning the support of powerful individuals in the School (e.g. Dean, Head of Department), in the University (e.g. Academic Registrar), and externally (e.g. Shipping Industry in the City; Corporation of London). Good examples of these are the MSc in Shipping Trade and Finance, and the MSc in Mathematical Trading and Finance.
- Gaining the support of individuals who would be most affected by the proposal if accepted. Overstretched academics are unlikely to welcome new degrees if it means a heavier teaching load for themselves. Hugh Murray tackled this by ensuring he had the support of his own Export Management Division (and sympathetic staff from other divisions) before putting forward his proposal for an Evening MBA.
- Drawing on a new source of lecturers so as not to attract the opposition of existing staff. The use of enthusiastic part-time lecturers to contribute to the Consortium MBA is an example.
- Highlighting the existence of an unfulfilled market related to the School's mission. All new degrees were examples of this.
- Creating self-funding degrees by obtaining pump-priming funds or sponsored posts so that initial costs would be externally financed, and therefore not a strain on School resources. This applied to the majority of postgraduate degrees for which UGC/HEFCE funds were not available. The initial funding from the Corporation of London for the degree in Mathematical Trading and Finance was one of several examples.
- Creating a semi-autonomous structure (administratively and financially) so that income generated strengthened one's independence within the School, and minimised 'bureaucratic interference' in subsequent developments. This is what happened in the early years of the Evening MBA degree, the shipping degrees, the undergraduate banking degree, and the investment and insurance degrees.

support, academic credibility, market know-how, financial independence, personal commitment and determination. Thus, innovators used a number of ways to influence the process of getting a proposal for a new degree through the committee structure (an uphill battle in the best of times!). These are illustrated in Box 15.1.

Deans as leaders

The history of the School has many examples of the innovative behaviours of academics that have affected the School/Environment (S/E) fit. These have been outlined elsewhere (see Chapters 9, 10 and 11) in relation to degrees and research centres. However, at the end of the day it is the Dean who has the greatest potential influence as to which innovations succeed or fail, and therefore carries the ultimate responsibility for the nature and outcomes of the S/E fit. Although Deans are expected to have more power than anyone else in a business school, one is only too well aware of the constraints they face when trying to bring about change. Joan Gallos (Gallos 2002) talks about 'the Dean's squeeze' to express the position that a Dean occupies between the internal world (own staff and students) and the external world (i.e. the rest of the university as well as the outside world). She points out that the Dean's job is a lonely one, and that tenure in the States is only five years (the average for the School is a little over four years). This she feels is not surprising given the intensity and inevitability of the Dean's squeeze – the conflict between internal and external demands in the Dean's job. Senior faculty in the School have always expected Deans to provide strategic leadership that would bring competitive advantage. The Dean is expected to behave as the CEO of a company, with the Vice-Chancellor equivalent to the Chairman of the Board. However, by chairing Senate and wielding substantial influence on Council, Vice-Chancellors have much more influence than the Chairman of a Board of Directors. The frequent formal and informal interactions with staff ensure that this is the case when they choose to exercise the power at their disposal.

In order to gain a better perspective on the challenges that Deans may face, a list of strategic choices or dilemmas from the School's history are listed in Box 15.2. These will be familiar to most Deans of university-based schools in the United Kingdom. Underlying these dilemmas are clashes between old and new cultures, that is, *academic values* relating to autonomy and knowledge generation and *management values* relating to competitiveness and financial control. Two things stand out from this list. First, they can be sub-divided into four categories: those concerned with the market, that is, programmes and their delivery; those focusing on the individual/School relationship; those concerned with structure; and those affecting School autonomy. Second, most of these dilemmas cannot be resolved by an either-or-solution because both choices are legitimate and potentially beneficial to the School's competitive strength. *It is in this process of managing (balancing) these dilemmas that Deans are expected to give a lead by initiating and/or supporting appropriate change, given the mission and objectives of the School.*

Deans are but one element in this change process, since their influence combines with other forces to make things happen. In the School's history there are examples of where a newly appointed Dean has found that the hard work in relation to an important issue had already been done by former Deans, and that all that remained was for the new Dean

Box 15.2 Leadership dilemmas.

- 'Postgraduate school' versus 'Postgraduate + undergraduate school'
- 'MBAs' versus 'MBAs + specialist MScs'
- 'Financial sector' versus 'General management' orientation
- 'Teaching' versus 'Learning'
- 'Face-to-face' versus 'Distance' learning techniques

- 'Teaching/learning' versus 'Research'
- 'Academic autonomy' versus 'Management direction'
- 'Moderate' versus 'Tight' financial control
- 'Entrepreneurial' versus 'Bureaucratic' climate

- 'Departmental' versus 'Faculty' structure
- 'Close' versus 'Distant' structure for executive education.

- 'Maximise student numbers' versus 'Quality of student intake'
- 'Dependence on parent university' versus 'School autonomy'
- 'State funding' versus 'Self-funding'

to reinforce previous decisions and to enjoy the fruits of their predecessors! In the context of premises this happened when Griffiths was appointed and the School moved into the Barbican; the hard work in relation to the UGC had already been completed by Lord Alport, Edward Parkes, Raoul Franklin and John Treasure. Similarly, when Lord Currie was appointed Dean most of the major decisions concerning the Bunhill Row building had already been taken under the David Kaye and Leslie Hannah Deanships.

One of the valuable learning experiences to emerge from longitudinal case studies is the process of facilitating transfer of learning from one formal leader to another. Transitions have been remarkably smooth in the School for several reasons. First, there was always a critical mass of senior staff to ensure continuity (e.g. deputy dean, heads of department, director of administration). Second, if there was no strong internal candidate and the initial external search had drawn a blank, the Vice-Chancellor and selection committee brought into operation a temporary 'steady as she goes' solution so as to give more time to find a suitable candidate. In the history of the School this has occurred on three occasions. Although nothing remarkable may have happened during these intervals, the things that were already in train continued to be nurtured and implemented. Thus the major decisions relating to the first undergraduate degree in the School took place at the end of David Glen's Deanship, and were implemented during the 'Triumvirate' and the Treasure Deanships.

Market related dilemmas

The first group of dilemmas in Box 15.2 almost resolved themselves. In other words, at the time when critical choices had to be made, the forces at work were sufficiently focused and energised to arouse similar perceptions (and hence beliefs) among the Dean and senior faculty. Although entering the undergraduate market was not something that all staff were enthusiastic about, the positive forces were overwhelming. They included: in the 1970s the University was geared more for undergraduate than postgraduate education; its culture was vocationally oriented; competitors were entering or planning to enter the market (i.e. apart from LBS, MBS and Cranfield); the market was ready as demonstrated by those already running such degrees; a former undergraduate of the University was keen to take the academic lead (Ivor Delafield); a nucleus of staff in finance, marketing and general management was sufficiently keen to get involved in designing and teaching on the degree; the opportunity to specialise in finance in the final year of the degree was compatible with the School's mission and strategies. The distinctive characteristic of the BSc in Business Studies was its dual specialisation (i.e. finance and marketing); and this has remained constant from 1978 to 2003. Only in 2004 was a more general stream introduced.

The launch into specialist MScs was compatible with the University and School's culture. In the very early days of the School there was an MSc in Information Science, and a little later an MSc in Systems Analysis and Design. Both of these migrated to become independent departments when they had reached 'maturity' (i.e. could stand on their own two feet financially, academically and administratively). Moreover, the MSc in Administrative Sciences and its MBA re-label, had itself developed specialist streams that were recognised on degree certificates (e.g. MBA Finance, MBA Marketing). The proposal some years later to introduce an MSc in Shipping Trade and Finance was consistent with the School's history, and was a 'natural' development when combined with the positive forces of support from the top and from the City, and the influential networks and commitment of the academic leader Costas Grammenos. The Vice-Chancellor's support was guaranteed so long as external pump-priming finance could be found, and Brian Griffiths' support was assured as he originally sponsored Costas Grammenos when he was first introduced to the School. All these factors, together with the degree's compatibility with the mission and strategy of the School, and the minimum demands the degree would make on existing staff, created forces that ensured the successful introduction of the degree. The numerous proposals to introduce MScs in the finance area during the 1990s were given impetus by an internal working party reporting in 1994/95. This report crystallised existing forces that were coming into play and stimulated the emergence of additional forces: new academic appointments (e.g. Elias Dinenis, Mark Salmon); School's need to augment its income to strengthen its push for a new building; markets waiting to be exploited; pump-priming funds from the Corporation and the Insurance industry.

The directional compatibility of forces in the examples just discussed may disqualify them as examples of dilemmas. However at the time, without the benefit of hindsight, they presented decision makers with the choice of remaining a postgraduate school or not, and of focusing primarily on an MBA programme or not. The dilemma 'Financial sector versus General management orientation' was more problematic. A succession of Deans from Brian Griffiths onwards have sought to give priority to strengthening the financial expertise of the School in keeping with the element in the School's strategy that most differentiates it from competitors. During the 1990s the financial orientation 'brand image' became particularly strong, and inevitably weakened the development of the MBA programme and the non-financial disciplines in the School. More recently there are signs that deteriorating numbers on the MBA programme, and the importance of this programme for the School's *FT* global ranking, have given new impetus to correcting the skewed balance of expertise within the School. The new MSc in Management is evidence of this awareness.

The dilemma 'Face-to-face versus Distance learning techniques' is one that the School has struggled with over a number of years. As part of his push for growth Dean Chambers had tried to enter the distance learning market in partnership with a correspondence college, but aroused the opposition of senior faculty. Under Kaye's Deanship discussion of the topic was almost taboo in case it prejudiced negotiations concerning new premises. The strategy for top of the range new premises in one of the most expensive areas of the world sat uncomfortably with a strategy that pointed in the direction of distance learning. Under Hannah's Deanship some preliminary discussion took place for a joint venture in distance learning with a City-based educational institution, but it failed to gain the support of the executive committee. However the School has now dipped its toes into distance learning through the China MBA degree launched in 2003. This was only done after considerable anguish and with a new Dean in place. Forces that tipped the scale included: it was designed to meet the needs of one main client (the Bank of China);

two powerful individuals fully supported the development (i.e. the Chairman of the Bank who was an alumni of the School's Evening MBA degree; and the University's Vice-Chancellor); the programme was to be delivered in conjunction with the prestigious Shanghai University of Finance and Economics; prolonged negotiations reduced the financial risks to the School; the programme was in effect a mixed delivery one, and incorporated a good deal of face-to-face teaching. Now that useful 'know how' and associated academic leadership (via Dr Hassan Hakimian) have been gained through the China MBA, this aspect of the School's products and services is likely to be expanded. The imaginative agenda of the School's Learning Laboratory under the direction of Clive Holtham may facilitate this expansion (see www.cass.city.ac.uk/tandl/learning_lab).

Individual/School related dilemmas

The dilemma 'Teaching versus research' relates as much to academic leadership as to corporate leadership. The problem here is that academics find themselves involved in a zero sum game – the more time one spends on research the less time is available for preparing and delivering teaching, and vice versa. There are of course occasions when the two overlap and a lecture is based on one's research, or research data is collected as part of the teaching process. Somehow a culture where both are equally valued needs to be created. While senior academics can contribute to this by acting as role models, the individual with the most influence over relevant systems affecting the behaviour of individual academics is the Dean.

Until the latter half of the 1980s academics enjoyed sufficient autonomy to decide for themselves whether their 'spare' energies went to improving their teaching or research performance. The new forces created by the introduction of the QAA and RAE have had profound effects on the management of the University and the School. Everyone recognised the importance of obtaining high positive ratings with respect to the learning experience of students and the research reputation of academics. Changes on the teaching side included: a formal 'teaching and learning' position was created so as to provide leadership in the area, and a sub-committee of the Board of Studies formed to oversee the function; appraisal systems and student feedback forms carried more weight; the form used for requesting a sabbatical had to specify what the individual proposed doing to improve their teaching as well as their research plans; seminars were organised on good practice in teaching and learning; poor teachers were encouraged to attend in-house and/or external courses; cash prizes were created for rewarding outstanding teachers. Also the recent 'learning laboratory' initiative of Holtham's is designed to accelerate the exploitation of technology for teaching and learning in the new School building and beyond.

Changes on the research side included: the research committee played a more interventionist role in rating individuals on their research performance on the basis of RAE criteria; the director of research became an ex-officio member of most selection committees; the School invested more in the infrastructure for research by allocating precious space for the use of PhD students and research staff, by providing administrative assistance in running the PhD programme and in advising on the preparation of research proposals; more money became available for research and for giving papers at conferences at home and abroad; a low research rating for those who had been at the School for sometime meant that they would have to do more teaching, or even encouraged to consider alternative employment. One of the solutions that is slowly emerging in relation to the teaching/research dilemma is creating a 'teaching only' category of staff to work alongside the traditional 'teaching cum research' category. The long-term consequences of this strategy for a school need to be thought through carefully (see Claire Sanders report on this topic in *THES*, 24 June 2005).

Other examples of leadership dilemmas represent additional fundamental challenges, for example, 'academic autonomy versus management direction'. Right up to the early 1990s, that is before Kaye's Deanship, many academics felt that one of the main attractions of working at the School was the opportunity and encouragement to develop and implement new ideas about courses, degrees, research and consultancy. This aspect of the School's culture enabled the more ambitious academics to develop along the lines that they felt most comfortable, and thereby to contribute to the development of the School in ways that they saw to be appropriate. This observation particularly applies to those seeking promotion to senior lecturer or professor inside the School, and there were many of these as shown in Part III. The weakness in this approach is that it gave equal autonomy to those who were more interested in augmenting their consultancy income than in developing themselves in line with the interests of the School. A legal and symbolic change in the contract of employment for academics was the legislation that abolished tenure for new appointments and for those who were subsequently promoted (e.g. from lecturer to senior lecturer or professor). Tenure essentially meant a job for life unless some exceptional misconduct was committed; the Education Reform Act of 1988 introduced a redundancy clause. In 2005 only two individuals in the School have retained their tenure (they achieved professorial status before the Act came into operation). Although the removal of tenure legally weakened the power of individual academics its long-term impact was minimal; however, in the short term it had an adverse effect on the morale of those already in post as a consequence of a change to the psychological contract (i.e. the mutual expectations created on appointment were unilaterally changed by the employer). Pressures were imposed by successive governments on universities to professionalise their management (e.g. introduction of performance appraisals was originally tied into a pay settlement). These together with the creations of new evaluative systems (e.g. institutional audits, research assessment exercises) have strengthened the arms of management to direct and control.

These external pressures on universities led them to develop management systems that could be 'imposed' on schools. Since the School had developed a culture of its own, occasional clashes with the University were inevitable. Over the years these clashes have been caused by what the School saw as the unnecessarily high level of bureaucracy emanating from the centre, and the unacceptably low level of service in some areas (e.g. computer services). The move to the new premises in Bunhill Row has provided an opportunity for the School to assume more direct responsibility for the finance and provision of several basic services.

Closely related to the last dilemma are those concerned with the level of control exercised by the Dean with respect to financial matters and conformity to formal procedures. The Dean largely has to operate under the constraints set by the University in these areas, but there is some freedom (including the freedom to oppose excessive bureaucratic proposals emanating from the University). For instance, the Dean may set a ceiling above which formal permission may have to be obtained for travel expenses before they are incurred. There is no doubt that paperwork procedures that accompany initiatives in course development and research have increased with the growth of the School and its increased 'professional management'. Maintaining a professional approach to management and at the same time encouraging academic entrepreneurialism is a real challenge for Deans.

Structure related dilemmas

The School has experienced several different structures; each one has brought advantages and disadvantages. Initially the School was one department with several informal sub-systems (i.e. divisions and centres); then it became two departments (Business Studies, and Banking and International Finance) plus Executive Education; then eight departments plus Executive Education; then two faculties (Management and Finance) plus Executive Education; and then three faculties (the third being Actuarial Science) plus Executive Education. As has already been pointed out departmental structures can strengthen forces for innovative behaviour, but adversely affect co-operation across the School. The full advantages and disadvantages of the three-faculty structure have yet to be discovered, but one of the favourable consequences has been a reduction in the numbers involved in the top management decision-making team. It can be argued that the current structure is more 'Dean friendly', and theoretically should be more effective in integrating mission, strategies and systems. Unintended consequences of these changes could be the additional strains exerted on the consultative and communication systems in the School.

One of the dilemmas that has proved difficult to resolve for most Deans of the School is that of 'Close versus distant structure for executive education'. In the early history of the School the precedent was set in running this activity separately from other activities; this was necessary because it was not financed by the UGC and therefore had to be run as a self-financing operation. In these early years the Post Experience Unit was relatively successful. Contributing factors included: the School was sufficiently small for everyone to know each other; faculty were a fairly cohesive group; the commitment to succeed was high; the head of the Unit was an academic; staff most closely involved in the Unit could identify with the City's culture and belonged to networks frequented by potential clients; the Gresham College location meant that one was in the heart of the City; competition from rivals was less severe. All these factors, together with supportive University Officers, School Deans, faculty and friends (e.g. Advisory Panels) of the School, enabled the Unit to be sufficiently successful to cover the cost of several appointments (lecturers, researchers, secretaries), and thus enabled the School to grow despite hard times within the University as a whole.

During the 1980s onwards executive education fortunes fluctuated. New conditions operating included: academics required to be paid for their contributions; the academic standards of the courses were no longer monitored and approved by the Board of Studies if qualifications were not involved; in the early 1990s the MDC (as it was then called) was formed into a limited company and, for a time, only one of the five directors was employed as an academic. This latter structure was meant to bring financial advantage, but an unpredictable consequence was a further distancing of executive education from the core of the School. Moreover, with hindsight some appointments made to head executive education were not suited to the conditions that prevailed (executive education being a part, and yet not a part, of the School!), and this was exacerbated by an unfavourable economic climate and increased competition.

The strategic leadership provided by successive Deans was not consistent across time, unlike the overall strategic leadership provided for the School as a whole. For instance: Was executive education primarily in the open course or in the company tailor-made market? Did it exist to generate extra income to subsidise other activities and to supplement the salaries of contributing academics, or was it intended to help shape the brand image of the School? For a time the MDC was responsible for delivering two part-time diploma/degree programmes, but these were terminated after a few years – one because the School and University were dissatisfied with quality safeguards and the poor financial returns being made (i.e. the Consortium MBA), and the other because the corporate client was unhappy with the hard-line approach the Centre was taking on academic standards. It is not surprising to find that in recent years executive education failed to generate a planned surplus income for the School. New initiatives taken in 2003/04 designed to bring executive education closer to the core of the School (both psychologically and physically) may achieve the desired transformation.

Autonomy related dilemmas

Underlying all three dilemmas in this group is the tension created by the School wanting to maximise its autonomy, and the University needing to exert control to ensure its compliance with UGC/HEFCE policies and guidelines and to protect the interests of the University as a whole. Deans, and their executive teams, have to steer a political pathway through this minefield. Maximising student numbers had the benefit of strengthening the School's arm in negotiations with the University and in building-up financial resources. On the other hand it threatened the longer term reputation or quality brand image that the School was trying to develop. One of the benefits of Deans initiating or supporting self-funding activities is that the School was able to cope more effectively than other parts of the University as State funding diminished. But the School has remained very much dependent upon the University for the capital expenditures involved in the leases and acquisition of premises.

Power

In the process of managing such dilemmas Deans have to draw on their sources of 'power'. This is particularly true where radical rather than evolutionary change is needed. It could be argued that the School's competitive standing would be greater today if Deans had been able to exercise greater power in the 1960s and 1970s (i.e. when the University's Engineering School was the most powerful group). A Dean acquires power through personal and situational factors. The most widely quoted framework for listing these sources of personal power is that of French and Raven (French and Raven 1959), and the framework still plays a prominent part in textbooks on organisational behaviour (Buchanan and Huczynski 2004). The five basic sources of power identified have been adapted for the present context in Box 15.3.

This perspective of power emphasises the influence of the perceptions, beliefs and desires of followers and others with whom one interacts. Deans draw on these sources of power to bring about needed change, particularly where an entrenched organisational culture is against proposed changes. This often means that they have to learn to cultivate their power; either covertly or overtly. Some may do this by learning about the dynamics of leadership through formal courses; all will do it by changing situational factors that experience has taught

Box 15.3 Sources of a Dean's power (after French and Raven 1959).

- *Reward-based power* refers to the Dean's perceived control over rewards valued by School staff such as titles (e.g. associate dean), promotion, salary and bonus payments, praise and recognition.
- *Coercive power* refers to the Dean's perceived control over punishments such as the termination of contract, admonishments and increase of teaching workload.
- *Legitimate authority* (positional power) refers to the power associated with the role of Dean to command the actions of others, and to influence decisions in structures in which the Dean is a member by virtue of their role (e.g. a member of the University Senate).
- *Expert power* refers to the perceived perception that the Dean has superior knowledge/skills for tackling tasks at hand (e.g. understands the University's formula for distributing HEFCE money to schools).
- *Personal power* (referent power) refers to those perceived attributes of a Dean that are attractive to others – a role model. Individuals well endowed with these characteristics early in their careers are often referred to as potential leaders.

Box 15.4 Examples of situational devices for enhancing a Dean's power.

- Deciding on the chairmanship of working parties. This attempt to 'load the dice' was more likely to happen in relation to bringing about change in existing degrees (e.g. improving the standing of the MBA programmes; building on the synergies existing, but not utilised, between the undergraduate degrees).
- Ensuring that they have the final say in appointing staff to key positions (e.g. those heading the MBA programme and research; the Deputy Dean).
- Imposing their authority in the selection of new recruits to senior positions so as to bring on board new blood with the 'right' knowledge, skills and attitudes.
- Creating an executive decision-making structure that can be effectively managed (e.g. it is easier to influence a meeting consisting of 3 or even 7 members than one with 15 members – especially if they consist of independently minded academics!).
- Nurturing informal coalitions of interests and alliances prior to critical decision-making meetings of, for instance, the Business School Council or the Board of Studies (this form of 'playing politics' is an everyday occurrence in academic settings where committees abound).
- Accumulating resources (e.g. finance, reputation) so as to lessen one's dependence on those with whom one is negotiating (e.g. School negotiating with the University over premises).
- Ensuring that one is appointed to influential decision-making bodies that can affect the School (e.g. University Council).
- Personally chairing influential committees when the choice exists (e.g. executive committee).
- Mobilising the expert and personal (referent) power of outsiders to support one's agenda (e.g. 'Three wise men' report; advisory bodies).

them affect their power. Typical examples of situational devices for enhancing power are given in Box 15.4.

The level of a Dean's power is less important in the management of evolutionary change, or when emergent forces are sufficiently strong so as to create a positive climate for change. Level of power becomes critical when radical change requires more determined and controversial actions, as were needed when the School's competitive standing in the business school world was slipping because others were moving ahead faster. This was not perceived as a problem in the low competitive climate during the first two Deanships (Shone and Glen). The need for radical change became more obvious in the eighties and nineties, particularly with respect to profitability, research performance and premises. It was in the highly competitive climate of these periods that Deans needed to be able to mobilise to the full their most appropriate sources of power to bring about change. Precise methods adopted reflected their most comfortable style of leadership, personality make-up and their reading of situational factors. For instance, Kaye drew on his legitimate power to the full when attempting to re-structure the School; whereas Hannah relied more on the persuasive power stemming from expert and referent sources when presenting the case to the University Council and its committees for a quality building of adequate size for the School.

Mental models as outcomes and determinants of organisational change

Power to introduce change does not guarantee that the choices made are the most appropriate from the point of view of a school's fit with its environment. Deans may be motivated to initiate or to drive change because they perceive an opportunity (e.g. as happened when the School entered the undergraduate market in 1978), or a shortfall (e.g. as happened when the School failed to get a '5' rating in the 1996 RAE). Why they experience the world in these ways is a complex process that psychologists and others have researched and theorised about. It is clear that perceptions are the result of an individual's own learning experiences that have shaped their attitudes, values, and beliefs. An example of organisational research illustrating the significance of this is Gabarro's study of 17 general managers who were taking charge of a situation new to them; one of the findings to stand out was the profound influence of a manager's prior experience (functional and industry-specific) on his actions and his priorities (Gabarro 1987). In the present case history Dean Kaye's approach to prioritising, re-structuring and the development of a mission statement bear all the hallmarks of a consultant from Andersons.

In order to draw practical knowledge from the research in this area, many management theorists use such terms as 'mental models' or 'mental sets' to account for the unique and consistent ways that individuals see and make sense of their world. Some of the dynamics of this process as they relate to the organisational setting, and the factors influencing them, have been explored by Weick in his discussion of 'sensemaking' (Weick 1995), and by Hodgkinson and Sparrow in their psychological analysis of the strategic management process (Hodgkinson and Sparrow 2002). Deans enact or construct their environment in the process of making sense of it. A leader's mental models will not only determine what is important, but what is the best way of approaching change and exercising power (see Boxes 15.1 and 15.3). One of the main tasks of management development programmes is to modify the mental models of participants in order to accommodate relevant environmental change (e.g. technological innovation, population trends, new competitors). Developing methods for codifying and modifying mental models of individuals and groups is a goal of many academics in business education (Eden and Spender 1998; Sparrow 1998; Williams *et al.* 2002).

Vice-Chancellors and their selection panels endeavour to select Deans who are likely to make the 'right choices' in relation to the opportunities/shortfalls that they perceive face their business school. The uncertainty and difficulty surrounding this task makes it all the more sensible to build diversity into a school's decision-making groups so as to avoid following an inappropriate 'groupthink' strategy made famous by the Bay of Pigs study of Janis (Janis 1972). The appointments to date of three businessmen as School Deans out of a total of nine were not a matter of chance. All three were intended to strengthen those areas that the selection committees felt were holding back the development of the School – the most obvious assets of these 'outsiders' (Glen from the oil industry, Treasure advertising, and Kaye consultancy) being their successful managerial background, the senior standing they had achieved in their industry, the networks they had developed in the City, and their relative immunity from the entrenched culture of the School.

Other studies of leadership in business schools

There are very few studies that focus on leadership in business schools as opposed to higher education in general. Reference has already been made to Gallos' study of the internal and external pressures experienced by Deans (Gallos 2002). Another recent study is that of Lorange (2002) who has been a successful Dean at IMD in Switzerland for several years. His book is largely based on his experiences in private schools focusing on postgraduate and executive education, and does not reflect an important contextual feature of the present study – being part of a university subject to interventions from the State. However, his main assertion that the Dean's role is critical to the effective management of business schools is amply reflected by the School's history. The forces pushing the School toward financial self-sufficiency have created a situation not too distant from those experienced by such private and independent schools as IMD and INSEAD. Managerialism and professionalism have been one of the strategic responses of the School in coping with competitive pressures and Government policies. These responses also conform to University practice.

Bareham (Bareham 2004) examined leadership in ten business schools – five in the United Kingdom and five in Australia. Many of the findings ring true in the present case history, suggesting that the Cass story is not atypical. They include: Resource pressures and accountability have meant an increase in managerialism and a decrease in collegial decision making; the tension between a business school and its parent university appears to be a common feature, and this is exacerbated when a school makes a financial surplus and seeks more autonomy; a Dean's primary role is the development and implementation of strategy.

Conclusions to Part IV

Given the continuing emphasis on the need to improve leadership in the United Kingdom (CEML 2002) and the high level of competition between business schools, it made sense to explore the role of leadership in the development of Cass. The 'strategic leadership' perspective adopted (as opposed for instance to 'team leadership') was in keeping with the longitudinal nature of the data collected. Building on the work of organisation theorists and consultants, a model was developed that incorporates open systems theory and those elements (e.g. 'structure'; 'products and services') known to have strategic significance (see Figure 14.1).

It is in the process of managing a business school's relationship with its environment that the contribution of the Dean comes into its own. Hence the importance of selecting the 'right' Dean for a particular set of circumstances. When Brian Griffiths was appointed he was seen as someone who would enhance the academic leadership of the School, as well as bring the School and the City closer together. His traditional academic 'mental set' influenced him to manage through the School's professoriate (small and manageable at that time). David Kaye's paradigm for giving a fillip to the School was that of the internal market – a philosophy he was familiar with when employed at Andersons the management consultants. The turnover of Deans may be disruptive, but it gives the opportunity for Vice-Chancellors and their selection committees to make appointments that may be more in tune with changed circumstances. An average tenure of a little over four years may be criticised in some quarters, but given the changing environment of the business school scene this has probably worked to the advantage of the School.

A unique characteristic of business schools (and their parent universities) is that a significant aspect of strategic leadership comes from the innovative behaviour of academics (via educational media and research initiatives). Deans have to learn to facilitate and encourage these initiatives without adversely affecting ongoing programmes. Dealing with conflicting demands is typical of the Dean's role, as illustrated in Box 15.2. Dilemmas may resolve themselves when there is a gradual accumulation of forces in support of one direction (e.g. the HEFCE intervention through the RAEs). At other times the direction of change is not so self-evident, and there is a need for the Dean to change the balance of forces in order to influence events in one particular direction. Altering the forces for change is a skill that a Dean can bring about by mastering the 'power game' within the School, the University and beyond.

Overall conclusions

The introduction in Part I highlighted the standing of the School in 2004/05 in contrast to its beginning in 1966. The gap was the stimulus to researching the history of the School with two aims in mind:

- *To give an account of the development of the School as accurately as possible so that current and future stakeholders will be more aware of what has gone before.* This knowledge is a prerequisite if these stakeholders are to experience the pride attached to past and future achievements. Parts I and II were primarily concerned with meeting this aim.
- *To share the story of Cass Business School with others in the business school world and in higher education.* A descriptive account of a single school is of limited interest to a wider audience, unless it is analysed and interpreted within theoretical frameworks that are relevant to that audience. The challenge here is to account for the developments, and to hypothesise or explain why certain things did or did not happen. Any insights to be gained can thereby be shared with those involved in the management of business schools. Parts III and IV were primarily concerned with this aim.

Reviewing the history of Cass through an open system perspective highlights the main role of a Dean as taking the lead in improving the School/Environment (S/E) fit. The major environmental changes the School encountered were new competitors and reduced State funding. Most universities realised that 'Business and administrative studies' was the main growth market for students and adapted accordingly. In the statistics published by the Higher Education Statistics Agency for student enrolments in 2001/02 'Business and Administrative Studies' was ranked first out of 19 subject groups in terms of total number of enrolments, and first out of 19 subject groups in terms of non-UK student enrolments.

The coping strategies followed by the School included: growth through innovation and expansion, City orientation, differentiating the School from City University in the eyes of the market, developing a quality culture (re research, teaching and learning, professional management), and occupying quality premises. Each of these strategies has had predictable and unpredictable consequences. For example, 'growth' in the early days brought along numerous problems, including: inadequate premises; overloaded academic staff; difficulties of recruiting and retaining high calibre staff on the basis of relatively low salaries; inadequate administrative support. This mix of adverse factors, not readily controllable by Deans, generated forces over time to make the School less dependent on the State, and to some extent, on the University. A growth strategy also increased the dependence of Deans on academic entrepreneurs – those academics with vision, expertise, energy and determination to propose and implement innovative degrees, courses and research programmes. Deans and others had to learn how to support these individuals without alienating those academics who were ensuring the success of existing programmes.

As the School has grown the need for a competent administrative subsystem to complement the academic sub-system has increased. In the 1960s academics were 'jack of all trades'; besides their teaching and research they fulfilled many administrative tasks such as acting as secretary to the Board of Studies, dealing with the routine paperwork involved in student recruitment and so on. Today the picture has completely changed, and those academics with special responsibilities have the assistance they require. The numbers now involved in both categories of staff are such that senior academics and administrators carry significant managerial responsibilities. This has meant that a need for a professional approach to management has accompanied growth; and this has been reinforced by government pressures to professionalize management within universities. The term 'new managerialism' has been used in some studies to encapsulate the cultural changes that have been taking place in the UK higher educational system for over a decade (Deem 2001). These developments have created a dilemma for Vice-Chancellors when appointing Deans of business schools – should they be appointed primarily for their managerial competencies or for their academic reputations? The choice is a real one because individuals with a high reputation for both are a rare commodity. On three occasions to date the University has chosen individuals for their achievements outside the academic world. Each brought with them knowledge of successful managerial practices from the commercial world, together with practical insights into the importance of following a clear mission and strategy.

One way of accounting for the success of the School is by portraying the story as a process of adapting the strategic elements of the School to each other, and to the prevailing environment. A business school will always have 'problem areas' where the S/E fit is less than satisfactory. Two frameworks have emerged in trying to codify the main environmental factors (see Figure 7.1), and the main School elements that affect the S/E fit (see Figure 14.1). They should prove useful analytical tools when reviewing progress and planning for the future. The need to master such models, and their underlying theories, emphasise the cognitive abilities and 'mental models' required of Deans. The history of Cass provides a concrete illustration of the process of strategic leadership in a developing business school, and as a case study it can be used as a powerful learning tool for others. Business schools can no longer rely on the academic expertise of their Dean to thrust them forward to the upper echelons of schools in the United Kingdom, Europe and the World.

One of the many practical insights to be gained from the Cass history is the importance of making external friends and nurturing networks among those who can make a difference to the School. Given the inadequate support from the State to finance the development of the School, there were many occasions when foundations, companies and individuals filled the vacuum to enable progress to be maintained. Voluntary generosity of this nature rarely falls from the sky – sponsors must feel that their 'investments' (i.e. expertise, time and money) will be worthwhile in terms of anticipated outcomes for students, professional bodies, the local community and the nation. There is no doubt that the various external advisory bodies formed by the School, and the many visiting staff appointed, have been able to provide useful market information and open doors to valuable networks, in addition to other more direct benefits that accompanied their association with the School. The numerous sponsored chairs (e.g. from financial institutions), named elements of premises (e.g. Lyons Suite, Cyril Kleinwort Learning Resource Centre, Cass Business School), and visiting professors (e.g. Sir Robert Shone) provide ample evidence of this. Deans and Vice-Chancellors have a critical role to play in this process as 'star' ambassadors, and this in no way devalues the contribution of academics in general in this process.

Strategic leadership is an iterative process that transcends individual Deanships. Hence the importance of a 'mission' as a unifying and bridging theme. It should be a humbling experience to realise that the successes of today were sewn by leaders of the past, and that today's actions will affect the outcomes of tomorrow's leaders. Deans come and go, but a school's culture persists and is slow to change. There is a danger that the analytical approach adopted when describing Figure 14.1 can be misleading. The complex, dynamic nature of the model is difficult to conjure up. Yet it is intended to portray a holistic system in which the whole is greater than the sum of the parts as the Gestalt psychologists would argue. One of the implications of 'holistic systems' is that the impact of change interventions is only partially predictable and controllable; and there can be a long 'time lag' before their full impact is realised. Orientating the School toward quality research, financial health and the City of London from its cultural heritage of a College of Advanced Technology, took many more years than Sir James Tait would have predicted. This reinforces the importance of Vice-Chancellors (and when appointed their Deans) adopting a combined historical and open systems perspective when providing strategic leadership for schools. A selection committee needs to have a clear vision of the mission and strategies for the business school for which they are selecting a Dean; recognise the strengths and weaknesses of the school in relation to that vision; and understand the main dilemmas that will have to be 'managed' by the appointed leader. The model of strategic organisational elements in Figure 14.1 can be a useful tool for posing the range of questions that need exploring.

Part V
Appendices

Appendix 1: Methodology

Methodological influences

Case histories need to record and recount as accurately as possible the unfolding history of the target institution, ensuring that significant events and personalities are covered, that is, those that have had a major influence on shaping the institution. *Case studies* as an example of a particular approach to research and theory building are more than case histories. The Cass history research straddles both categories. The case study as a research tool for challenging existing theory, and for gaining new insights and building new theory, has become respectable as a result of the efforts of several academics (Yin 1984; Pettigrew 1985; Eisenhardt 1989). Since case studies are examples of qualitative research there are dangers that the degree of subjectivity involved may result in unintended errors in data collection, analysis and interpretation. Precautionary measures can be taken by using several methods of data collection (e.g. 'triangulation'), by recognising the theoretical assumptions being made when interpreting the data, and by checking the consistency and plausibility of findings against the relevant literature and other researchers.

While the single case study has the disadvantage of lacking comparative data, it has the advantage of being able to research into much greater depth. This is even more so in the present case study given that the author was an 'acting observer'. There were no formal hypotheses, and as such the study may be seen as a piece of 'grounded research' (Glaser and Strauss 1967). The hope was that a longitudinal study of a business school would lead to new insights into organisational behaviour. However, it would be incorrect to claim that theoretical assumptions were being repressed in the interest of keeping an open mind. One of the recognised difficulties in historical research is the near infinite amount of data available. This means that the researcher must select what to attend to and what to ignore. In such a situation the beliefs and 'mental models' of the researcher affects the outcomes. Hence the importance of others (particularly fellow researchers) being made aware of the theoretical frameworks affecting data collection and interpretation, and the precautions taken to increase their validity. Figure A1.1 fulfils this task. It shows the main theoretical approaches interacting with the main data collection methods. A distinctive characteristic of the single case study that is designed to yield new insights is its iterative nature, where elements influence each other and where interpretations are continually up-dated as new data is accumulated and new insights developed (Eisenhardt 1989). This is reflected in Figure A1.1.

Methodological framework

Objectives. These should play the main part in determining the methods used, and were: (1) To record the Cass Business School history and to share it with

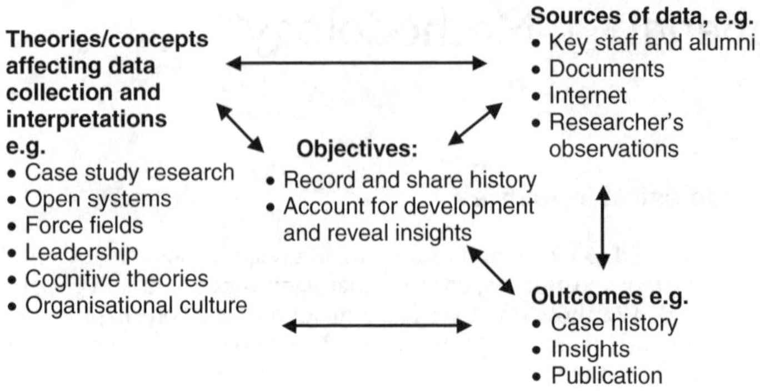

Figure A1.1 Methodological framework

stakeholders, thereby enhancing their sense of identity; (2) To account for factors affecting the School's development, and to reveal any insights gained, so as to enhance the learning of those concerned with leading and managing business schools in a competitive environment.

Theories and concepts. As an organisational psychologist there are certain theories and concepts that the author has drawn upon when trying to explain organisational behaviour, particularly in the context of change. All these are elaborated earlier or in the text.

Sources of data. In order to be as rigorous as possible several sources of data were used and these were cross-checked whenever possible. This approach minimised perceptual differences and memory failures when describing specific events. 63 current and alumni staff were interviewed, mainly face-to-face but a few by telephone (e.g. those living some distance from London such as France or Wales). The interview schedule was used in a flexible manner taking into account the unique roles and experiences of respondents. Topics covered in the schedule included: Background questions (e.g. dates and reasons for joining); perceived mission, strategies and changes in the School under different Deans; roles experienced at the School and factors facilitating/inhibiting performance; 'critical incidents' in the development of the School; other factors relating to the School (e.g. relationships with the University, the City; executive education; advisory panels; premises; decision-making structures).

All living academics who had held senior positions or responsible roles in the School post 1966 were interviewed, as were many of the University Officers. All Deans, except for the first two (who are no longer with us), were interviewed. Academics who had joined the School under the present Dean were not interviewed, but most academic and administrative staff holding senior management roles were interviewed.

Apart from the interviews the most important sources of information were: the Minutes of Northampton College's Board of Governors, the University's Council, the Business School Council; GBC/CUBS News; University's Annual Reports; Degree Congregation brochures; undergraduate and postgraduate brochures;

internal and external reports relating to the School; media rankings. Extracting information from documents was not always straightforward. For instance early annual reports contained data relevant to the study (e.g. number of academic staff employed by the School), but later ones catered more for their promotional value than their archival value. In more recent years some relevant material has been available on the School's website (e.g. alumni achievements). Internal documents have been supplemented by external ones where it was important to understand contextual issues. Examples include the archival material of the Association of Business Schools, and various governmental and institutionally sponsored reports.

The researcher/author was an active participant from 1963 to 2001, and an observer from that date. He held managerial roles for various periods in the School (e.g. Director of Research, Head of Business Studies, Deputy Dean) and in the University (e.g. Pro-Vice Chancellor) while at the same time carrying out normal academic roles as a researcher and teacher. Being a researcher 'on the inside' has enabled critical incidents, and their meaning and significance in the development of the School, to be identified in ways that a researcher 'on the outside' would have found difficult. Indeed the political subtleties of some incidents can only be understood if the context of the incident is understood. The author is only too well aware that he has inadequate insight into the less visible factors influencing events in the last few years than in the previous 38 years. Set against the advantages of having been an insider are the possible disadvantages of interpreting and accounting the School's history in an idiosyncratic manner. Information from the interviews, and the feedback obtained from relevant individuals reading drafts of sections of the manuscript, helped to avoid idiosyncratic interpretations. The *outcome* elements in the framework speak for themselves.

Appendix 2: Milestones in the History of Cass

1957 Dr James Tait, first Principal of Northampton CAT, appoints Mr Alvin Leyton to initiate courses in liberal studies and the principles of industrial administration into all recognised courses.

1961 Approval obtained from the Ministry of Education and the London County Council for a Department of Social and Industrial Studies. Leyton made Head of Department.

1962/63 Pressure from advisory committee (Chaired by Sir Walter Puckey) results in change of title to Department of Management and Social Sciences, and its primary mission to promote management studies of the highest standard.

1963 Recruitment of Douglas Vaughan (economist) and Dr Allan Williams (Industrial Psychologist) – first external appointments to lecture on the new Diploma in Management Studies. Sir Michael Turner (former Chairman of Hong Kong & Shanghai Bank) the first financier appointed to the College's governing body.

1965 Corporation's Court of Common Council approves a motion to establish a Faculty of Business Studies within the boundaries of the City.

1966 Department of Management and Social Sciences splits into two departments. Professor Kenneth Shone (an industrial engineer before entering academia) appointed to head new Department of Management Studies. First cohort of students recruited to the MSc in Administrative Sciences (an MBA in all but title).

1967 MSc Administrative Sciences team move to Gresham College building and form the Graduate Business Centre. Sir Robert Shone (first director general of NEDC) becomes first Visiting Professor. He initiates short courses in the financial area, and Basil Taylor is appointed as a research fellow to assist him (post funded by Esmee Fairbairn Trust).

1968 Mr David Glen OBE (headed corporate planning at Shell) appointed Dean. Lord Poole (Chairman of Lazard Brothers) heads University's development appeal, with a new building for the School on the menu.

1969 University receives first grant from UGC for business and management.

1970 The *FT*/City courses aimed at overseas bankers are launched.

1971 Second site in Lionel Denny House opened. City Advisory Panel formed with Sir Cyril Kleinwort as Chairman. The first Laurie Milbank Centenary Lecture is given by the President of Bank of London and South America Sir George Bolton in the Livery Hall of Guildhall. Post-experience courses given a boost by the appointment of John Bruce Lockhart as an adviser. Hugh Cockerell appointed to first senior academic fellowship in insurance.

1973 Diploma in Systems Analysis and Design launched as demand for computer skills increases.

1974/75 An MSc in Finance introduced, based mainly on the MSc Administrative Sciences. Peter Grinyer is promoted to a Chair in Business Strategy (partly funded by the FME) – the School's first internal promotion to a Chair. The School's Advisory Panel becomes the City Advisory Panel (chaired by Malcolm Wilcox Chief General Manager of Midland Bank), and an Industrial Advisory Panel is formed (chaired by the Chief Executive of London Borough of Camden). The first of the City/Whitehall Seminars (chaired by Sir Philip de Zulueta), and the Barclays Bank courses in industrial relations and human resource management (jointly chaired by Sid Kessler and Allan Williams).

1976 School is reviewed by the Dunn Committee, and changes its name to City University Business School (from Graduate Business Centre) in preparation for an undergraduate degree.

1977 BSc Business Studies is launched.

1978 Dr John Treasure (an economist and former Chairman of J.Walter Thompson) becomes Professor of Marketing and Dean. The School's first University recognised research centre (Centre for Personnel Research & Enterprise Development) established under the direction of Dr Allan Williams. Midland Bank funds a chair in export management, with the support of the Institute of Export Management.

1979 Hugh Murray appointed Professor of Export Management. MSc in Administrative Sciences rebranded as the internationally recognised MBA. Agreement (after 4 years of negotiation) between University, UGC and Corporation that the School will occupy space in Frobisher Crescent. Insurance Advisory Panel established.

1980 A chair in consumer studies is endowed by the Sir John and Lady Cohen Charitable Foundation, and Gerald Goodhardt is appointed to the chair.

1981 School moves into Frobisher Crescent. Michael Beenstock appointed to the Chair in Finance (funded by Esmee Fairbairn Trust).

1982 Professor Brian Griffiths (an economist heading the University's Centre for Banking and International Finance) becomes Dean, and within a year his Centre becomes part of the School. Evening MBA launched. Second major research centre formed under Beenstock – City Institute for Financial and Economic Research.

1983 Launch of the School's first academic journal edited by Beenstock – *The Economic Review*.

1984 The Centre for Shipping and International Finance, under the direction of Professor Costas Grammenos, is launched by Geoffrey Howe (Foreign Secretary) at the Baltic Exchange.

1985 The MScs in Shipping Trade & Finance, and Internal Auditing & Management, are launched. Griffiths and Murray publish their controversial pamphlet advocating the privatisation of business schools. School appoints its first placement and alumnus officer.

1986 Griffiths becomes Thatcher's chief policy adviser in 10 Downing Street, and Andrew Chambers succeeds him as Dean.

1987/88 Sponsorship of new chairs achieved: Price Waterhouse in Corporate Finance, Honeywell Bull in IT, Morgan Grenfell in Financial Markets, Market Research Society in that subject, National Westminster Bank in

Personal Banking. First Peat Marwick Lecture given by Anita Roddick, managing director of the Body Shop.

1989 MBA specialisation in IT launched.

1990 BSc in Insurance and Investment is launched. ESCP and School hold discussions leading to formation of AMSEC.

1991 Professor Gerald Goodhardt (Deputy Dean) appointed Dean for one year. VOLPROF launched under Visiting Professor Ian Bruce (Director General of RNIB) with support from NatWest Bank and BT.

1992 David Kaye (former partner of Anderson Consulting) appointed Dean. Department of Property Valuation and Management merged into School.

1994 MSc in Investment Management launched.

1995 Corporation funding enables the MSc in Mathematical Trading and Finance to be launched. MSc in Insurance & Risk Management also launched.

1996 Management of Technology MBA specialisation (emphasising telecoms and biotech) is launched. School's Business Studies Department restructured into five departments and the Head (Allan Williams) becomes Deputy Dean.

1997 First two-day 'Team development' residential meeting at Danbury Management Centre for School's executive committee. Professor Leslie Hannah (formerly Pro-Director of LSE) becomes Dean. Relaunch of MSc in Finance under Professor Mario Levis. Major part of Systems Science Department (BSc Management & Systems) merged into School.

1998 The first *FT* ranking of business schools – School in Europe's top ten. Financial Econometrics Research Centre formed under Professor Mark Salmon. Second 'Team development' residential meeting of executive committee at Swallow Hotel Waltham Abbey. Professor David Rhind succeeds Professor Raoul Franklin as Vice-Chancellor of University.

1999 MScs in Banking & International Finance, and Finance Economics & Econometrics, launched. University commits £42m to new building for School in Bunhill Row. Third 'Team development' meeting at Hitchin Priory.

2000 Michael Teacher (MBA 1971) becomes School's first Executive in Residence. International Board of Overseers replaces Business School Council.

2001 Lord David Currie (formerly Deputy Dean of LBS) appointed Dean. School restructured into two faculties.

2002 Lord Currie becomes part-time Dean following his appointment as Chairman of OFCOM. School's name changes to Cass Business School in recognition of the significant donation of the Sir John Cass Foundation. Department of Actuarial Science mergers into the School, and Professor Steve Haberman becomes Deputy Dean. School restructured into three faculties. In the Autumn the School begins the move into Bunhill Row.

2003 The Queen formerly opens the new building in May.
Launch of MSc in Management.

Appendix 3: Successive Advisory Bodies to the School

External membership of the City and Industrial Advisory Panels in 1976/77

City Advisory Panel

Chairman: M.G. Wilcox
Director & Chief General Manager
Midland Bank

C.T. Blackmore
Head of Administration
Lloyd's of London

G. Blunden
Executive Director
Bank of England

R.B. Botcherby
Managing Director
European Arab Bank

Sir Kingsley Collett
City of London Corporation

J.G.W. Davies
Formerly Executive Director
of Bank of England, member
of City University Council

J. Dukes
Director
The Financial Times

R.C. Hughes
Director
The British Federation of
Commodity Associations

G. Ross Russell
Director
Laurence Prust & Co.,
Member of the Stock Exchange
Council

Industrial Advisory Panel

Chairman: B.H. Wilson
Town Clerk & Chief Executive
London Borough of Camden

J.M. Beales
Corporate Planning Manager
John Laing & Sons

A.M. Fraser
Board of Customs & Excise

W.K. Gardner
Finance Director
Dunlop Group

I.R.G. Manning
Managing Director
Masson, Scott Thrissell Engineering

A.M. O'Malley
Director & General Manager
International Pinchin Johnson

M. Pattinson
Senior Commercial Executive, BP

Barbara Sloman
Head of Civil Service College

D.P. Wratten
Senior Director
Telecommunications
Post Office

L.T.G. Preston
Director
Standard Chartered Bank

A.R.N. Ratcliff
Chief General Manager
Eagle Star Insurance Company

C.R. Reeves
Deputy Chairman
Morgan Grenfell & Co.

R. Perkins
Managing Director
Ransomes & Rapier

F. Waterhouse
Chief Accountant
ICI Plant Protection Division

External membership of City and Insurance Advisory Panels 1986–87

City Advisory Panel

Chairman: C Brandon Gough, Senior partner, Coopers & Lybrand
C.T. Blackmore, former Head of Corporate Services, Lloyd's of London
J.G.W Davies, Former Director, Bank of England
J.H. Farr, Director, Federation of Commodity Associations
R.T. Fox, Vice-Chairman, Kleinwort Benson Ltd.
H.R.J. Human, Partner, Linklaters & Paines
E.P.T. Roney, former Chief Commoner for the City of London; Senior Partner, Roneys
N.O. Taube, Chief Executive, Rothschild Investment Management
D.N. Vermont, Director, E.W. Payne Companies Ltd.
R.J. Woodley, Divisional Chief of Corporate Services (Personnel), Bank of England
J.R.C. Young, Director, Policy and Planning, Stock Exchange

Insurance Advisory Panel

Chairman: A.R.N. Ratcliffe, Chief Executive, Eagle Star Insurance Co Ltd; also representing the Association of British Insurers General Insurance Council
S. Benjamin, Partner, Bacon & Woodrow; also representing the Institute of Actuaries Research Committee
D. Longbottom, Director of Training, Lloyd's of London
M.J.B. Lovegrove, Secretary (Technical) Chartered Insurance Institute
G. Newton, Directing Actuary, Government Actuary's Department
A.G. O'Leary, Actuary and Secretary, Clerical, Medical & General Life Assurance Society, also representing the Association of British Insurers Life Insurance Council
D.N. Vermont, Director, E.W. Payne Companies Ltd.
In addition to these seven external members there were three based in other parts of the University: Professors Haberman (Head of Actuarial Science), Kennedy (Head of Centre for Research in Insurance and Investment), and Wynn (Dean of the School of Mathematics, Statistics and Actuarial Science).

Table A3.1 External membership of the International Board of Overseers in 2000

Name	City University Degree (where applicable)	Position
Mr Ralph Arditti	MSc/MBA, 1970	Managing Director, Sanayi Yatirimlari Veticaret AS, Turkey.
The Hon Mr Apurv Bagri	BSc, 1980	Managing Director, Metdist Group; Member of British Invisibles South Asia Committee; Vice Chairman, International Wrought Copper Council; Commissioner, Crown Estate Paving Commission; Member of Executive Committee of Asia House.
Mr Stephen Barclay		Executive Chairman, Talisman House Plc Group.
Mr Richard Barnfield	MSc/MBA, 1973	Formerly Personnel Director, Bristol & West Building Society. Now Managing Director & Chief Executive, Western Training & Enterprise Council and Director, Rowen Dartington Stockbrokers.
Mr Roger Brooke		Life President, Candover plc; Chairman, Business School Capital Development Campaign.
Mr Richard Caruso		Chairman, Integra Life Sciences Corporation, New Jersey.
Mr Michael Cassidy	MBA, 1985	Formerly Chairman, City Corporation Policy & Resources Committee. Now Senior Partner, Maxwell Batley Solicitors; Director, British Land and Chairman, Linc; Chairman, City University Development Fund.
Mme. Veronique de Chantérac-Lamielle		Formerly Dean, Ecole Supérieure de Commerce de Paris (ESCP).
Mr Geoffrey Cooper	BSc, 1975	Finance Director, Alliance Unichem plc (France and United Kingdom).
Mr Peter Cullum	MSc/MBA, 1976	Formerly Managing Director, Economic Insurance Company and Marketing Director, Hiscox plc; now Chairman and Chief Executive, Towergate Underwriting Group Ltd.
Mr Michael Cunnane	MSc/MBA 1973	Executive Deputy Chairman, Sutherlands Ltd (Stockbrokers).

Continued

Table A3.1 Continued

Name	City University Degree (where applicable)	Position
Ms Karen Earp		General Manager, Four Seasons Hotel, Canary Wharf.
Mr David Essex	MSc/MBA, 1972	Chairman of Bemrose Group & Executive in Residence, CUBS. Formerly Managing Director, Finance & Planning of Vickers plc.
Mr Richard Exley	BSc, 1989	Director, MEPC UK Ltd and Managing Director, MEPC's Business Space Sector.
Mr Robin Fox CBE		Recently retired as Chairman, Dresdner Kleinwort Benson, currently with Lombard Risk Systems Ltd; Chairman, Whiteaway Laidlaw Bank and Centro Internationale Handelsbank AG, Vienna. Formerly Chairman, previous Business School Council; founding Chairman, International Board of Overseers.
Mr Eloy Garcia		Treasurer Elect, Inter-American Development Bank, Washing DC.
Mr Brandon Gough		Chairman, De La Rue plc and Yorkshire Water plc. Formerly Chairman, Higher Education Funding Council and of the Business School Council.
Mr Stelios Haji-Ioannou	MSc, 1988	Chairman, Easy Group including EasyJet and EasyEverything.
Mr Stephen Hodge		Group Treasurer, Shell Group.
Mr Robert Legget	MSc/MBA, 1974	Director, Quayle Munro Holdings plc, Edinburgh-based investment bank. Formerly Senior Finance Executive, Mitchell Cotts plc and Delta Group plc.
Mr Ron Lis	MSc/MBA, 1972	Formerly Director, Schroders plc and European Representative, Bashcreditbank, Russia.
Dr Julius Tawona Makoni	MSc/MBA, 1980	Formerly with Morgan Grenfell, the World Bank and Bankers' Trust. Founder and Chief Executive, National Merchant Bank of Zimbabwe.

Continued

Table A3.1 Continued

Name	City University Degree (where applicable)	Position
Mr Eric Moonman		Former MP and PPS. Now Group Chairman, DMG Radio; Visiting Professor in Marketing at City University and Vice President of the Board of Deputies.
Dr Takashi Nozu	D.Sc, 1996	Chairman, Nozu Group & Board of Trustees at Gyosei Intern. College.
Mr Andrew Pople	MBA, 1988	Managing Director, Retail Division, Abbey National plc.
Ms Fiona Price	MBA, 1983	Founded Fiona Price & Partners, 1988. Described by Harpers & Queen as 'first lady of financial advice for women'.
Mr Nicholas Roditi	MSc/MBA, 1971	Principal, N. Roditi & Co; Chairman, Plantation & General Holdings plc.
Mr Derek Sach	MSc/MBA, 1972	Formerly Managing Director, 3i and Head of Tesco Personal Finance. Now Director, Associated British Ports Holdings plc; Director, Berkeley Group plc; Director, Special Projects, Royal Bank of Scotland.
Ms Carol Sergeant	MBA, 1979	Formerly with the Bank of England. Now Director of Banks & Building Societies, Financial Services Authority; Deputy Chairperson, Building Societies Commission.
Mr John Sherrington	MSc/MBA, 1972	Senior Vice President, Scotia McLeod, Bank of Nova Scotia, Canada.
Mr Aram Shishmanian	MSc/MBA, 1977	Partner, Andersen Consulting.
Robert Shrager	MSc/MBA, 1971	Formerly with Morgan Grenfell and Finance Director, Dixons Group plc. Now Chairman, Tempo Holdings Ltd; Non-executive Director, Matalan plc and RJB Mining plc.
Ms Ruth Storm	MBA, 1988	Partner, Phildrew Ventures and their representative on Boards of Sitex, Hammicks, United Texon and B & M.
Mr Michael Teacher	MSc/MBA, 1972	Formerly Managing Director, Hillsdown Holdings plc. Now Entrepreneur and Executive in Residence, City University Business School.

Continued

Table A3.1 Continued

Name	**City University Degree (where applicable)**	**Position**
Mr David Turner FRICS		Founder and Director, Riva Group plc; Director, WSP Group plc. Formerly Chief Executive, Barclays Property Holdings Co. Currently Chairman, City University Business School new building Project Executive.
Mr David Watson	BSc, 1981	Finance Director, M & G Group plc (now part of the Prudential Group).

Updates at 2004–05. This body is now called the 'International Advisory Board', and it is chaired by Lord Currie the Dean of the School. The following are no longer members: Geoffrey Cooper, David Essex, Brandon Gough and Nicholas Roditi. New members include: Peter Ford (a former senior member of London Transport), Alistair Johnston (Vice Chairman, KPMG, UK, and Visiting Professor at the School), Dr Ann Robinson (former member of the University Council), Sandy Scott (Director General, the Chartered Insurance Institute), Stephen Sklaroff (Association of British Insurers), and Simon Brocklebank-Fowler (Cubitt Consulting). Recently other members may have changed their positions (e.g. Carol Sergeant is now Chief Risk Director, Lloyds TSB Group).

Appendix 4: The Mais Lectures 1978–2005

1. Reflections on the Conduct of Monetary Policy
   Rt Hon Gordon Richardson, 1978
2. Objectives of Monetary Policy: Past and Present
   Lord Lionel Robbins, 1979
3. The Fight against Inflation
   Rt Hon Sir Geoffrey Howe QC MP, 1981
4. Science and Ethics
   Professor F.A. Hayek, 1983
5. The British Experiment
   Rt Hon Nigel Lawson MP, 1984
6. The International Financial Scene: Can Sense be plucked out of Danger
   Rt Hon Roy Jenkins MP, 1986
7. The Instruments of Monetary Policy
   Rt Hon Robin Leigh-Pemberton, 1987
8. The IMF in a Changing World
   Mr M. Camdessus, Managing Director, IMF, 1988
9. A Restatement of Economic Liberalism
   Sir Samuel Brittan, 1989
10. Monetary Policy – A Post-mortem and Proposal
    Gordon Pepper, CBE, 1990
11. Economic and Monetary Union: The Case for Central Bank Independence
    Erik Hoffmeyer, 1992
12. Benefits and Costs: Securing the Future of Social Security
    Rt Hon Peter Lilley MP, 1993
13. The Changing World of Work in the 1990s
    Rt Hon Kenneth Clarke QC MP, 1994
14. The Economic Framework for New Labour
    Rt Hon Tony Blair MP, 1995
15. Achieving Competitiveness in a Global Economy
    Rt Hon Michael Heseltine MP, 1996
16. Monetary Policy in Britain and Europe
    Sir Edward George, Governor, Bank of England, 1997
17. Financial and Monetary Integration: Benefits, Opportunities and Pitfalls
    Dr Hans Tietmeyer, President, Bundesbank, 1998
18. The Conditions for Full Employment
    Rt Hon Gordon Brown MP, 1999
19. Markets, Governments and Virtues
    Chief Rabbi Jonathan Sacks, 2000
20. The New European Debate: The Euro-zone and the Greater Europe
    President Valery Giscard d'Estaing, 2001

21. Reflections on European Monetary Policy
    Professor Dr Ernst Welteke, 2003
22. The Euro – the First Five Years
    Professor Dr Otmar Issing, 2004
23. Monetary Policy: Practice ahead of Theory
    Mervyn King, Governor, Bank of England, 2005

Appendix 5: Milestones Relating to the School's New Building in Bunhill Row

Note: These notes are virtually those prepared by Michael O'Hara, University Secretary. He points out that the chronology is mainly based on the consolidated reports to University Council. Consequently the dates reflect the times at which particular actions were achieved rather than when work started.

- June 87: Working party set up to assess development potential of Northampton Hall (NH) land.
- January 88: Report to Council that there was an opportunity to realise the development potential of the site replacing NH with new student and academic accommodation. Appointment of development adviser recommended.
- April 89: Healey & Baker selected as development adviser.
- January 90: Joint development with Islington's City and East London College (CELC) explored.
- July 89: Further report from working party: identified marriage value of linking with adjacent City and East London College (CELC) site and constraints affecting development. Development options stated as speculative office and/or Business School; both implied finding alternative sites to replace student accommodation.
- January 90: Joint development with CELC/Islington explored. Sheppard Robson instructed to make outline planning application for offices. Healey & Baker take soundings from potential developers.
- March 90: Council advised that restrictive covenant had to be dealt with by application to Land Tribunal and resolved by April 91 in order to establish open market value of NH site. Outline application for 100% office use.
- May 90: Dialogue with Islington planners: office space plus Business School. No planning consent granted within statutory period; City appeals.
- November 90: Short list of student housing sites established.
- February 91: Public Planning Inquiry. City proposed office space. Islington argued over-development, no mixed use, too much traffic.
- March 91: Land Tribunal sets aside restrictive covenant on development of NH site.
- July 91: City's Planning Appeal upheld on all counts by Inspector.
- June 92: Substantial progress reported to council on alternative student housing sites weak property market gives opportunity to acquire freehold building in City fringe for conversion to Business School.
- October 92: Funding for alternative student accommodation (Graham Street) authorised (a prerequisite for the development of NH site was that alternative student accommodation would have to be found).
- March 93: Albion Place acquired to supplement Graham Street to provide accommodation equivalent to NH.

- November 93: Deterioration of property market means some delay in realising the value of NH site. But action taken to resolve complications for development – rights of light, archaeology, HEFCE agreement to retain proceeds of development gain.
- November 94: Preparations to market NH land.
- March 95: Preliminary archaeological survey raised no problems. Sheppard Robson to prepare detailed office planning application.
- August 95: Planning application made.
- October 95: Project manager appointed for demolition of NH.
- November 95: Detailed planning consent granted. Preferred development option agreed: select developer as partner to share risk. HEFCE confirmed City could retain proceeds of development. City Corporation proposes Barbican Exhibition Hall as expansion space to complement Frobisher; but feasibility study rejects.
- December 95: NH closes as student accommodation. Chiswell Street Executive appointed (University/School body to oversee developments).
- June 96: Lynton plc selected as Development Partner. Corporation proposes Bastion House in London Wall for Business School. Bennetts Associates undertake feasibility study; school's detailed requirements committed to paper for first time. Building did not fit requirements.
- September 96: Merrill Lynch search for new European HQ; NH + City and Islington College combined site a possibility.
- November 96: Lynton wanting to renegotiate Heads of Terms.
- March 97: Joint NH/City & Islington College site comes second in Merrill Lynch's choice for the location of its European HQ. Chiswell Street Executive recommends severing relationship with Lyton plc (Development Partner) who wanted to transfer risk back to University.
- July 97: Bellway Homes Ltd appointed as new Development Partner reflecting strength of residential market (idea of business school on lower floors and private and social housing above). Bennett Associates appointed as architects. Frobisher leases reviewed to achieve orderly withdrawal.
- September 97: GTMS appointed project manager. Joint investigation of development with Bellway. Strengthening of commercial property market brings office developers back into the frame.
- November 97: Firm interest from Helical Bar plc. City considers rival merits of office and Bellway schemes. Business School asked to produce 10-year business plan. Bellway scheme dropped.
- May/July 98: Development agreement with Helical Bar exchanged, land transfer providing site for new Business School plus £14.5 capital premium (total value of £25.5m). Bennetts take business school scheme to outline planning stage. Overall development arrangement links city and Islington College vacating site for new business school to ability to move into Alice Owen School by September 01 at latest.
- September 98: London Borough of Islington (LBI) grant planning consent subject to reserve matters. Rights of Light negotiations with Roman Catholic Church.
- November 98: NH demolition commences. Vacant possession of business school site put back to 31 August 2000.
- December 98: Planning consent issued.

- March 99: Rights of Light resolved on paying compensation (£0.35m) to Roman Catholic Church.
- April 99: Transfer of NH title. £13.9m (net of all rights of light payments) to University.
- November/December 99: City commits £28.5m to fund development of new business school; size of development authorised as basement, ground + 6 floors.
- May 00: Bennetts scheme design approved.
- July 00: Exterior appointed construction manager.
- August 00: City & Islington College (CIC) vacate their Bunhill Row site.
- September 00: Demolition of CIC buildings.
- November 00: City gains entry to cleared site. New business school Dean: final revisions to layouts.
- May 01: Inauguration of new building by Lord Mayor, Chancellor of University.
- October 02: Some lectures take place in the new building.
- December 02: Academic and administrative staff move into the building.
- May 03: Her Majesty the Queen and the Duke of Edinburgh officially open the new building.

References

Bareham, J. (2004). 'The leadership and management of business schools'. *Occasional/Working paper series* (BBSO3-2): 1–32.

Barnes, W. (1989). *Managerial Catalyst: The Story of London Business School, 1964–1989*. London, Paul Chapman.

Barsoux, J.-L. (2000). *Insead: From Intuition to Institution*. Basingstoke, Macmillan.

Bass, B.M. (1998). *Transformational Leadership: Industry, Military and Educational Impact*. Mahwah, NJ, Epilbaum.

Bessant, J. (2003). 'The state of the field in UK management research: reflections of the research assessment exercise (RAE) panel'. *British Journal of Management* **14**(1): 51–68.

Boswell, J. (1973). *The Rise and Decline of Small Firms*. London, Allen & Unwin.

Brech, E. (2002). *The Evolution of Modern Management: 1852–1979*. Bristol, Thoemmes Press.

Buchanan, D. and A. Huczynski (2004). *Organisational Behaviour: An Introductory Text*. Harlow, Pearson Education Ltd.

Capie, F. and G. Wood, Eds (1996). *Monetary Economics in the 1990s: the Henry Thornton Lectures 9–17*. Basingstoke, Macmillan.

Capie, F. and G. Wood, Eds (2001). *Policy makers on Policy: The Mais Lectures*. London, Routledge.

CEML (2002). *Managers and Leaders: Raising our Game*. London, Council for Excellence in Management and Leadership.

Chan, K.C. *et al.* (2002). 'Production in finance literature, institutional reputation, and labor mobility in academia: a global perspective'. *Financial Management* **31**(4): 131–156.

Chartres, R. and D. Vermont (1998). *A Brief History of Gresham College 1597–1997*. London, Gresham College.

Constable, J. and R. McCormick (1987). *The Making of British Managers*. London, BIM/CBI.

Dahrendorf, R. (1995). *A History of the London School of Economics and Political Science 1895–1995*. Oxford, Oxford University Press.

Deem, R. (2001). *'New Managerialism' and Management of UK Universities*. Lancaster, Lancaster University.

Dickinson, G. and H. Cockerell (1980). *Motor Insurance and the Consumer*. Cambridge, Woodhead-Faulkner.

Eden, C. and J.C. Spender (1998). *Managerial and Organisational Cognition: Theory, Methods and Research*. London, Sage.

Eisenhardt, K.M. (1989). 'Building theories from case study research'. *Academy of Management Review* **14**(4): 532–550.

ESRC (1994). *Commission on Management Research*. London, ESRC.

Franks, L. (1963). *British Business Schools*. London, HMSO.

Fraser, E. (2004). *The Worshipful Company of Management Consultants: The Road to Livery*. London, Worshipful Company of Management Consultants.

French, J.R.P. and B.H. Raven (1959). 'The bases of social power', in *Studies in Social Power*, edited by D. Cartwright. Ann Arbor, MI, Institute for Social Research.

Gabarro, J. (1987). *The Dynamics of Taking Charge*. Boston, Harvard Business School Press.

Gallos, J. (2002). 'The dean's squeeze: the myths and realities of academic leadership in the middle'. *Academy of Management Learning and Education* **1**(2): 174–184.

Glaser, B.G. and A.L. Strauss (1967). *The Discovery of Grounded Theory: Strategies for Qualitative Research*. Chicago, Aldine.

Griffiths, B. and H. Murray (1985). Whose business? A radical proposal to privatise British Business Schools. *Hobart Paper*. London, Institute of Economic Affairs.

Grinyer, P. and J.C. Spender (1979). *Turnaround: the Fall and Rise of the Newton Chambers Group*. London, Associated Business Press.

Handy, C. *et al.* (1987). *The Making of Managers*. London, NDEC/MSC/BIM.

Hodgkinson, G.P. and P. Sparrow (2002). *The Competent Organisation: A Psychological Analysis of the Strategic Management Process*. Buckingham, Open University Press.

Janis, I.L. (1972). *Victims of Groupthink: A Psychological Study of Foreign Policy Decisions and Fiascoes*. Boston, MA, Houghton Mifflin.

Katz, D. and R.L. Kahn (1966). *The Social Psychology of Organisations*. New York, Wiley.

Kessler, S. and A. Williams (1978). 'How industrial democracy works in banks abroad'. *The Bankers' Magazine* **222**: 8–10.

Lambert, R. (2002). *Lambert Review of Business–University Collaboration*. London, Treasury.

Leavitt, H. (1965). 'Applied organisational change in industry: structural, technological, and humanistic approaches' in *Handbook of Organisations*, edited by J. March. Chicago, Rand McNally.

Lewin, K. (1951). *Field Theory in Social Science*. New York, Harper and Row.

Lorange, P. (2002). *New Vision for Management Education: Leadership Challengers*. Oxford, Pergamom/Elsevier, Science.

Mant, A. (1969). *The Experienced Manager – a Major Resource*. London, BIM.

Mathur, S. and A. Kenyon (1997). *Creating Value: Shaping Tomorrow's Business*. London, Butterworth Heinemann.

Miles, R.E. and C.C. Snow (1978). *Organisational Strategy, Structure and Process*. New York, McGraw-Hill.

NEDC (1963). *Management Education?* London, NEDC.

Nind, P. (1985). *A Firm Foundation: the Story of the Foundation for Management Education*. London, FME.

Owen, T. (1970). *Business Schools: the Requirements of British Manufacturing Industry*. London, BIM.

Peters, T. and R. Waterman (1982). *In Search of Excellence*. New York, Harper and Row.

Pettigrew, A. (1985). *The Awakening Giant: Continuity and Change at ICI*. Oxford, Blackwell.

Pfeffer, J. and G.R. Salancik (1978). *The External Control of Organisations: a Resource Dependence Perspective*. New York, Harper and Row.

Pidwill, S. (2003). Bennetts Associates' Cass Business School. *Architecture Today*.
Porter, L. and E. Lawler (1968). *Managerial Attitudes and Performance*. Homewood, Dorsey-Irwin.
Porter, L. and L. McKibbin (1988). *Management Education and Development Drift or Thrust into the 21 Century*. New York, McGraw-Hill.
Pullan, B. and M. Abendstern (2000). *A History of the University of Manchester 1951–73*. Manchester, Manchester University Press.
Revans, R. (1983). *The ABC of Action Learning*. Bickley, Kent, Chartwell-Bratt.
Robbins, L. (1963). *Report of the Committee on Higher Education*. London, HMSO.
Roethlisberger, L.F. and W.J. Dickson (1939). *Management and the Worker*. Boston, MA, Harvard University Press.
Rose, H. (1970). *Management Education in the 1970s*. London, HMSO.
Rowe, K. (1964). 'An appraisal of appraisals'. *Journal of Management Studies* **1**(1): 1–25.
Schalk, R. and D.M. Rousseau (2001). 'Psychological contracts in employment: theory, methods and applications', in *Handbook of Industrial, Work and Organisational Psychology: Organisational Psychology*, edited by N. Anderson, D.S. Ones, H.K. Sinangil and C. Viswesvaran. London, Sage. **2**.
Schein, E.H. (1992). *Organisational Culture and Leadership*. San Francisco, CA, Jossey-Bass.
Servan-Schreiber, S. (1994). *Les Epices de la Republique: ESCP Itinerire d'une grande ecole, 1819–1994*. Paris, CpL.
Sparrow, J. (1998). *Knowledge in Organisations: Access to Thinking at Work*. London, Sage.
Stewart, R. (1967). *Managers and Their Jobs*. Basingstoke, Macmillan.
Stewart, R. (1970). *The Reality of Organisations*. Basingstoke, Macmillan.
Teague, J. (1980). *The City University: A History*. London, City University.
Weick, K. (1995). *Sensemaking in Organisations*. London, Sage.
Williams, A.P.O. (1980). 'Integrating individual and organisational learning: a model and a case study'. *Management Education and Development* **11**(1): 7–20.
Williams, A.P.O. (1993). 'Strategies for the success of full-time MBAs'. *British Academy of Management Newsletter* 8–9.
Williams, A.P.O. (1998). 'Organisational learning and the role of attitude surveys'. *Human Resource Management Journal* **8**(4): 51–65.
Williams, A.P.O. and S. Woodward (1994). *The Competitive Consultant: a Client-oriented Approach for Achieving Superior Performance*. Basingstoke, Macmillan.
Williams, A.P.O. *et al.*, 'Participative Practices in European banks'. *Industrial Relations Journal* **7**(4): 21–40.
Williams, A.P.O. *et al.* (1993). *Changing Culture: New Organisational Approaches*. London, Institute of Personnel and Development.
Williams, A.P.O. *et al.* (2002). *Managing Change Successfully: Using Theory and Experience to Implement Change*. London, Thomson Learning.
Wilson, J.F. (1992). *The Manchester Experiment: A History of Manchester Business School 1965–1990*. London, Paul Chapman.
Yin, R.K. (1984). *Case Study Research: Design and Methods*. London, Sage.
Yukl, G. (2001). *Leadership in Organisations*. London, Prentice Hall.

Index